How to Do
Everything™

iPad™

D0128599

4/11

About the Author

Joli Ballew is a technical author, technology trainer, community college instructor, and self-proclaimed "gadget expert," residing in Dallas, Texas. She holds several certifications including MCSE, MCTS, and MCDST. Joli has written over three dozen books on technologies ranging from Photoshop to operating systems to phones, and her work has been published in over 10 languages.

In addition to writing and teaching, Joli works as a network administrator and web designer for North Texas Graphics, writes web pages for Microsoft, and writes articles for various online communities, including BrightHub. In her free time, she enjoys golfing, yard work, exercising at the local gym, and teaching her cats, Pico and Lucy, tricks.

Joli welcomes all correspondence and can be contacted via email at Joli_Ballew@hotmail.com.

About the Technical Editor

Donald Bell is a senior editor for CNET.com, covering portable media players and tablets. He is the writer responsible for CNET's official iPad review, and regularly publishes tutorials for CNET's iPad Atlas blog. You can also hear him each week on CNET's Crave podcast. When he's not testing the latest gadgets, he enjoys playing guitar, listening to old records, and being a dad.

iPad™

Joli Ballew

New York Chicago San Francisco Lisbon
London Madrid Mexico City Milan New Delhi
San Juan Seoul Singapore Sydney Toronto

The McGraw·Hill Companies

Cataloging-in-Publication Data is on file with the Library of Congress

McGraw-Hill books are available at special quantity discounts to use as premiums and sales promotions, or for use in corporate training programs. To contact a representative, please e-mail us at bulksales@mcgraw-hill.com.

How to Do Everything™: iPad™

iPad image used by permission from Apple, Inc. iPad product shot used by permission from Peter Belanger © 2010 www.peterbelanger.com; iPad background photo of Pyramid Lake (at Night) by Richard Misrach © 2004.

1234567890 WFR WFR 109876543210

ISBN   978-0-07-174869-8
MHID   0-07-174869-5

Sponsoring Editor Megg Morin	**Technical Editor** Donald Bell, Senior Editor, CNET	**Production Supervisor** Jean Bodeaux
Editorial Supervisor Patty Mon	**Copy Editor** Margaret Berson	**Composition** Glyph International
Project Manager Rajni Pisharody, Glyph International	**Proofreader** Julie Searls	**Illustration** Glyph International
Acquisitions Coordinator Meghan Riley	**Indexer** Jack Lewis	**Art Director, Cover** Jeff Weeks **Cover Designer** Jeff Weeks

For Cosmo, who loves me and loves my iPad.

Contents at a Glance

Contents

x Contents

Acknowledgments

I've written four *How to Do Everything*™ books now, and have worked with just about everyone at McGraw-Hill. This book was the most special of them all, though. Everyone came together, at the same time, and with the same gusto. My Sponsoring Editor, Megg Morin, even purchased her own iPad, and we spent lots of time swapping stories and sharing our views on the latest and greatest apps. We both love iBooks; we both love Netflix. We both think watching TV on the iPad is awesome, and that Maps is the bomb. We've both spent way too much money on movies, books, and apps, even though we could have opted for free ones, but neither of us cares. I don't normally have such a close relationship with the people I work with, and I have a feeling Megg and I will remain friends for many years to come.

To get this book to market as soon as possible, we all worked long days and long nights. Everyone was crunching numbers, and everyone was pushed to their limits with regard to how much they could do within a given window of time. The people who worked directly with me on this book include Megg Morin, Donald Bell, Meghan Riley, Patty Mon, and Rajni Pisharody, and I'd like to thank them for all their hard work.

I'd like to call out Donald Bell for a moment, though. I can't recall ever having a more informed technical editor. And because we were in a rush, I gave Donald permission to simply write over my words, if he felt so inclined. He did so occasionally, and I always kept the words he wrote. The man knows his iPad, there's no doubt about that, and he's not a bad writer, either.

Book writing takes a bit of family support too, and I'd like to thank mine for sticking by me through the months that I'm overworked, and the various times when I'm not. I put in some incredibly long 12-hour days toward the end of this journey, and my family left me alone and let me be. They let me slide on Monday and Thursday night dinners and didn't complain when I spent all day Saturday or Sunday at my computer.

I miss my mom, who passed away in 2009, and the sadness was especially heavy while writing this book. I know she would have loved the iPad, and I often wanted to call her on the phone and say something like "Hey Mom, you have to try iBooks!" or "Mom, check it out, I can see your house on Maps!" She was always a bit afraid of the computer, with all its pop-ups about updating antivirus software, installing operating system updates, and the thing freezing up from time to time, and toward the end she was just too sick to even care to try. iPhones and the like were too small for her, so she never got into that either. She would have loved the iPad, though, I know it. I wish she were here for this.

I'm proud of my dad, who at almost 90 still lives alone, drives, does his own shopping, and maintains his swimming pool all by himself. I'm only about 15 minutes away if he needs me, though, and he has a Jitterbug phone he's quite comfortable with. He's a happy guy, and it's nice to see him getting along on his own. He never complains and always agrees with me, and he trusts the decisions I make for him. Believe me, I know how blessed my life has been and continues to be, even with the tragedies that must occur because life is, well, life, and things will and do happen.

The rest of my family includes Jennifer, my daughter, a recent graduate of the University of Texas and a civil engineer (I never get tired of saying that); my son-in-law Andrew, a black belt in Karate and awesome physical education teacher; and Cosmo, my best friend and partner in life, who like Dad, always has a smile on her face and happiness in her heart. I don't know how all of these people put up with me, because I'm not generally that easy to get along with and I'm not always as happy as they seem to be. I'm thankful, though, you can count on that.

Finally, I'd like to thank my agent, Neil Salkind, who continues to surprise me with his talents, tact, personal support, and connections, and how he goes out of his way to keep me busy. He's a great friend, my biggest fan, and for some reason, thinks I can do no wrong. I'm sure I wouldn't be where I am today without him. I enjoy our emails, our phone calls, and our friendship, and am glad to have him on my side.

The publisher would like to add special thanks to Sue Carroll at Apple, Inc. for her help in securing the green light to use the iPad image on this book's cover, and thanks to Peter Belanger Photography for taking the great iPad product shot. Richard Misrach captured the beauty of Pyramid Lake in 2004, and gets our thanks for the iPad background image and granting permission for our use.

Introduction

Congratulations on the purchase of your new iPad. You're going to be amazed at how versatile this device is, how many ways you can use it to stay in touch with others, and how many apps are available for you to play and work with. You'll love surfing the Internet on the go and on a screen you can actually see; you'll appreciate Maps when you need to get somewhere fast or find information about a business or restaurant; and in your downtime, you'll enjoy shopping at the iTunes Store for movies, podcasts, music, TV shows, and just about any other media imaginable and watching and listening to that media on your iPad.

Here at McGraw-Hill, we're all amazed with the iPad. We're amazed at how great an HD movie looks in the Videos app, we're stunned at how fast we can surf the Internet, and we love all of the different ways we can share our photos. Picture Frame is awesome, and we can create slideshows on the fly. iTunes offers iTunes U, where we can listen to lectures for free from colleges and universities all over the United States, including Stanford, Yale, and Berkeley, and we're all happy that for only about $30 a month, we can have always-on Internet access using an iPad 3G.

The third-party apps are incredible too. iBooks offers a lot of free books, and we have full bookshelves. Netflix lets us watch movies, and the ABC Player lets us watch TV shows we missed the night before. We can sit on the couch and answer our email on a keyboard that we can actually see, touch, and use effectively, and we can open all kinds of documents and pictures. With iWork apps, we can even work from anywhere.

We all sincerely hope that you are just as excited as we are. In this book we vow to teach you "all you need to know." In fact, I'm pretty sure we've introduced everything there is to the iPad here, with the exclusion of all of the third-party apps, of course. If we've left anything out or if you have any questions or comments, feel free to email me directly at joli_ballew@hotmail.com, or visit my Facebook group, How to Do Everything: iPad. It's open and everyone can join.

Without further ado then, let's get started. Here's what you'll learn in this book:

Chapter 1, "Set Up and Discover Your iPad," helps get you through the setup process, learn the parts of the iPad Home screen, sync your iPad, and learn touch techniques. You'll discover what's on the outside of your iPad, what model iPad you have, and what kind of data plan might be right for you (if you have the Wi-Fi + 3G model).

Chapter 2, "iPad Basics," shows you how to personalize your iPad, turn on Wi-Fi and connect to a free hotspot or your home network, connect via cellular connections using a Wi-Fi + 3G iPad, use Spotlight Search to find data on your iPad, and how to type effectively, or at least well enough for now!

Chapter 3, "Safari," instructs you on using Safari to surf the Internet, using gestures to zoom and otherwise navigate a page, creating shortcuts to web pages (called web clips) on your Home screens, bookmarking sites you visit often, and organizing those bookmarks. There's a lot more to Safari than you may have expected, and we'll cover it all here.

Chapter 4, "Communicate with Mail," walks you through setting up your email accounts in Mail, the iPad's email app. With accounts configured, you'll learn to send, receive, compose, organize, and work with mail. You'll also learn how to send pictures in an email, open an attachment, and add senders to your address book.

Chapter 5, "Go Digital with iBooks," shows you how to get iBooks, how to use iBooks, and how to browse and shop the iBookstore. You'll learn about Top Charts, where you can download free books, like *The War of the Worlds* by H.G. Wells and *Pride and Prejudice* by Jane Austen. You'll also explore all of the iBooks controls, including changing the font and font size for any book.

Chapter 6, "Read News and Commentary, and Use Social Networks," shows you how to locate your local newspaper online, read the *New York Times*, read blogs and listen to podcasts, and participate in social networking web sites like Facebook. You'll also learn to text with a popular third-party app and exchange instant messages with others using an app like AIM.

Chapter 7, "Get and Use Apps from the App Store," helps you learn how to locate, purchase, download, and install apps, and how to read reviews and ratings for apps or write your own. We'll introduce some of our favorite apps, and show you how to manage the apps you keep by backing them up, repositioning them on your Home screens, and deleting apps you don't want from both your iPad and your computer.

Chapter 8, "Use Your iPod App," shows you how to do virtually everything with your iPad's music player, from syncing to creating playlists to enabling and using Genius. You'll learn how to browse your music by category, and how to play, pause, and skip songs, and use onscreen controls, to name a few.

Chapter 9, "Shop the iTunes Store," shows you how to get what you want from the iTunes Store including music, movies, TV shows, podcasts, audiobooks, and media from iTunes U. You'll learn how to rent and preorder movies too, and how to back up and sync your data to your computer. There's a lot more to iTunes than music!

Chapter 10, "View, Manage, and Share Photos," teaches you how to use the Photos app to...well...view, manage, and share your photos! You can create slideshows, pinch to zoom, skim all your photos quickly, set a photo as wallpaper, assign a photo to a contact, and copy a photo so you can paste it in an email, and lots, lots more. With the optional Camera Connection Kit, you can also upload photos directly to your iPad, skipping the need to sync photos from your computer.

Chapter 11, "View, Manage, and Share Videos," teaches you how to use the Videos app to watch movies you buy and rent from iTunes, watch music videos or podcasts you've acquired, and access media you've downloaded from iTunes U. You'll learn how to use the video controls and how to enable closed captioning too, should your media include closed captions. Of course, there's YouTube, and third-party apps such as Netflix and the ABC Player to explore too.

Chapter 12, "Manage Contacts," shows you how to input, sync, and manage contacts using the Contacts app. You can add contact information that's considered outside the box too, like birthdays and anniversaries. If you add an address, you can even tap the address on the Contact card to open Maps to view the location, or tap an email address to open a new message in Mail. It all works together!

Chapter 13, "Manage Your Schedule," teaches you how to use the Calendar app to sync calendars you already use, add events to a specific calendar, and even create new calendars on your computer and sync those to your iPad. You can create events that repeat, and you can create alerts too. You can even subscribe to others' calendars like those from your favorite sports team, your child's school cafeteria, and more.

Chapter 14, "Use Maps," guides you through the process of searching for locations, getting directions, and finding driving, walking, and even public transportation routes. You can view locations in various views too, including Classic, Satellite, Hybrid, and Terrain, and if a location has a picture for Street View, you can view it with a full 360-degree angle, so you'll know what you're looking for when you get there. You can also save bookmarks, share locations, and mark new locations on maps, as well as find a business's web site and phone number.

Chapter 15, "Use Notes," introduces the Notes app you'll use to create personal notes you can type quickly. There's no need to save a note, because they're all saved by default, and they are easy to delete or share, when applicable.

Chapter 16, "Accessibility," offers guidance on using the available Accessibility options on your iPad, including VoiceOver, Zoom, white-on-black display, mono audio, and others. Other options are introduced, which, while they are not true Accessibility options, will make the iPad easier to use for those who have visual, hearing, or mobility issues.

Chapter 17, "Security," shows you how to secure your iPad with a Passcode Lock, Restrictions, and parental controls. You'll also learn about securing Safari, avoiding phishing scams, and more.

Appendix A, "Settings," lists all the things you can do in settings from enabling and disabling Wi-Fi to signing out of the App Store.

Appendix B, "Troubleshooting," describes some of the most common problems that iPad users encounter and their solutions.

PART I

Introduction to the iPad

1

Set Up and Discover Your iPad

HOW TO...

- Install iTunes on your computer
- Understand sync options
- Perform your first sync (or not)
- Configure default connection options
- Add headphones, microphones, and speakers
- Use the Sleep, Volume, and Rotation Lock buttons
- Navigate the Home screen
- Explore accessories
- Understand the differences between iPad models (Wi-Fi only and Wi-Fi + 3G)
- Choose a data plan for the iPad 3G
- Understand the Status icons
- Create your first backup

Congratulations on your new iPad! If you've ever used an iPhone, or an iPod Touch, you'll recognize that the iPad has similar features (except for its size). Once you've set it up, you'll see the familiar Home screen and applications like Mail and Safari, and you'll find you can touch the screen to interact with it, just as you can with many of Apple's devices. If you've never used an "iDevice," you're in for a real treat. Set it up, turn it on, and hold it in your hands; it's a nice fit! You'll marvel at how a simple touch can manipulate such a fantastic device, and begin to uncover all of the things you can do with it.

In this chapter you'll set up and discover your iPad, including connecting it to your computer and downloading the proper software so you can register, sync, and back up your iPad. You'll learn how to use the external jacks and ports and what you can and cannot connect, how to navigate the Home screen, and how to connect Bluetooth devices, to name a few. You'll learn about some of the accessories you can purchase to make the iPad uniquely yours, and what data plans are available for the Wi-Fi + 3G model. Finally, you'll discover a little bit about some technical stuff too, like what an "accelerometer" is and what the iPad's "OS" consists of.

First Steps

There are a few things you have to do with (and to) your iPad before you can use it. You can't just open the box and turn it on. There aren't any directions in the box (at least we didn't get any), so we will carefully outline the required *first steps* here. They include

- Connecting the iPad to your computer
- Installing iTunes
- Registering your iPad

Connect Your iPad to Your Computer

You have to connect your iPad to a computer to set it up. You can't use your iPad until you set it up, so this is a must-do thing. If you have more than one computer available to you, you should choose the one that contains your music, pictures, data, videos, and other items you want to put on your iPad once it's up and running. The computer you select should be the computer you use most often, and one that is always available to you.

The computer you use will also have to have iTunes, a software program you download and install from Apple. Don't worry, it's free, and it's easy to install. You'll use your computer along with iTunes to sync your data between your computer and your iPad, and to back up your iPad's settings and application data.

Additionally, you will have to have the following in place before you can get started:

- You must have Administrator rights on the computer so you can download and install iTunes to it.
- You must have the ability to obtain an iTunes store account, which includes having a PayPal account or a valid credit card.

- You must use a computer that
  - Has an available USB port
  - Is either a Mac and runs Mac OS X v. 10.5.8 or later, or is a Windows PC and runs Windows 7, Windows Vista, or Windows XP with SP3 or later
  - Is currently connected to the Internet

 Your iPad should arrive fully charged, or at least charged enough to get started. If it isn't charged, refer to the section later in this chapter, "Charge Your iPad."

Now you're ready to connect your iPad to your computer. Because a majority of readers will have a Windows-based PC (Windows XP, Vista, or 7), we'll outline the steps for connecting to a PC here. However, connecting with a Mac is similar.

To connect your iPad to your Windows-based PC:

1. Connect the included white USB cable connector to the iPad and the computer. Plug the larger end into the iPad with the icon facing upward; plug the smaller end into an available USB port on your computer.
2. Press the Home button on the iPad. That's the round button toward the bottom of the iPad.
   a. If you see the iTunes icon, iTunes is not installed on your computer. Install iTunes as outlined in the next section.
   b. If iTunes is installed on the computer, the iPad Home screen will appear. Skip the next section, "Install iTunes," and go directly to "Register Your iPad."

 The iPad can be associated with only one computer at a time. Attempting to plug the iPad into a different computer than the one used for setup could result in the loss of data.

Install iTunes

If iTunes is not yet installed on your computer, you'll have to install it. You'll also need an iTunes Store account. You'll use the iTunes program (which will soon be on your computer) to manage and sync data between your computer and your iPad. Some things you may opt to sync are your media (including music, videos, movies, pictures, music videos, TV shows, podcasts, and so on), and contacts, calendar appointments, and other data. You'll also need iTunes on your computer to back up and restore your iPad. If you already have and use a current version of iTunes and have an iTunes account that you use with another iDevice such as an iPod or iPhone, you can skip this section, although you may want to check iTunes for updates.

Chapter 9 shows you how to obtain media from the iTunes store using the iTunes app installed on your iPad.

To download, install, and set up iTunes and obtain an iTunes Store account on a Windows-based PC (the steps for a Mac are similar but not exactly the same), follow these steps:

1. From your computer, visit www.apple.com/itunes/download.
2. Verify whether you want to leave the two options selected to receive email notifications from Apple (and if so, input your email address). If you do not want to receive email from Apple, deselect these items.
3. Click Download Now, shown in Figure 1-1.
4. Click Run, and when the download has completed, click Run again.
5. Click Next to get started.
6. Click I Accept the Terms in This License Agreement, and click Next.
7. Configure installation options, including whether or not you want a shortcut to iTunes placed on your Desktop and to use iTunes as the default player for audio files. Do not change the location of the iTunes folder unless you know what you're doing!
8. Click Install. You may have to input administrator credentials or otherwise allow the installation on your PC.
9. Leave Open iTunes After the Installer Exits selected. Click Finish.
10. When iTunes starts, you'll be prompted to agree to more terms of service. Click Agree.
11. When prompted to create an account, click Continue (and if you aren't prompted, click Store and Create Account).

Download iTunes Now

iTunes 9.1.1 for Windows XP, Vista or Windows 7

☑ Email me New on iTunes and special iTunes offers.

☑ Keep me up to date with Apple news, software updates, and the latest information on products and services.

Apple Customer Privacy Policy

Email Address

Download Now ⊙

FIGURE 1-1 Click Download Now to start the download process.

12. Tick I Have Read and Agree to the iTunes Terms and Conditions (and you may actually want to read these); click Continue.
13. Click Next to begin the iTunes setup.
14. If you want iTunes to find and incorporate your music files, leave the default options selected, shown in Figure 1-2. Click Next.
15. If you want iTunes to keep your media folder organized, click Yes, keep my iTunes folder organized. Otherwise, click No, I'll Change the File and Folder Names Myself. (We opted for Yes.)
16. Click Finish. Wait while iTunes adds your media files.
17. Click Done.

Register Your iPad

After iTunes is installed on your computer, you can connect your iPad. When you touch the Home button (that's the round button on the iPad itself in the center of the bottom of the iPad), the Home screen will appear. Use your finger to move the slide to the right to unlock the iPad.

The first time you unlock your iPad, you'll see a helpful hint about editing the Home screen icons. You can tap Dismiss to make this tip disappear.

Now, take a look at iTunes on your computer. You'll notice a prompt to register your iPad, shown in Figure 1-3.

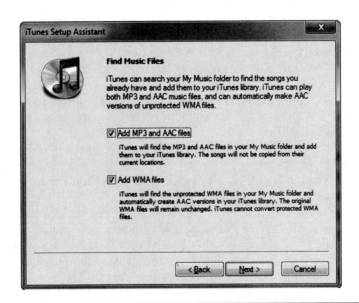

FIGURE 1-2   You have to set up iTunes after installation, and you should let iTunes find your existing music files.

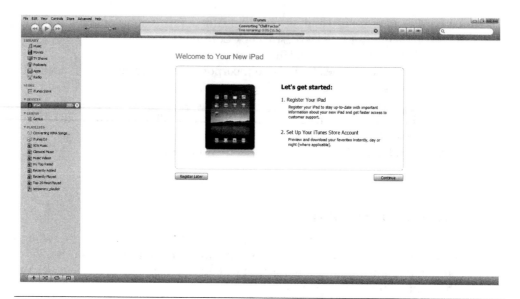

FIGURE 1-3   You'll want to register your iPad right away.

To register your iPad and to create a new iTunes Store Account (Apple ID):

1. With your iPad connected to your computer, at the iTunes Welcome page, click Continue. See Figure 1-3.
2. Tick I Have Read and Agree to the iPad Software License Agreement, and click Continue. (You can read this if you like.)
3. On the iTunes Account (Apple ID) page, either log in with an existing Apple ID or tick I Do Not Have an Apple ID. Click Continue.
4. If you do not have an Apple ID, work through the steps to create one. You'll also have to input a form of payment for future purchases. Click Continue when finished.
5. At the Register Your iPad page, fill in the required information. Click Submit when finished.
6. If prompted to try MobileMe, click Not Now. You'll learn about MobileMe later in this book.
7. On the Set Up iPad page, type a name for your iPad. On that same page decide how you'd like to sync your music, photos, and applications. If you're unsure if you want to sync your iPad with every song and photo on your computer, deselect all three. You'll learn to set up syncing in the next section, and you can choose then exactly what you want to sync and what you do not.
8. Click Done.
9. The iPad's screen will come on, and it will show that syncing is in progress. If you have not selected anything to sync, it won't take it long to complete.
10. To make sure you have the latest software on your iPad, go to iTunes on your computer, and from the Summary tab, click Check for Update. See Figure 1-4.

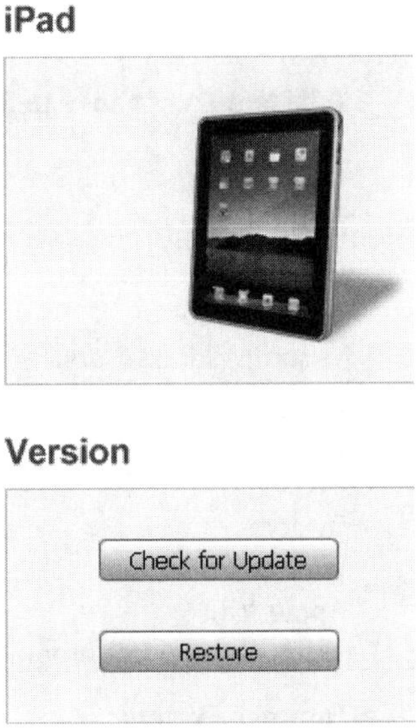

iPad

Version

[Check for Update]

[Restore]

FIGURE 1-4   Make sure your iPad is updated with the latest software.

Note   If you already have an iTunes account that has not yet been authorized on the computer you're using, in iTunes, click Store, and click Authorize Computer.

Set Up Syncing and Perform Your First Sync

With your iPad connected and registered, and with iTunes open, you can now begin to configure how you'd like syncing to occur between your computer and iTunes. Syncing, at this particular moment anyway, is the process of copying data from your computer to your iPad, so that the data, pictures, music, movies, calendar appointments, contacts, and the like are on both your computer and your iPad. Once data has been copied to your iPad, any changes that occur later, either on your iPad or on your computer, will be synced back to your PC and the reverse, the next time you connect. You can configure syncing now or later, but we suggest you set up syncing now.

Tip   If you have duplicate songs in your Music folder, duplicate songs will be copied to your iPad. If you have duplicate contacts in your contact list, the same holds true. It's best to clean up your computer before syncing your iPad.

You can opt to sync certain types of data automatically, manually, or not at all. There are lots of options. Several of these options have their own tabs in iTunes, while a few are listed together under one tab. (For instance, the Info tab offers a place to sync, or not sync, contacts, calendars, mail accounts, and the like). Table 1-1 summarizes the options.

TABLE 1-1   iTunes Tabs and Options

iTunes Tab	Data You Can Choose to Sync If Desired
Info	
Contacts from:	Outlook Google Contacts Windows Contacts Yahoo! Address Book
Calendars from:	Outlook Third-party calendars as applicable
Mail accounts from:	Outlook Windows Mail Apple Mail Third-party email programs as applicable
Bookmarks (Favorites) from:	Internet Explorer Safari Third-party web browsers as applicable
Notes from:	Outlook Third-party applications if applicable You can also replace information already on your iPad including contacts, calendars, mail accounts, bookmarks, and notes.
Apps	All apps or only apps you handpick
Music	Your entire music library Only the songs you select or only selected music from artists, playlists, and genres Music videos Voice memos
Movies	All movies (your entire movie library) Only movies you select or the most recent movies on your computer
TV Shows	Sync all TV shows Sync only TV shows you've yet to watch, most recent, or by other criteria
Podcasts	Sync all podcasts Sync only podcasts you've yet to hear, most recent, or by other criteria
iTunes U	Sync all iTunes U collections Sync only collections you've yet to hear, most recent, or by other criteria

TABLE 1-1   iTunes Tabs and Options *(continued)*

iTunes Tab	Data You Can Choose to Sync If Desired
Books	Sync all books Sync selected books Sync all audiobooks Sync selected audiobooks
Photos	Sync all photos from a specific folder Sync only selected picture folders Include (or not) videos in those folders

 Note that many of these options in the Info tab are different on a Mac computer and some vary on a PC depending on what software you have installed.

After you've decided what you'd like to sync and how, configure those options in iTunes:

1. Open iTunes on your computer.
2. Connect your iPad to your computer.
3. In the left pane, click to select your iPad, as shown in the following illustration.

4. Next, you'll click each tab to configure sync options. Most tabs work similarly, so we'll start with the Music tab:
   a. Click the Music tab.
   b. Tick Sync Music.
   c. Choose syncing options. If you opt to sync only selected playlists, artists, and genres, more options will appear, where you can handpick the music to sync.
5. Click the Photos tab.
   a. Click Sync Photos From.
   b. Note the default picture folder. In Windows, it's the Pictures folder, but you can select a different folder using the arrows.
   c. To select only certain picture folders, tick Selected Folders. You'll see something similar to what's shown in Figure 1-5.
6. Repeat these steps to configure syncing options for the rest of the tabs.
7. When finished, click Apply.
8. If your iPad is still connected to your computer, the sync will begin immediately. If the iPad is not connected, syncing will occur the next time you connect it.

| Summary | Info | Apps | Music | Movies | TV Shows | Podcasts | iTunes U | Books | **Photos** |

☑ **Sync Photos from:** | My Pictures ▾ |

○ All folders
◉ Selected folders
☐ Include videos

Folders:

☐ 📁 BlackBerry	
☑ 📁 Cats	124
☐ 📁 Cosmo's Camera Card	
☐ 📁 Cosmo Family	
☐ 📁 Friends	
☑ 📁 Houses	157
☐ 📁 iPad 1	
☑ 📁 Jennifer and my family	145
☑ 📁 Joli	18
☑ 📁 Mom and Dad	16
☐ 📁 My Favorites	
☐ 📁 ReadyPyrographics	
☐ 📁 T-Shirts for eBay	
☑ 📁 UK	73
☑ 📁 Vacations	68
☐ 📁 Wi Fi Screenshots	

FIGURE 1-5 You can select exactly the folders you want and no others.

Tip

Once syncing is set up, syncing will occur automatically each time you connect your iPad to your computer.

Note

You can prevent syncing from automatically occurring between a computer and an iPad. The configuration change can be made in the Preferences dialog box from iTunes. On a Mac, in iTunes, click iTunes, and then Preferences; on a PC, in iTunes, click Edit, and then Preferences. In the Preferences dialog box, tick the following option: Prevent iPods, iPhones, and iPads from Syncing Automatically. If you ever decide to sync data, you can do so manually.

Charge Your iPad

Your iPad has a built-in battery that has to be charged to use it. To charge it, you connect the USB dock connector and a power adapter that shipped with it, and let it sit for a while to get a full charge. A charge should last a full day (10 hours or so) if you use it constantly, or for a month if you rarely use it. It's okay to keep the iPad connected to the charger when you aren't using it. It'll charge when it needs to and be ready when you need it. Understand, though, that a rechargeable battery's life is defined by how many times it is charged, and your iPad's battery won't last forever. That said, I'll add a few tips later to help you get the most from your battery.

To charge your iPad:

1. Locate the charging port on the outside of the iPad. It's a 30-pin connection and is located at the bottom of your iPad.
2. Locate the dock connector that came with the iPad and connect it to the adapter.
3. Plug the adapter into a wall outlet.

To get the most from your battery while at the same time extending the battery's life:

- If you know you won't be using your iPad for a while, turn it completely off by holding down the screen lock button until a red Power Off slider appears. Move the slider to turn off the device.
- Lower the screen brightness by opening the Settings app and selecting the Brightness and Wallpaper menu option.

Note   For more information on the Settings app and available options, refer to Appendix A.

- When you aren't using Wi-Fi and/or Bluetooth, turn those features off. You can access these settings in the Settings app, under Wi-Fi for Wi-Fi settings, and General for Bluetooth.
- Turn off Push notifications. Again, look to the Settings app under Mail, Contacts, Calendars.

Explore the Hardware

Your iPad is registered and ready to use, congratulations! So let's get going. First things first, though; spend a minute or two exploring the outside of your iPad before you start touching and tapping items on the Home screen, because you may want to connect something or adjust the volume while you explore.

There are several things on the outside of your iPad. There's a docking port that allows you to charge your iPad or connect it to your computer, a jack to connect headphones, a switch to lock the screen rotation, a Volume Rocker to turn the volume up and down, and a sleep button that also works to power the iPad on and off.

Add Headphones or Speakers

Your iPad has the required port for connecting generic (non-proprietary) headphones and external speakers, neither of which are included with the iPad. You'll likely use headphones when listening to music, an audiobook, or when on an airplane; you might opt for a headset with an integrated microphone when using Skype or voice-chatting with contacts using another medium; and you can use external speakers when watching a video (although the speaker built into the iPad is pretty good). You'll use speakers when watching a movie or video, or listening to music or podcasts.

Note Although the iPad comes with a powerful speaker with rich, full, sound, external speakers can improve on this. As you might guess, two or four (or more) speakers are better than one. However, you'll lose the portability when you opt for this type of setup.

Carefully turn your iPad in all directions and look for the following ports and features:

- **Built-in speaker** The speaker is located at the bottom of the iPad, on the right side.
- **Audio** A 3.5mm stereo headphone jack that accepts generic headphones and headsets is located at the top of the iPad on the left.
- **Microphone** The pinhole microphone is located on the top of the iPad next to the headphone and speaker jack.
- **Dock Connector** The dock connector is located on the bottom of the iPad, in the center. This is where you connect accessories, such as Apple's Keyboard dock, docking stations, the Camera Connection Kit (optional), and other devices.
- **Screen Rotation Lock** This lock is located on the right side of the iPad near the top.
- **Volume** The volume rocker is located on the right side of the iPad underneath the Screen Rotation Lock.
- **Sleep/Wake** The Sleep/Wake button is located on the top of the iPad on the right. You can use this button to turn off and on the iPad as well.

Locate and Use the Sleep and Volume Buttons

Look straight at the iPad Home screen and locate the physical Sleep/Wake button on the top-right corner of the device. It's at the top on the thinnest part of the iPad, the part that is facing the ceiling as you hold it in portrait view. Now, locate the Volume Rocker on the right side, also near the top.

Use the Sleep/Wake button to lock your iPad when you aren't using it, to prevent it from waking up when you touch it. While sleeping, you can still listen to music and use the volume buttons. To wake the iPad, press the Sleep/Wake button and the Home button to bring up the unlock screen. Press and hold the Sleep/Wake button to shut the iPad completely off and turn it on again.

FIGURE 1-6   You'll see this icon on the screen when you increase or decrease the volume.

 If you haven't used the iPad for a few minutes, it'll lock itself automatically. You can lengthen or shorten the AutoLock duration by opening the Settings app, tapping General, and tapping the AutoLock option. For more information, refer to Appendix A.

The Sleep/Wake button can also be used to put the iPad to sleep or to wake it up. When the iPad is asleep, it uses minimal battery power, and is ready to use when you press the Sleep/Wake button again. In this state, the iPad can hold its charge for a long time, so it's okay to use this mode as often as you like. You'll put the iPad to sleep when you want to blacken the screen and use the device again in the near future. In contrast, you'll completely power off the iPad when you know you won't be using it for a few days, or if you intend to pack it for travel.

The Volume Rocker is used as you might guess; you press and hold the top part to increase the volume and the bottom part to decrease the volume. To quickly mute the iPad, you simply hold the Volume Rocker's bottom button until the device is silent. You'll see an icon on the screen when you press the Volume Rocker. See Figure 1-6.

Tip   You can configure the maximum volume in Settings, under iPod.

Explore the Home Screen

The Home screen is what you see when you turn on your iPad, and it gives you one-tap access to everything that's available on it. In Chapter 2 you'll learn how to personalize this screen by moving the icons, and how to add or remove icons to make the iPad uniquely yours. For now though, you'll want to explore what's on the Home screen already, and learn to navigate around in it. The Home screen icons are shown in Figure 1-7.

FIGURE 1-7   The Home screen comes with preconfigured icons for Apple's own apps.

These are the icons you'll see on the Home screen when you first turn it on:

- **Calendar**   A fully functional calendar that allows you to create and manage events; configure reminders for events; and view the calendar by day, month, and lists of events. You can also access calendars you sync from third-party applications, like Microsoft Office Outlook.
- **Contacts**   An application you use to manage the contacts you create or add. You can easily add new or edit existing contacts and share contact information with others.
- **Notes**   An application that allows you to take notes easily. The Notes app looks like a yellow lined steno pad that allows you to create notes with a virtual keyboard, and then email them, delete them, or access them later.
- **Maps**   A full-fledged application for getting directions to and from local restaurants or points of interest, your contact's physical addresses, your current position (where you are), and for showing traffic, satellite views, directions, and more.
- **Videos**   An option for managing the videos you own, and watching videos you get from iTunes.

- **YouTube**   An application that allows you to quickly view video content from YouTube, watch the most popular videos of the day, and search for videos you want to view. With the YouTube app, you can also mark your favorite videos so you can access them later or view similar videos easily.
- **iTunes**   An application that allows you to preview and purchase music and media on your iPad. (As with some of the other apps, you need to be online to access the iTunes Store.)
- **App Store**   The App Store is where you purchase and download apps, including those that enable you to make social networking easier, manage your finances, obtain additional information about products you plan to buy, play games, share data, and more. Think of anything you'd like to do with your iPad; there's likely an app for that!
- **Settings**   An application that enables you to turn on and off Wi-Fi; change sounds, brightness, and wallpaper; configure email, contacts, and calendar options; change Safari defaults; change iPod defaults; and more. The Settings options are detailed throughout this book and in Appendix A.

There are also four icons located across the bottom of the screen:

- **Safari**   A web browser for surfing the Internet. With it you can create bookmarks, set a home page, and perform common tasks associated with the Internet.
- **Mail**   The email client included with the iPad. With Mail, you can send and receive email, delete, move, and manage email, and perform common tasks associated with emailing.
- **Photos**   An application for viewing and managing photos. With Photos, you can view slideshows, view photos individually, organize your photos, and even upload photos from a digital camera or media card (provided you purchase the Apple Camera Connection Kit).
- **iPod**   A complete music player that enables you to play and manage music. You can create playlists of your favorite songs or access playlists that have been synced from your home computer, such as Most Played.

Navigate the Home Screen

Navigation isn't difficult; just touch any icon on the screen to open it. To return to the Home screen, press the Home button. The Home button is the small button on the iPad itself, located on the bottom center of the device, and has a rounded rectangle on it. That's it. It's what you do after you open an application that can change from app to app. Go ahead, touch any icon on the screen to open it, and tap the Home button to return to the Home screen.

You'll probably notice quickly that applications respond differently from each other, once opened. For instance, if you open the Notes app (included with your iPad), you touch once to bring up the keyboard, and use it to create your note, shown in Figure 1-8. Touch the keyboard icon on the virtual keyboard to make the keyboard disappear, and then use your finger to share the note, delete it, or otherwise manage it. It won't take long for you to get the hang of it.

FIGURE 1-8   The Notes app is one of the easiest apps to use.

Click the Home button to return to the Home screen, if you haven't already, and this time click Photos. If you synced photos earlier in this chapter, they will appear here. Continue experimenting as desired, noting that some apps require you to connect to the Internet to use them (Maps, YouTube, iTunes, the App Store, Safari, and Mail).

Learn Touch Techniques

There's more to navigating the icons and applications besides touching an area of the screen. You can "flick" up or down to scroll up and down in a screen, for instance. You can flick left and right to move between pages in an iBook. You can "pinch" (spread a finger and thumb outward or inward) to zoom in and zoom out on a photo, web page, email or other item. You can "tap" to open a stack of photos in the Photo application, and you can "double-tap" to switch between full-screen and wide-screen mode in the Video application or to zoom in on something. You can also *tap and hold* to select items, and *tap and drag* to move icons and data.

 Tap and touch are used often in this book and are generally exchangeable terms.

How to... **Tap and Touch**

The best way to get to know your iPad is to explore it. Perform these steps to learn how to use the touch techniques introduced in this section:

1. Touch the Photos icon to open Photos. If you have photos, you can
   a. Double-tap one to make it full screen.
   b. Double-tap again to zoom in.
   c. Use a pinching motion with your thumb and forefinger by pulling them together on the photo to make the photo small again.
2. Touch and hold an app icon on the Home screen for a few seconds. Once the icons begin to "jiggle," you can
   a. Drag to rearrange the icons on the screen.
   b. Press the Home button to stop the icons from "jiggling" and accept the new arrangement.
3. Touch and hold an app icon again to enable the "jiggle" mode, and then
   a. Drag to move an icon to the right until you have moved it "off" the screen.
   b. A new, blank screen will appear. Drop the icon.
   c. Click the Home button when finished.
   d. To visit additional Home screens, flick left or right.
4. Flick right to open the Spotlight Search screen.
5. Tap any icon to open the app associated with it; tap the Home screen to close the app.

Understand the iPhone OS

The iPad uses the iPhone OS. Although the iPad was initially touted as a tablet *computer*, it simply isn't. A tablet computer should, in the minds of most experts at least, run a full-fledged operating system, like the one used in an Apple Mac computer or a Windows-based PC and run multiple applications at once. A full-fledged operating system allows the user to manipulate the computer at the disk level, restructure the files and folders stored on it (if desired), and install compatible hardware and their drivers, as well as any compatible software. You can't do much of that with the iPad; you can't manipulate the file structure, for instance, or install device drivers for hardware that may be connectable physically, but will not work.

Your iPad does have an operating system, though. While it does not run any version of the Mac OS X software that a Mac computer would run, it does run an OS. It runs a version of the iPhone's operating system. This operating system is locked down and heavily restricted; it can't be modified in the way you'd modify a computer, and it can't fulfill many of the specialized tasks we ask of computers. So understand that when you want to do something with your iPad, like manage music, videos, or photos, you'll need to rely on what Apple provides, at first at least, and then you can move on to more fully featured apps as you gain experience with the iPad.

When you start to explore apps, note that a few notable apps can really improve what you can do with your iPad, like iWork's Numbers, Keynote, and Pages, and can help you be more productive. iBooks, another app, enables you to turn your iPad into a digital book reader, complete with a built-in store for purchasing books. And Netflix enables you to watch movies on demand if you have a Netflix subscription.

 Earlier in this chapter you learned a little about the applications located on the Home screen, including but not limited to Maps, Videos, and Contacts. There are additional features, though, like Spotlight for searching for data. As you work through this book, you'll learn about these things and others.

Explore and Purchase Accessories

Your iPad came in a box with a USB adapter, and a power adapter. As you may know already, though, there are other Apple accessories you can purchase, including a Camera Connection Kit, Keyboard Dock, and a Standard Dock. In this last section, you'll learn about some of the additional accessories you can obtain, and what to look for when you do.

When you get a chance, visit www.apple.com and click the Store tab. There, you can take a look at all of the accessories available from Apple. Take a look at each of the following while at the store. You may find something you can't live without:

- Apple's wireless Bluetooth keyboard
- Video adapters for an external monitor or projector
- Carrying case that also serves as a stand
- Bluetooth-compatible speakers
- Camera Connection Kit
- Apple's in-ear headphones with compatible remote

Connect a USB Component

There's no USB port on the iPad. There is a USB Camera Connection Kit you can purchase, though, which allows you to connect a USB digital camera to your iPad. If you can connect a USB digital camera, physically at least, you may also think that you can

 iWork Is Available for Your iPad

Apple's popular iWork suite of productivity applications is also available for your iPad. iWork apps include special editions of Keynote, Pages, and Numbers, software you can use to create and manage presentations, spreadsheets, and documents. The three apps are priced individually at $9.99 each, and can be downloaded directly through the iPad's App Store or through iTunes on your home computer.

also connect a USB printer, USB scanner, USB mouse, or any other USB device. That's not the case at the moment, although you never know what the future holds.

Let's start with something we know will work, and connect a digital camera using the USB Camera Connection Kit. With that done, you can experiment with other USB devices.

To use the USB Camera Connection Kit to connect a USB digital camera:

1. Purchase the USB Camera Connection Kit from any Apple store, authorized reseller, or third party.
2. Connect the adapter to the 30-pin connection at the bottom of your iPad.
3. Using the camera's USB cable, connect the camera to the new hardware, or if you opt to use the Media Card Reader adapter instead, insert a media card. Turn on the camera, if applicable.
4. Click the Home button and move the slider to unlock the iPad, if necessary.
5. Note that the pictures appear automatically on your screen.
6. To select images, tap them one time. Note that you can choose to import all of the pictures if desired. See Figure 1-9.
7. After selecting the images, click Import. You can then select Import All or Import Selected.

FIGURE 1-9 It's easy to import images using the optional Camera Connection Kit.

8. Wait while the import process completes.
9. When the import process is complete, you can opt to delete or keep the images on your card.

 Images imported directly to the iPad can be transferred back to your computer when you sync.

Connect a Bluetooth Device

A compatible Bluetooth device is a wireless device you can use with your iPad, such as a wireless headset, wireless speakers, or wireless keyboard. Because these devices are wireless, connecting them requires a little more effort than connecting devices that simply plug in (like headphones). Specifically, you have to "pair" the device with the iPad, and it is this process of pairing that allows the iPad to recognize and use the device. Pairing also allows the device and the iPad to agree on a Bluetooth frequency, so that they can communicate effectively without "crossing signals" with any other Bluetooth devices you may have installed. To connect a new Bluetooth device the first time (and you shouldn't have to repeat these steps):

1. Turn on your new Bluetooth device, insert batteries, or perform any other step to power the device.
2. Follow the directions for the device to make it discoverable.
3. Locate and tap the Settings icon on the Home screen.
4. Tap General.
5. Tap Bluetooth and move the slider to On.
6. Wait while the iPad searches for Bluetooth devices.
7. When it finds the device, type the device's passkey or PIN when prompted.
8. To turn off Bluetooth, again click Settings, then General, then Bluetooth. Move the virtual switch into the off position.

Note If you're in the market for a Bluetooth device, make sure it's iPad compatible; not all devices will be.

Understand Wi-Fi and Wi-Fi + 3G iPad Models

iPads come in two models, each with varying amounts of internal memory. There's a Wi-Fi only model and a Wi-Fi + 3G model. The Wi-Fi only model enables you to get online via wireless routers, including those found in home and work networks and free Wi-Fi hotspots. Wi-Fi only models don't allow you to sign up for a data plan from AT&T so that you can have additional Internet access using an integrated cellular connection. Thus, although you can access free Wi-Fi hotspots in coffee shops, hotel lobbies, libraries, pubs, gyms, and the like with your Wi-Fi only iPad, if you're away from these types of networks you won't be able to get online. This limits your ability to use the iPad on the go. When you're within range of a Wi-Fi network and you attempt to access the Internet, you'll be prompted to join the network, as shown in Figure 1-10.

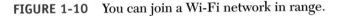

FIGURE 1-10   You can join a Wi-Fi network in range.

The Wi-Fi + 3G model allows you to access the Internet over a conventional Wi-Fi connection, but also gives you the option of using AT&T's prepaid Internet data service, which works over a 3G cellular network. This means that when you're travelling in a car, commuting on a bus, or away from a Wi-Fi network, you can get online using AT&T's 3G cellular network (provided you have 3G coverage in your area). Additionally, with Wi-Fi + 3G, you'll be able to use Assisted GPS (Global Positioning System) thanks to an integrated chipset not included on Wi-Fi only models. Of course, you'll have to pay for a monthly data plan to make this happen. A $14.99 plan offers a limit of 250MB each month, while a $29.99 plan gives you unlimited data. The great thing about these particular plans is that you can turn them on and off at will. This means you can turn on 3G service when you leave on vacation, and turn it off when you get home.

Note There are, of course, downsides to 3G service through AT&T. You can't get access everywhere, and coverage can be spotty. When 3G is enabled, you'll use quite a bit of battery life, too. And don't forget that a 3G model costs $130 more than a Wi-Fi only model. However, to get the most from your iPad, you really do need to be connected to the Internet most of the time.

Choose a Data Plan for Your Wi-Fi + 3G iPad

To get the most from your iPad, you really need always-on Internet access. You'll need Internet access to get your email, to use Maps to get directions, and to surf the web. To get Internet access, you have two options. The first option is to access the Internet via your wireless home and work networks and free Wi-Fi hotspots. You can do this on all models of the iPad. While this option isn't necessarily convenient (you may have to trek to your local coffee shop to get online), it is probably something you're already paying for, or maybe it's free.

 Tip Perform a Google search for free Wi-Fi hotspots in your area and you will likely find them in nearby hotel lobbies, gyms, libraries, and coffee shops.

You can also sign up and pay for a *data plan* so you can have Internet access from AT&T's 3G cellular network. If you opt for a paid data plan, you have two choices. The data plan you choose depends on how much time you plan to spend on the Internet, and what you plan to do while there. Note that to sign up for a data plan you must have a Wi-Fi + 3G model.

The first time you try to access the Internet and you aren't connected to a Wi-Fi network, you'll be prompted to consider a cellular data plan. If you choose Now, you can sign up right from your iPad. See Figure 1-11.

There are two plans available from AT&T:

- $14.99 a month for 250MB of data
- $29.99 a month for unlimited data

Both of these plans can be activated from your iPad (no computer or phone call required), do not require a contract (most cell phone data plans require two years), and also offer free Internet access at any of the thousands of AT&T Wi-Fi hotspots. All plans allow you to enable and disable the plan at will without incurring penalties. So, how do you decide which plan is right for you?

If you have a Wi-Fi + 3G iPad model and a data plan, you can connect to the Internet the same way a cell phone does, which means you can get Internet access even if no Wi-Fi service is available.

If you only want to check email, read online newspapers and blogs, and occasionally watch a video from YouTube, you might be able to get away with the first option, 250MB. Many experts refer to this plan as "your mother's plan." Having 250MB of data will allow you to access the Internet, but with limited access. If you're unsure what 250MB is, consider this: One email with a large attachment can be somewhere around 2MB; a single song can be 3 to 4MB, and a video can be 8 to 10MB (or more). An hour of web browsing consumes about 40MB of data; watching a single high-definition video can consume upwards of 300MB. As you can see, this type of data usage can add up pretty quickly. Note that when you connect to the Internet on your iPad from a home Wi-Fi network or from a free AT&T Wi-Fi hotspot, you will not be charged for your data usage, though, so if you can work this into your surfing regimen, this plan may work.

FIGURE 1-11   You can sign up for a data plan right from your iPad.

AT&T will warn you when you're getting close to your monthly limit, and offer an available upgrade to unlimited service.

You can also opt for the unlimited plan. That's just what you'd think, unlimited Internet access all the time. You don't have to worry about Wi-Fi hotspots or home networks. Just pay your monthly fees and you're good to go. I am of the opinion that this is the plan that will suit most iPad users.

Understand the Built-in Sensors

Your iPad came with various sensors to help it perform tasks. The accelerometer, for instance, can sense when you turn the iPad from landscape to portrait view, and change the view of what's on the screen accordingly. The accelerometer, because it senses and understands the movement of the device, also enhances game play. You can move the iPad to simulate a movement, such as driving really fast around a sharp curve, and the game will respond accordingly.

There are other sensors you might not think too much about, but they are there. There's a sensor that identifies the current lighting, be it a sunny sky or a dark tunnel, and then adjusts the brightness of the screen to accommodate. And of course, Multi-Touch is a sensor. *Multi-Touch* technology is what enables you to tap or touch the iPad and have it respond.

GPS (Global Positioning System) is another sensor. With it, the iPad can access information from earth-orbiting satellites to find your current location or the location of another place (like a restaurant or library). Only the iPad 3G models have true GPS capability, due to the use of an integrated chip. Wi-Fi models of the iPad can also be used to provide a ballpark guess of your location by gathering information on nearby Wi-Fi hotspots.

Your iPad also has a built-in digital compass. With it you can discover your direction, but the best part of the digital compass is that it automatically repositions maps to match the direction you're facing.

Understand the Status Icons

While you're using your iPad, various status icons will appear and disappear on the Home screen. The icons tell you how you are connected to the Internet, how much battery life you have left, and a few other things, all of which are summarized in Table 1-2.

Did You Know?

There's an iPad User Guide on Your iPad

To view the iPad User Guide, tap Safari, tap the Bookmarks icon, and then tap the iPad User Guide bookmark. While viewing the guide, you can also tap Add to Home Screen to make the guide easily accessible. You can even view the guide in other languages.

TABLE 1-2 Status Icons on the iPad

Status Icon	Meaning
Airplane Mode	Shows that Airplane Mode is enabled. When this mode is enabled, you can't access the Internet or use Bluetooth devices. This option is only available on the Wi-Fi + 3G iPad models.
3G	Shows that your carrier's 3G network is available and is currently being used to connect to the Internet. This option is only available on the Wi-Fi + 3G iPad models.
EDGE	Shows that your carrier's EDGE network is available and is currently being used to connect to the Internet. This is available on Wi-Fi + 3G iPad models.
GPRS	Shows that your carrier's GPRS network is available and is currently being used to connect to the Internet. This is available on Wi-Fi + 3G iPad models.
Wi-Fi	Shows that your iPad is connected to the Internet via Wi-Fi. The more bars, the stronger the connection.
Activity	Shows that there is activity. The activity can be network activity or app activity.
VPN	Shows that you are connected to a VPN (virtual private network). Generally, this is a network you use in an enterprise at work.
Lock	Shows that the iPad is locked.
Screen Rotation Lock	Shows that the screen's orientation is locked.
Play	Shows that something is playing, perhaps a song, audiobook, or podcast.
Bluetooth	Shows the status of a Bluetooth connection. If the icon is white, Bluetooth is enabled and a device is connected. If the icon is gray, Bluetooth is enabled but no device is connected. If the icon is not showing, Bluetooth is not enabled.
Battery	Shows the status of the battery and/or its charging status.

Connect and Create Your First Backup

If you've worked through this chapter from beginning to end, you now have some data on your iPad. If your iPad is still connected to your computer, disconnect it. Now, reconnect it. Your iPad will sync automatically (if that's what you've configured) and a backup will begin automatically as well, as shown in the following illustration.

2

iPad Basics

HOW TO...

- Reposition icons on the Home screen
- Move icons off the Home screen
- Delete icons for third-party apps
- Change the wallpaper
- Turn on Wi-Fi
- Locate and connect to a free, public Wi-Fi hotspot
- Connect to a private network
- Access the Internet using 3G
- Change your data plan
- Use Spotlight Search
- Type effectively
- Restore your iPad to its previous settings

You're eager to get started with your iPad by making it uniquely yours with new wallpaper, rearranging the icons to meet your needs, getting online, learning to type, and finding stuff! After you've worked through the exercises in this chapter, you'll be well on your way to understanding how to navigate all parts of your iPad. You can then use this knowledge to work through the rest of the book in any order you like.

 Chapters 1 and 2 should be read in sequential order. After you've finished Chapter 2, feel free to skip around.

Personalize the Home Screen

The Home screen on your iPad has several icons, all placed in a specific order out of the box, and a beautiful picture of a lake, mountains, and sky set as its wallpaper. You can change just about everything about this, though, by repositioning apps on the Home screen or moving apps to another screen (and out of your way), deleting icons for third-party apps you've decided you don't need or like, and by replacing the wallpaper with something else.

Manage Icons

Just because the icons are positioned a certain way when you unpacked your iPad doesn't mean they have to stay that way! If you aren't perfectly happy with the order of the icons on the Home screen, you can do a little tweaking. If you write a lot of notes, for instance, you can put the Notes app in the top-left corner of the Home screen for easy access; if you use Maps quite a bit, you can opt to put the Maps app at the bottom of the screen, and replace one of the four there currently or add it to them (you can have up to six); if you rarely access the Contacts app, you can move it off the main Home screen to a secondary screen with other apps you rarely use so that it's not in your way.

Tip Yes, you can have multiple Home screens! You access any additional Home screens you create by flicking your finger to the left or right while on a Home screen.

If you read Chapter 1, you may have already tried the tap-hold-and-drag technique for repositioning icons, but we'll go over it here in more detail, just to make sure it's clear. Because there's a lot you can do with hiding, moving, and repositioning icons, there are four scenarios we'll cover:

- You want to reposition the icons on the Home screen.
- You want to change something about the four icons that appear across the bottom of the screen.
- You want to hide icons by moving them to a secondary Home screen.
- You want to delete an icon for an app you've downloaded and installed.

To reposition an icon on the Home screen:

1. On the Home screen, touch and hold your finger on any icon.
2. Once the icons all start "wiggling," drag any icon to any area of the Home screen to move it there. See Figure 2-1.
3. Repeat Step 2 as often as desired, and then click the Home button to set the icons.

FIGURE 2-1   To reposition the icons on the Home screen, tap, hold, and drag.

To change which four icons appear across the bottom of the screen:

1. On the Home screen, touch and hold your finger on any icon.
2. Once the icons all start "wiggling," drag one icon from the lower area of the screen to the upper area. Repeat if desired.
3. From the upper area of the Home screen, drag an icon to the bottom area to add it there. Repeat as desired. You can have up to six icons on the bottom of the screen.
4. Click the Home button to set the icons.

To hide icons by moving them to a secondary Home screen:

1. On the Home screen, touch and hold your finger on any icon.
2. Once the icons all start "wiggling," flick any icon to the far right of the screen, as if you were trying to flick it off the iPad.
3. A new screen will appear, where you can "drop" the icon.
4. Flick left to return to the main Home screen, and repeat as desired. You can have multiple Home screens.

You can also delete icons for third-party apps you've acquired. When you delete the icon, the app is also removed from your iPad (and thus frees up space on your iPad for other things). Deleting icons and their apps from your iPad can help you keep it uncluttered and organized. It's important to note that the iTunes program on your computer will retain copies of apps you've acquired, including those downloaded directly on the iPad, which get automatically transferred to your iTunes collection when you sync your iPad. If you ever want to reinstall an app you've deleted on your iPad, connect your iPad to your computer, and in iTunes under the App tab, select the app to sync.

To remove an icon for a third-party app you've downloaded and installed:

1. On the screen that shows the third-party app, touch and hold your finger on any icon.
2. Once the icons all start "wiggling," look for any icon that offers a little X on it. These are the only icons you can delete.
3. Touch the X on the app to delete, and when prompted to delete it, touch Delete. See Figure 2-2.
4. Repeat Steps 2 and 3 as often as desired, and then click the Home button to set them.

Change the Wallpaper

As noted earlier, the picture on the Home screen is called the wallpaper. You can change the wallpaper to any picture you can get onto your iPad (like a picture you've taken with a digital camera), or any picture that Apple has provided for you (and there are several). If you don't have any of your own pictures yet, that's okay. You can always return here to set your favorite image as wallpaper when you do.

FIGURE 2-2 You can delete icons for third-party apps you've downloaded by clicking the X in the top corner of the icon.

FIGURE 2-3   The Lock screen with a new image applied.

You can also assign a picture to the Lock screen. That's the image you see when the screen is locked, but the display is on. In other words, it's the picture you see on the page that shows the slider to unlock the iPad before using it. The Lock screen is shown in Figure 2-3. I've already changed the image here, and it shows the familiar world wallpaper.

To change the wallpaper for the Home screen, the Lock screen, or both on your iPad:

1. On the Home screen, touch Settings.

 If you created an additional Home screen page, you may have to flick left or right to find the Settings icon.

2. In the Settings page, touch Brightness & Wallpaper. See Figure 2-4.

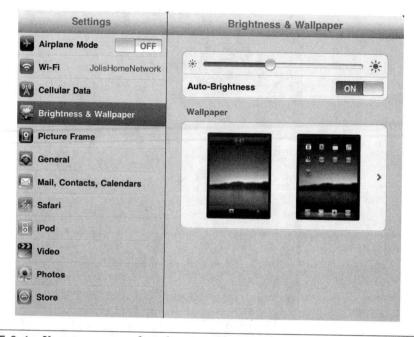

FIGURE 2-4 You can access a lot of options from Settings, including Brightness & Wallpaper.

3. In the right pane, touch the sample wallpaper or the arrow next to it, also shown in Figure 2-4.
4. If you have pictures on your iPad, you'll see them in the resulting screen. If you do not have your own pictures yet, you'll only see the Wallpaper option. Click any folder to view the pictures in it. See Figure 2-5. Any other folders shown below Wallpaper are your own personal photos you've synced or imported.
5. If you see a picture you like, tap it, and click one of the following options:
   - **Set Lock Screen** This is the screen you see when the computer is locked.
   - **Set Home Screen** This is the image you see on the Home screen, under the Home screen icons.
   - **Set Both**
6. To return to the Settings window, click Back, and then click Wallpaper. You can see the Wallpaper option (it looks like a backward arrow at the top of the screen) in Figure 2-5. To return to the Home screen, click the Home button on the iPad.

To set different pictures for both the Lock screen and the Home screen, perform these steps twice.

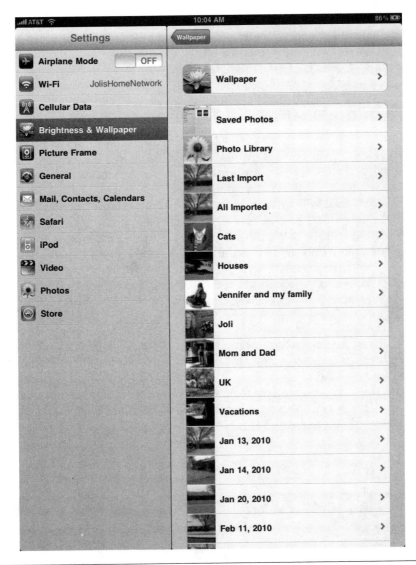

FIGURE 2-5 The Wallpaper option, located here on the top right, includes the Wallpaper provided by Apple.

Access the Internet with Wi-Fi

If you read Chapter 1, you know the difference between Wi-Fi and Wi-Fi + 3G iPad models, and you understand the differences between connecting to the Internet using a Wi-Fi connection versus using a 3G connection. If you didn't read Chapter 1, the sidebar here provides an explanation. That said, in this section you'll learn about connecting to a Wi-Fi network to gain Internet access, something you can do with either the Wi-Fi only or the Wi-Fi + 3G iPad model. In the next section you'll learn about connecting to the Internet with 3G, something you can only do if you have the Wi-Fi + 3G iPad model and sign up and pay for a data package from AT&T.

Turn on Wi-Fi

Your iPad has an option that enables you to turn on and off the Wi-Fi feature at will. When Wi-Fi is enabled, you're telling your iPad "Hey, I want you to look for Wi-Fi networks, and keep searching until you find one!" Because the iPad then constantly searches for networks, battery power is drained more quickly than if it isn't. So, when you don't need Wi-Fi access, it's best to turn this feature off. You'll be asked to disable Wi-Fi when you're on a plane too, so you need to know where this feature is and how to get to it quickly. (It's easiest to just enable Airplane Mode, and that option is also in Settings, but Airplane Mode is only available on the Wi-Fi + 3G model.)

Caution   Wi-Fi must be enabled to see and connect to wireless networks like the one in your home or your local library.

If you have a home network and have already opened Safari or YouTube while exploring, you may have already connected to your own home network. That's because by default, Wi-Fi is on, and when you try to access the Internet, your iPad will let you know about available wireless networks. If you were prompted about your own network and input your security code or passphrase, you're ahead of the game and already connected!

Wi-Fi vs. Wi-Fi + 3G

There are two models of the iPad. The first is Wi-Fi only and the second is Wi-Fi + 3G.

The Wi-Fi model connects to the Internet only one way, when you are within range of and have permission to use a Wi-Fi network. You may have a Wi-Fi network in your home or at work, and you can locate free Wi-Fi networks in coffee shops, hotels, libraries, and similar establishments. You must be within range of a Wi-Fi network to get Internet access. There is no other way to get online.

The Wi-Fi + 3G model connects to the Internet in two ways. One is through a Wi-Fi connection, described in the preceding paragraph. The other is through a 3G connection available via cellular networks, access to which is offered by a company like AT&T, a cellular phone and Internet provider. If you have a Wi-Fi + 3G model, you can get online at free Wi-Fi hotspots, at your wireless network at work and home, and, when those aren't available, from a cellular network. Note that you have to pay for a 3G data plan to obtain cellular access.

To turn on and off Wi-Fi and to connect to an available network:

1. From the Home screen, click Settings. (To view the Home screen at any time, click the Home button.)
2. In the left pane, tap Wi-Fi.
3. Move the slider for Wi-Fi to Off or On, as desired. Remember, Wi-Fi must be turned on to connect to Wi-Fi networks. See Figure 2-6.
4. If you want to be notified when Wi-Fi networks are available, move the slider for Ask to Join Networks to On. This is also shown in Figure 2-6.
5. If networks are available, you'll see them under Choose a Network. If you see a network you'd like to join now, you can
   a. Tap the network in the list.
   b. Enter the password, if applicable, and click Join.
6. Click the Home button to return to the Home screen.

Locate a Free Hotspot

With Wi-Fi enabled you can now seek out and join free, unsecured Wi-Fi networks in public places like your local coffee shop. These free and open networks are called Wi-Fi hotspots. Before you can connect you have to find a local hotspot, though, and that's detailed here.

To locate a free hotspot near you:

1. Visit www.google.com and search for Free Wi-Fi Hotspots, followed by your zip code. You'll probably see several results.
2. Browse through the results to locate a Wi-Fi hotspot near you.
3. If Step 2 does not result in a viable hotspot, try any of the following:
   a. Navigate to www.free-hotspot.com and type your zip code to see the results.
   b. Navigate to www.jiwire.com, drill into Wi-Fi users, Wi-Fi Finder, and use the menus to locate your state, city, and area.
   c. Navigate to www.openwifispots.com, and enter location information to see the results.

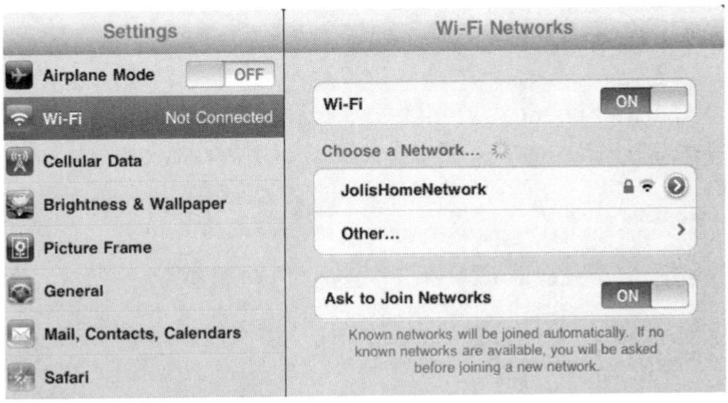

FIGURE 2-6   Wi-Fi must be enabled to choose and connect to a network.

Connect to a Free Hotspot

With a free Wi-Fi hotspot in your sights, it's time to take a walk or a drive and learn how to connect to it. Keep in mind that some establishments will require you to purchase a cup of coffee, a beer, or a bite to eat for the privilege of using the hotspot (or maybe you have to get a library card), so once you get there, inquire about the rules. When you're ready to connect, verify that the following settings are enabled:

- In Settings, for Wi-Fi, Wi-Fi is set to On.
- In Settings, for Wi-Fi, Ask to Join Networks is set to On.

When you're sure you are within range, and you've verified that the settings are properly enabled, from the Home screen, tap Safari on the Home screen. You should see a notification that a network is available. Tap it to join the network. The next time you're within range, you should be connected automatically.

If you don't see a prompt, tap Settings, tap Wi-Fi, and under Choose a Network, tap the network to join. Here, 3802 is the desired network.

Note On the slim chance the network is not listed under Choose a Network, click Other. Then type the name and password for the network.

Connect to a Private Network

If you have a wireless network in your home, you can connect to it with your iPad. If there is a secured wireless network where you work, at your parent's house, or at a friend's, and the owner or administrator of that network will give you the information required to connect, you can access the Internet from that network too. So before you try to connect to any private network, obtain the required information for the personal Wi-Fi network you want to connect to (which is generally referred to as a passcode, password, or something similar). You'll need to input this information when prompted during the authentication process the first time you connect. You should not need to input it again unless the security information for the network changes.

With the security information at hand, you can connect to a secure, personal network:

1. From the Home screen, tap Settings.
2. Tap Wi-Fi.
3. Verify that Wi-Fi is enabled.
4. Under Choose a Network, tap the arrow beside the network you'd like to connect to. (If it's not listed, tap Other.)
5. Type a name, if required, and type the password.
6. Click Join.

Because the iPad is not a computer, you won't be able to access files and folders on resources connected to the network. You will be able to access the Internet, though, and for free! You will not be charged for nor will you accumulate data usage on any prepaid plan when you're connected to a local wireless network like this one.

 You'll learn about Safari in Chapter 3.

Access the Internet with 3G

If you have a Wi-Fi + 3G iPad and pay for a data plan from AT&T, you can access the Internet when you're away from private wireless networks and Wi-Fi hotspots (provided you are in an area with coverage). With this combination, you can access the Internet from anywhere, at any time. If you choose the plan that only allows 250MB of data usage per month, you'll want to watch just how often you use the 3G service, but if you have the unlimited plan, there's no need to worry about usage. Either way, leave Wi-Fi enabled at all times with the 3G plan, so that you can use Wi-Fi when it's available.

Note If you have a Wi-Fi only iPad but now want 3G service, there's no way to upgrade. The 3G model has an embedded SIM card, which is not part of the Wi-Fi only design and cannot be added.

There is a very good reason to leave Wi-Fi enabled, even when you have a cellular data plan. Wi-Fi is faster than 3G, so not only will Wi-Fi give you a better surfing experience, but it will also limit your 3G usage if data usage management is an issue. The only time you'll surf the Internet with 3G is when a Wi-Fi network is not available. This transition should be seamless to you, but you will notice the 3G icon on the Home screen.

If you choose a limited data plan, AT&T will warn you when you're close to using up your data allotment for the month so that you can plan accordingly.

Tip To sign up for a data plan with AT&T, click Settings, click Cellular Data, and fill in the required information to sign up.

Enable or Disable Cellular Data on the Wi-Fi + 3G Only

You know you can enable and disable the Wi-Fi feature on your iPad when you aren't using it. Generally you do this to save battery power. You can also enable and disable cellular data. You will want to disable cellular data when you've met your data usage limit for the month, so you won't incur additional data charges, or if you're out of the country and aren't sure what charges you'll incur if you leave it on.

You may also opt to disable cellular data when you don't need to access the Internet and don't want data to be sent to your iPad automatically. Some apps receive data from the Internet routinely, like a social networking app that gets status updates from your friends behind the scenes. If you don't need to view these updates and are keeping an eye on your data usage, you can disable the cellular data feature when you aren't using the iPad.

To disable cellular data and enable it when you need it again:

1. Tap Settings.
2. Tap Cellular Data.
3. Use the slider for Cellular Data to switch from On to Off. See Figure 2-7.
4. Click the Home button to return to the Home screen.

Settings		Cellular Data	
✈ Airplane Mode	OFF		
🛜 Wi-Fi	3802	**Cellular Data**	ON
📶 Cellular Data		**Data Roaming**	OFF
🖼 Brightness & Wallpaper		Turn data roaming off when abroad to avoid substantial roaming charges when using email, web browsing, and other data services.	
🖼 Picture Frame		**View Account**	
⚙ General		View account information or add more data.	

FIGURE 2-7 You can easily turn off the cellular data feature.

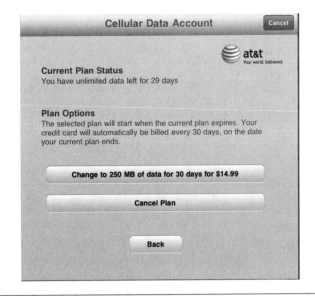

FIGURE 2-8   On the Cellular Data Account page, you can view your account details with your cellular provider.

Change Your Data Plan

You may have noticed on the Cellular Data page that you saw in Figure 2-7 that you can also tap View Account. You'll see this if you have already signed up for a cellular data plan with AT&T. You can change your plan from here too, so if you ever decide to cancel your plan or change the data usage, do it here. Figure 2-8 shows what you might see.

 If you haven't yet signed up for a data plan and you want to, do it at the Cellular Data page in Settings.

Search for Anything

Spotlight Search is a built-in feature on the iPad, and you'll find the small Spotlight Search window in several iPad app windows like Calendar, Contacts, Maps, YouTube, App Store, iTunes, iPod, and Mail (when you're in an account's Inbox). You can use this window to search inside an app for something specific, like a song or an artist, or a specific contact or event. You use the search window the same way you'd use a search engine on the Internet; you simply type in keywords. As you type, results are filtered automatically in apps that contain personal data, and suggestions are offered for apps like iTunes that offer data you can download.

Try it in Contacts:

1. Open Contacts.
2. Tap once in the Spotlight Search window.
3. Use the keyboard to type a contact's name. Note how, the more you type, the shorter the results list becomes.
4. Click the Home button to exit Contacts.

Now, try the Spotlight Search option in the iPod.

1. Open iPod.
2. Tap once in the Spotlight Search window.
3. Use the keyboard to type the last name of any artist in your library and view the results.
4. Click the X in the Spotlight Search window to clear the results.
5. Type a word you know is in a specific song title. View the results. This time, all of the songs with that word in the title appear (and perhaps other data, if it matches an album title or band name). See Figure 2-9.

You can access the full Spotlight Search page by flicking right while on the Home screen. You can also click the Home button if you're on the Home screen to access this page. From here you can search the iPad for data. Results in this list will offer contacts, events, notes, and music.

To use the Spotlight Search page to search your iPad:

1. While on the Home screen, flick right. (Note you can also click once on the Home button.)
2. In the Spotlight Search window at the top, type any keyword.

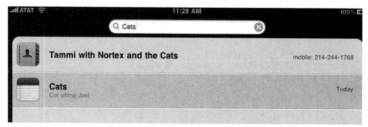

3. The results will appear automatically.
4. To perform another search, use the back key on the keyboard to erase what's in the Spotlight Search window, and type another keyword.

Whenever you tap somewhere that requires you to type, the virtual keyboard will appear. For information on how to type effectively, see the next section, "Type Effectively."

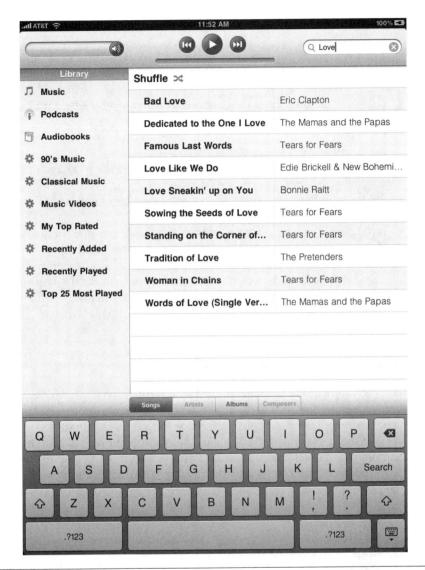

FIGURE 2-9   Type any word that's in a song title to see all songs with that word.

Type Effectively

When you search for something on your iPad, you have to type what you're looking for in the Spotlight Search window. Typing a word or two is pretty easy, and doesn't require much instruction. However, as you progress, you'll do more and more typing, and will need to know how to type effectively. Here are a few tips now to get you started, and we'll scatter other tips throughout the book as needed.

To type effectively, try these tips and tricks:

- When typing, if you press the wrong key on the virtual keyboard, simply slide your finger to the correct one and tap it. A letter is not input until you lift your finger from the screen.
- Tap the up arrow (that's the SHIFT key) on the virtual keyboard before typing a letter to capitalize it.
- Tap the up arrow key and slide to a letter to capitalize it. To type a period and a space, quickly tap the space bar two times.
- If you've enabled Caps Lock in Settings, in General, in Keyboard, double-tap the SHIFT key (up arrow) to enable Caps Lock.
- Tap the number key (.?123) to access a secondary keyboard that includes numbers, and then type a number.
- Tap the symbol key to access a secondary keyboard that includes symbols and punctuation. To access this key, click the number key first.
- While you're typing, the Dictionary may suggest a word before you've finished typing the word. To accept the word, tap a space or hit the RETURN key, or hit any punctuation key. To reject the word, continue typing the word as you want it. (Tap the X next to the word to help your iPad learn the word.)

Restore Your iPad's Settings

Your iPad offers a way to revert to previous settings, so if you've made changes to the Home screen and want it to look as it did out of the box, you can reset Home screen icons. You may have also input network settings you're unhappy with now, and you can reset those easily as well. You can also reset other things, like the Keyboard Dictionary, and even erase all content and all settings.

To reset any of the settings you've changed so far, and to reconfigure the settings to work like they did out of the box:

1. Tap Settings.
2. Tap General.
3. At the bottom of the screen, tap Reset.
4. Tap the settings to change. Note that opting to erase all content and settings will remove all of the personal data you've added so far, and chances are you don't want to do that.
5. Click Reset to apply the changes.

So when would you want to erase all of your personal data and settings? When you sell your iPad, of course! You can be sure that new models of iPads will be released, and you may want to trade up. That's why the iPad offers the option of erasing all content and settings. The next model of the iPad may have a camera, a web cam, or a media card slot. Future models may also support Flash, have a paper-thin slide-out keyboard, or even offer a built-in app for Voice over IP (VOIP) for making

Internet-based phone calls. Whatever happens, there will likely come a time when you want to sell your current model and purchase something better. Before you do, you'll need to restore your iPad to its factory settings.

When you restore the iPad to factory settings, you make it appear brand new again, at least on the inside! After it's restored, there will be no trace of your email accounts, messages, photos, videos, applications, iBooks, or anything else; it's returned to the state it was in when you purchased it. You must do this before selling it to erase all of your personal data, and to make it easier for the next person to personalize.

To restore your iPad to factory settings:

1. Click Settings.
2. Click General.
3. At the bottom of the right pane, click Reset.
4. To reset your iPad to factory settings, tap Erase All Content and Settings.
5. Click Erase to verify.

PART II

Internet and Email

3

Safari

HOW TO...

- Open Safari and visit a web page
- Navigate with Multi-Touch
- Change the view, use zoom, and scroll
- View History
- Save a web site as a Home screen icon
- Personalize a web page
- View web media
- Save a bookmark
- Create a new bookmark folder
- Sync bookmarks with your computer
- Configure Safari settings

Safari is the web browser that comes preinstalled on your iPad and you can use it to surf the Internet. It's a full browser; with it you can locate anything on the web, view just about any web page, view lots of types of web media, save and manage bookmarks for web sites you visit often, and lots more. You can explore varying views, you can zoom in and out of a page, and, you can have multiple web pages open at once.

If you've never used Safari and have always used a browser like Internet Explorer, Safari won't take much getting used to. The navigation bar is clean and contains easy-to-recognize icons, and there are some pretty smart features that just might take you by surprise. For instance, Safari keeps track of the web sites you've visited in the past, and when you type in a web address, Safari offers addresses that start with the letters you've typed. If you see what you want in the resulting list, you can click the suggestion to go there.

You can also add icons for web pages you visit often right on a Home screen. You may want to add an icon (called a web clip) for Facebook, MySpace, CNN, or any other page you visit regularly.

Safari is available from the Home screen by default, and is one of the four icons across the bottom of the screen. It's ready to use, so there's no muss and no fuss!

Get to Know Safari

Before you can use Safari to surf the web, you have to be somewhere that offers Internet access. You can access the Internet with any iPad model, and in Chapter 2 you learned how to connect to the Internet from a Wi-Fi hotspot, using your own home wireless network, or using a 3G connection from a provider like AT&T. If you aren't sure what model you have or how to get connected to the Internet, refer to that chapter before continuing here. When you're ready to get started and are sure you are in a location where you can connect to the Internet, touch the Safari icon, shown here.

If you're within range of a Wi-Fi network or have paid for 3G coverage, you'll be connected to a web page automatically. The first page you'll see is the Apple home page.

 If you're sure you're within range of a free Wi-Fi hotspot but can't access the Internet, verify Wi-Fi is enabled via Settings | Wi-Fi.

Understand the Safari Interface

Everything you need to know about Safari's interface is located in the top part of the browser, called the navigation bar. As shown in Figure 3-1, there are several buttons and areas to explore.

The icons on Safari's navigation bar are detailed in order from left to right here.

- **Back and Forward buttons** To return to the previously visited web page. The Back button will only be available if you've clicked a link in one page to go to another. After you click the Back button, the Forward button will become available. If you've visited lots of pages, you can click the Back and Forward buttons as many times as necessary to return to pages you've recently visited.

FIGURE 3-1 Safari's navigation bar contains icons, an address bar, and a search window.

- **Thumbnail view** To turn the page you're currently viewing into a thumbnail, and to have access to a new, blank, page in Safari, as well as any other open web pages. See Figure 3-2.

Tip You can have up to nine web pages open at a time.

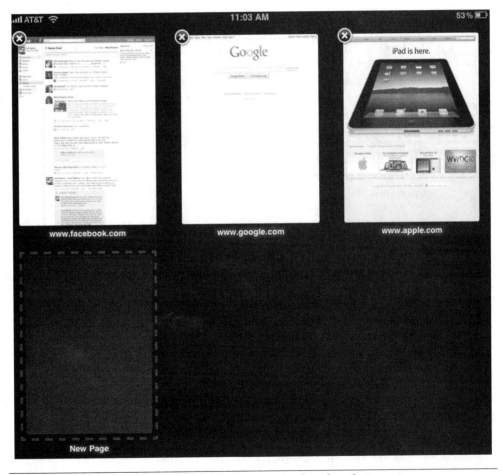

FIGURE 3-2 You can view all open web pages in thumbnail view, open a new page, or close an unwanted open page.

- **Bookmarks**   To view bookmarks included with your iPad, including Apple's web site and the link to the iPad User Guide. You can tap any item in the list to go to the bookmarked page, or view your History (web sites you've recently visited), or to view the Bookmarks Bar (a place to organize some of the bookmarks you keep), which is shown in this illustration.

- **Add a bookmark (the + sign)**   To add a bookmark for the current page so that you can access the same page later from a list of bookmarks. You can also add a web clip (icon) to your Home screen or email a link for this page to a friend.
- **Address window**   To type a web address and navigate to it. The keyboard appears when you tap inside this window, and an X allows you to delete what's already there quickly.
- **Reload (the circular arrow in the address bar)**   To refresh and reload the current web page. Generally you reload a page when you want to view changes to the page, for instance, to read the latest headlines or get the most recent weather forecast. This icon is replaced with an X when you're typing inside the address bar.
- **Search box**   To type keywords and search criteria to locate data on the Internet. Searches can be composed of a few words, a short question, or a complete sentence. By default, the search engine is Google. You can choose Yahoo! if you desire.

From the Apple.com start page, feel free to explore these buttons and menus. Since you're probably already familiar with web surfing, type a few keywords in the Search window, or touch the preconfigured bookmarks to navigate to their pages. Don't worry, you can't hurt anything, and you can easily reset your iPad's settings should you ever desire to.

Tip   If you're holding the iPad in Portrait view, hold it in Landscape view. If you're in Landscape view, try Portrait.

Navigate with Multi-Touch

You interact with Safari using your finger. You can scroll, pinch, tap, flip, and flick. You can also type with the virtual keyboard anytime you tap inside a window or form that requires it. While connected to Apple.com (or any other web page), try these moves to navigate to and through a web page:

- To move from page to page, touch any link in any page. The Back button will become available the first time you do this in a new page.
- To return to a previous page, touch the Back button. After you've used the Back button once, the Forward button becomes available.
- Tap the bookmark icon and tap any existing bookmark to navigate there.

- Tap inside the address bar, search window, or Internet form to access the keyboard. You can then type a new web address, query, keywords, or other information.
- Tap the Thumbnail View icon (the two rectangles). Tap the last page in the list, which is black, to create a new page. Now, type a keyword into the Search window to obtain results.
- If you're on a page that runs longer than the length of the screen, use a flick to scroll up or down.
- To zoom in on a page, use a reverse pinching motion with a finger and thumb. Pinch to zoom back out.
- To zoom in or out of a web page without pinching, tap the screen twice to zoom in. Tap twice again to zoom back out.
- To show a web page to someone sitting across from you, flip the entire iPad upside down.

View History

You can view web sites you've recently visited but did not bookmark using the History option. You can access your History from the Bookmarks icon. Click History to see where you've been. By default, Safari keeps your History for the last ten days, as shown in the following illustration.

Tip Click Clear History to remove all items listed there.

To access, view, use, and clear History data:

1. Touch the Bookmark icon on the Safari navigation bar.
2. Tap History. (Notice that when you tap History, a new option appears in the History window, Bookmarks. Click it to return to the Bookmarks list.)
3. Tap any item in the History list, or touch the desired day in the History list.
4. After you tap a link, the History list will disappear back into the navigation bar.

In the Bookmark list and others, when you tap to access a subfolder, a button appears that will let you return to the previous list or menu. Tap that to return to the previous category.

Personalize Safari

There aren't as many personalization options as you might expect in Safari, and certainly not as many as you're used to in Safari on a Mac or PC. There's no "Action" or "Tools" menu where you can change the default font size, view additional toolbars, or change the color and appearance of web pages. However, there are a few things you can do, including saving web clips for your favorite pages on any Home screen and configuring web sites to log you in automatically. You can even personalize web sites to suit your personal needs, such as inputting your zip code for weather and news, or changing the layout of content shown on a web page. These personalization options are offered by web sites, though, and differ from site to site. Options like the latter are not created by Safari or your iPad.

Note If you can't view Safari because of a visual impairment, refer to Chapter 16.

Save a Web Site as a Home Screen Icon

If there's a web site you visit often, you can put an icon for that page on your Home screen. This is called a "web clip." Doing this gives you one-tap access to the page. If you use a web-based mail program, or have a customized web page from a provider like Time Warner or Verizon, this may be just what you need. This is also a great option if you use a specific social network site regularly, or if you have a blog you write to daily.

To save a web page as a Home screen icon:

1. Open Safari and navigate to your favorite web page.
2. Tap the Add Bookmark icon (+). Click Add to Home Screen.
3. If desired, change the name offered, and then click Add.
4. Safari will close and the new web clip will appear on your Home screen. See Figure 3-3, which shows Facebook available from one of the Home screens. Note the other icons for apps we've added. You'll learn about adding apps in Chapter 7.

Set Web Pages to Log You in Automatically

If you protect your iPad with a password as detailed in a sidebar at the end of this chapter, it's probably okay to configure web sites to log you in automatically and to keep you logged in. If you don't want to input a password each time you unlock your iPad,

FIGURE 3-3   Here, Facebook and My Yahoo! are available from one of the Home screens.

you may want to reconsider this. If you let web sites log you in automatically and keep you logged in for two weeks (a common option), then anyone with access to your iPad will also have access to your favorite sites. If these sites include Facebook or a page where you access your email, someone could do quite a bit of damage to your reputation and online activities if they gained unauthorized access.

Options to keep you logged in to a site for a long period of time or to remember your password are specific to a web page. Not all web sites offer this, and of course, this does not apply to web sites you don't log in to. However, for web sites you log in to often, here's how it works:

1. Open Safari and navigate to the site.
2. Log in, and look for an option to stay logged in or for the site to remember your password.
3. Tick the appropriate box to enable this feature on this web page, as shown in the following illustration.

Tip   If you type something incorrectly, tap and hold your finger on the area of the misspelling. When the magnifying glass appears, shown here, drag it to the area to retype.

Personalize a Web Page You Visit Often

Some web pages allow you to personalize them with content, select a font color or apply a theme, change what part of the page you want to view and what part you want to hide, set your zip code for local information like weather and news, and more. For instance, you can visit Google.com and tap iGoogle in the right corner, and create your own page "in less than 30 seconds." This is shown in Figure 3-4.

FIGURE 3-4   You can personalize many of the web pages that you visit.

You can also configure Weather.com with your zip code, Facebook with friends you want to view and hide, and personalize Yahoo! with content and themes.

 Not all web sites are compatible with the iPad, since it doesn't currently run **Adobe** Flash, a popular web program for adding interactivity to Web pages. However, you can do quite a bit. It's fun to experiment with it anyway!

Here's an example of how you can configure Google with colors, themes, fonts, content, and more:

1. Open Safari and visit www.google.com.
2. Tap iGoogle in the top-right corner.
3. Tap the content you'd like to see on your page. There are lots of options to choose from including News, Entertainment, Sports, Weather, and Technology.
4. Select a theme from the available options.
5. Continue until finished and click I'm Done.
6. You can now save this page to your Home screen if desired.

Tip Some web sites require you to create a user name and password to configure and save a page. When creating user names and passwords, avoid the _ (underscore) character. It takes three taps on the keyboard to get to that symbol. As an alternative, use a period (only one tap), or the – (two taps).

View Web Media

You can't view all of the media on the web, because you can't view media that plays with Adobe Flash. However, you can view lots and lots of media, and it looks good on the iPad. To see how good it looks, watch a video about Safari from the Apple web site:

1. Open Safari and navigate to www.apple.com.
2. Click the iPad tab across the top of the page.
3. In the iPad web page, click View the Guided Tours.
4. Tap Safari in the left pane.
5. Click the arrow on the video to play it. See Figure 3-5.
6. To stop or pause the video, tap the video. Controls will appear that you can use to stop, pause, play, or replay the video.

FIGURE 3-5 You can view lots of kinds of web videos on your iPad.

Work with Bookmarks

You've heard a little about bookmarks already in this chapter, and have likely surmised that a Bookmark offers a quick link to a web site you visit or plan to visit often. You already know how to add a web clip, which is a sort of bookmark available from a Home screen, but the bookmarks we'll talk about here appear in lists, and can be organized into folders. You can save bookmarks in two places, the Bookmarks list and the Bookmarks Bar.

Add Bookmarks

There are some bookmarks already in place, including Apple, Google, and Yahoo!. These bookmarks appear in the Bookmarks list, available with a single tap after you tap the Bookmarks icon. The Bookmarks list includes the iPad User Guide too, along with any bookmarks you've added already, like Facebook shown here. You'll notice two options too, History (sites you've recently visited but did not bookmark) and Bookmarks Bar. You can save bookmarks to the Bookmarks Bar folder. All bookmarks stored in the Bookmarks Bar folder are also revealed beneath the Navigation bar when you tap either the Search field or URL field within the Navigation bar. You can change this in the Settings app (select Safari), to make the Bookmarks Bar permanent, instead of appearing only when you touch the URL or search fields.

To add a bookmark to the Bookmarks list:

1. Open Safari and navigate to the page for which you'd like to add a bookmark to the Bookmarks list, as shown in Figure 3-6.
2. Click the Add Bookmark icon (+) and click Add Bookmark.
3. If you like the name of the bookmark given by Safari, that's great; if you'd like to change the name, simply use the back key on the keyboard to erase what's there and type in something more favorable.
4. Verify that Bookmarks is selected underneath that. If it shows Bookmarks Bar instead, click Bookmarks Bar and then select Bookmarks.
5. Click Save.

Tip   If you're an avid Internet Explorer user, a Bookmark is the same as a Favorite.

To add a bookmark to the Bookmarks Bar:

1. Open Safari and navigate to the page for which you'd like to add a bookmark to the Bookmarks Bar. (We'll add iGoogle.)
2. Click the Add Bookmark icon (+) and click Add Bookmark.
3. If you like the name of the bookmark given by Safari, that's great; if you'd like to change the name, simply use the back key on the keyboard to erase what's there and type in something more favorable.
4. Verify that Bookmarks Bar is selected underneath that. If it shows Bookmarks instead, click Bookmarks and then select Bookmarks Bar.

FIGURE 3-6   The Bookmarks list

5. Click Save.
6. To view this new bookmark in the Bookmarks Bar:
   a. Click the Bookmarks icon on the toolbar.
   b. Click Bookmarks Bar.
   c. Note the new bookmark, shown in the following illustration. Also note that you can edit this bookmark or return to the Bookmarks list. You'll learn more about this next.

Organize Bookmarks

The Bookmarks Library holds your bookmarks. With it, you can organize your bookmarks by saving them in a long list, or by creating folders to hold similar bookmarks. You could create a folder named, Travel, say, and put links to all of your favorite web sites that offer information about travel there. You could create additional folders named Help Pages, Apple, Job Hunting, Real Estate, or any other topic, to organize other bookmarks you want to keep.

To create a new bookmark folder on the Bookmarks list:

1. Tap the Bookmarks icon on the toolbar.
2. Tap Edit.
3. Tap New Folder.
4. Type a name for the folder.
5. Verify that Bookmarks is showing, as shown in the following illustration. If Bookmarks Bar is showing instead, tap it and then tap Bookmarks.

6. Click Bookmarks.
7. Click Done.
8. Note the new folder in the Bookmarks list.

To create a new bookmark folder on the Bookmarks Bar:

1. Tap the Bookmarks icon on the toolbar.
2. Tap Edit.
3. Tap New Folder.
4. Type a name for the folder.

5. Verify that Bookmarks Bar is showing. If Bookmarks is showing instead, tap it and then tap Bookmarks Bar.
6. Click Bookmarks.
7. Click Done.
8. In the Bookmarks list, tap Bookmarks Bar.
9. Note the new folder in the Bookmarks list. Here, we've added Personal and Travel folders, and the iGoogle web site, as shown in the following illustration.

To move a bookmark into a folder:

1. Tap the bookmark icon.
2. Locate the screen that contains the bookmark to move. You may have to click Bookmarks Bar or a folder you've created.
3. Tap Edit.
4. Tap a bookmark *you created* that you'd like to move.
5. In the Edit Bookmark window, tap Bookmarks or Bookmarks Bar, or whatever appears at the bottom of that window.
6. Tap the folder to move the bookmark to.
7. Tap Bookmarks to return to the Bookmarks list.
8. Tap Done.

Sync Bookmarks

Depending on how you set up bookmark syncing in Chapter 1, you may or may not be set up to sync the bookmarks you create on your iPad with your computer. You may have decided now that you want to sync them, or you may want to keep the bookmarks you configure on your iPad on your iPad and not sync them.

To find out how your settings are configured and to make changes if desired, and to sync bookmarks if applicable:

1. Open iTunes on your computer.
2. Connect your iPad to your computer.
3. While iTunes backs up your iPad, in iTunes, click the iPad source pane.
4. In iTunes, click the Info tab.
5. Scroll down to Other. Change the sync options as desired. See Figure 3-7.

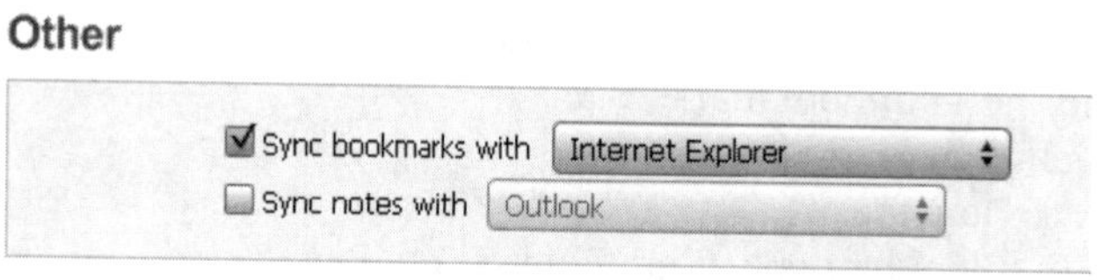

Other

FIGURE 3-7 You can opt to sync or not to sync bookmarks in iTunes, after connecting your iPad to your computer.

Tweak Safari Settings and Preferences

You can change settings and preferences related to Safari for a better browsing experience from Settings on the Home screen. You can configure preferences, including what search engine to use, whether or not to automatically fill in web forms with your name, address, and the like, and whether or not you want to *show* the Bookmarks Bar permanently in Safari. Figure 3-7 shows what the Bookmarks Bar looks like when enabled. Notice that the folders that have been created previously for the Bookmarks Bar under the Bookmark icon appear, as do the individual bookmarks you've created there.

Safari helps you maintain your safety and privacy while on the Internet too. Settings that Safari deems optimal are already set, but it's always a good idea to review them. You can also clear your History, Cookies, and Cache, among other things. Safari's settings are shown in Figure 3-8.

The following security settings are enabled by default:

- **Fraud Warning** To warn you when you visit a fraudulent site that may try to get you to input personal information or information about your bank or credit cards. Some fraudulent web sites also try to infect computers and devices with adware, spyware, and viruses.
- **Block Pop-ups** To block pop-ups from web sites that initiate them. Pop-ups are generally advertisements, and open in a new window.
- **Accept Cookies** To accept cookies from web sites you visit. Cookies are small text files that are stored on your iPad that tell a web site what you prefer when visiting. Cookies can include your name, browsing history on the site, and information about items you've purchased.

AutoFill is not enabled by default. When you enable AutoFill, you tell your iPad and Safari that you want it to populate web forms automatically. While this is a convenience, it can also create a security hole. If your iPad is stolen and is not protected by a passcode, the thief can access Safari and populate the forms themselves.

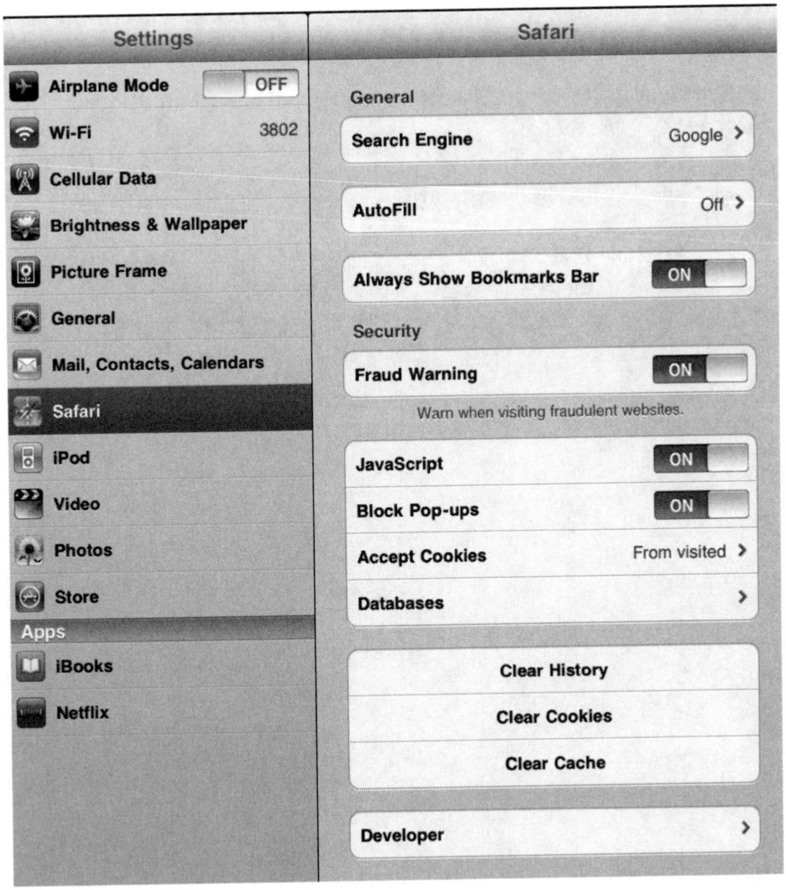

Settings	Safari
Airplane Mode OFF	**General**
Wi-Fi 3802	Search Engine Google >
Cellular Data	
Brightness & Wallpaper	AutoFill Off >
Picture Frame	
General	Always Show Bookmarks Bar ON
Mail, Contacts, Calendars	**Security**
Safari	Fraud Warning ON
iPod	Warn when visiting fraudulent websites.
Video	JavaScript ON
Photos	Block Pop-ups ON
Store	Accept Cookies From visited >
Apps	Databases >
iBooks	Clear History
Netflix	Clear Cookies
	Clear Cache
	Developer >

FIGURE 3-8   From the Settings app, you can access settings for Safari.

There are also a few things you can do to erase the information that Safari has thus far stored about your web browsing. With only a couple of taps you can clear the following information:

- **History**   A list of web sites you've recently visited.
- **Cookies**   Information about you regarding your preferences at specific web sites, like what you generally shop for, your name, and other information.
- **Cache**   What the iPad stores regarding the web pages you visit. The iPad and Safari store information about a web page the first time you load it, save some of that data, and reuse it the next time you visit. This helps pages you've previously visited load faster. You may want to clear the cache if the data on web pages is outdated, and new data isn't being loaded.

How to... Secure Your iPad with a Passcode

If you really want to secure Safari, create a passcode to unlock your iPad.
To create a passcode:

1. Tap Settings on the Home screen.
2. Tap General.
3. Tap Passcode Lock.
4. Tap Turn Passcode On.
5. Type a four-number passcode, and type it again when prompted.

4

Communicate with Mail

HOW TO...

- Configure a web-based email account
- Configure a POP3 email account
- Incorporate MobileMe
- Verify that all email accounts are configured properly
- Explore Mail's interface
- Compose an email and insert a photo
- Do more with cut, copy, and paste
- View incoming email and respond to it
- Open an attachment
- Use gestures to manage email
- Search email folders with Spotlight
- Explore Mail Settings

The iPad comes with Mail, an email management program already built in and ready to use, and available from the Home screen. You have to tell Mail about your email accounts before you can use it, though, including your email address, password, and associated settings, and you need to test the email accounts you configure to make sure they're working properly. It's notable that Mail integrates with several types of email almost seamlessly, including Yahoo! Mail, Gmail, AOL (America Online), and MobileMe, as well as Microsoft Exchange accounts, which are used in larger enterprises. This helps make the setup for these types of accounts a simple and generally flawless task. Mail also allows you to configure email accounts from Internet Service Providers (ISPs), such as Time Warner, Comcast, Verizon, and the like, as well as email accounts you've acquired from schools, businesses, and other various email providers, although setting up these accounts sometimes takes a little more effort than the supported email accounts previously mentioned.

Once your email addresses are configured, you're ready to use Mail. Of course, you'll need to be within range of a wireless hotspot or your home network, or you'll need a data plan from a service provider like AT&T if you're out of their range to send and receive mail, but you knew that!

 Note You can't receive new email unless you can connect to the Internet.

So without further ado, let's get your email addresses configured, send a few test emails, and then focus on what you need to know to use Mail on your iPad.

Set Up Mail

As mentioned in the introduction, you need to tell Mail about your email addresses. If you're used to setting up email accounts on a computer, this is a little different. While you can set up your first email account in the Mail program easily, if you want to set up a second or third account, you'll want to do that in Settings.

Tip Mail knows the configuration settings for several types of accounts. So, it's generally best to type in the most basic information, and see if the iPad and Mail can do the rest. Before you start, make sure you're within range of and can connect to a Wi-Fi or 3G network.

Configure a Web-Based Email Account

A web-based email account is an account provided by an online entity, which is often a search provider as well, such as Google, AOL, or Yahoo!. With web-based email, your email data is stored on web servers and you can access that data using a web browser. Because of this, you can get your email from anywhere and any computer, as long as the computer offers Internet access. For instance, if you have a Gmail account from Google, you can go to www.google.com from any computer, sign in, and access your email easily.

You don't have to use the provider's web site, though. You can get email from web-based providers on your iPad with Mail. Additionally, Mail knows the settings and can automatically configure email accounts for these and other web-based email accounts, which makes setting up these types of email accounts a breeze.

If you're worried that you'll receive email on your iPad and won't receive it on your computer at home, have no fear. You can get email on your iPad and then retrieve the messages again at your home or office computer the next time you log on, even if you delete them in Mail.

Tip If you're in the market for a new email address, consider one from Google, Hotmail (also known as Windows Live), AOL, or Yahoo! With it, you can easily configure your iPad and access mail from any computer you have access to (that also has access to the Internet).

To configure a web-based email account like Yahoo! Mail, Gmail, or MobileMe (MobileMe is a subscription service that we'll introduce later):

1. On the Home screen, tap Mail.
2. Tap the option that matches the type of account you want to configure. See Figure 4-1. If your web-based email account isn't listed (Hotmail or Windows Live, for example), click Other.

Note If you don't see this screen, open Settings and tap Mail, Contacts, Calendars to access the option to add a new account.

3. Fill out the required information:
   a. **Name** Type your name as you'd like others to see it when you send them mail.
   b. **Address** Type your email address.
   c. **Password** Type your email account password, and remember that passwords are case-sensitive.
   d. **Description** Type a description for the account (such as AOL, Hotmail, or Yahoo!).
4. Click Save. The Inbox for this account will appear.

Now, send a test email to yourself to verify the account has been set up correctly:

1. Tap the New Mail icon in the top-right corner of the Mail interface.
2. In the To line, type the email address for this account. For example, if you just set up an account for yourname@yahoo.com, type that.
3. Tap the Subject line.
4. Type Test.
5. Tap the Send button in the upper-right corner. Wait a few seconds for the email to be sent and received.

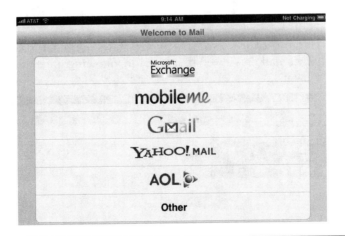

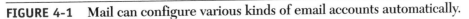

FIGURE 4-1 Mail can configure various kinds of email accounts automatically.

Did You Know?

There Are Special Keys Available on Your iPad's Virtual Keyboard

If you've never used a virtual keyboard, typing the information required to set up your email account may be a tad difficult. If you're having trouble inputting the required information, try these typing tips:

- If you need to capitalize a letter, touch the up arrow.
- If you need to locate an underscore, dash, or similar character, click the .?123 key. Note that you may have to touch the #+= key to access additional characters.

6. To verify the mail has arrived, you need to locate it. Mail offers a different interface depending on the view:

   a. **In Portrait view**   Tap Inbox. Then tap the email to view it (see the following illustration).

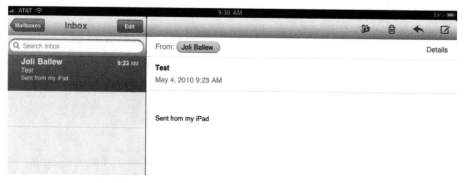

   b. **In Landscape view**   The Inbox shows in the left pane, and you can see the new email previewed in it (see the following illustration). Tap the email to view it.

If you receive errors, from the Home screen, tap Settings. Tap Mail, Contacts, Calendars to access the account and edit it. If you do see errors, those errors are probably related to an incorrect email address or password.

Configure a POP3 Email Account

POP3 email accounts differ from web-based accounts in many ways. POP3 email accounts are commonly provided by companies that offer Internet service you pay for, such as Time Warner, Comcast, Verizon, and the like. You can also have a POP3 email account from a place where you work or go to school, or from a dedicated email host. These are often referred to as email providers, but can still be POP3 in nature. Email providers like these have their own mail servers, and unlike web-based servers, they often delete email after you've downloaded it to your computer. If you download email to your home or office PC before it can be downloaded to your iPad, then you won't get it on your iPad.

So, if you have your home or work PC configured to automatically download your messages from your provider's POP3 email server, and you have not changed the default settings on that computer to *leave a copy of the messages on the server* for a specified period of time, you won't get those same messages on your iPad. That's because those email messages, once downloaded to your home or work computer, are no longer available on your email provider's servers when you log on with your iPad. If you want to receive all of your email messages on your iPad as they arrive at the server, you'll have to change the settings on your home or work PC.

It's important to note that configuring your computer's email program to leave a copy of your email messages on the server differs depending on what email program you use and what type of computer you use at home and at work. This makes it difficult to give you specific instructions for making the change on your home or work PC. However, because it's important to configure your computer to leave a copy of your messages on the email provider's server, here are some generic instructions to do so:

1. On your home and/or work PC, and any laptop you use to obtain your email, open your email program. This may be Outlook Express, Apple Mail, Windows Mail, Windows Live Mail, Thunderbird, or something else.
2. Locate a Help menu or Help button. Here are some suggestions:
   a. If you don't see any menus, click the ALT key.
   b. If you don't see a Help menu, look for a question mark.
   c. If you don't see either, click F1.
3. Click the option to get help regarding your email program.
4. In the Help window, search for *read pop3 email messages on multiple computers*.
5. Follow the directions to leave a copy of the messages on the POP3 mail server. See Figure 4-2, which shows Microsoft Outlook.

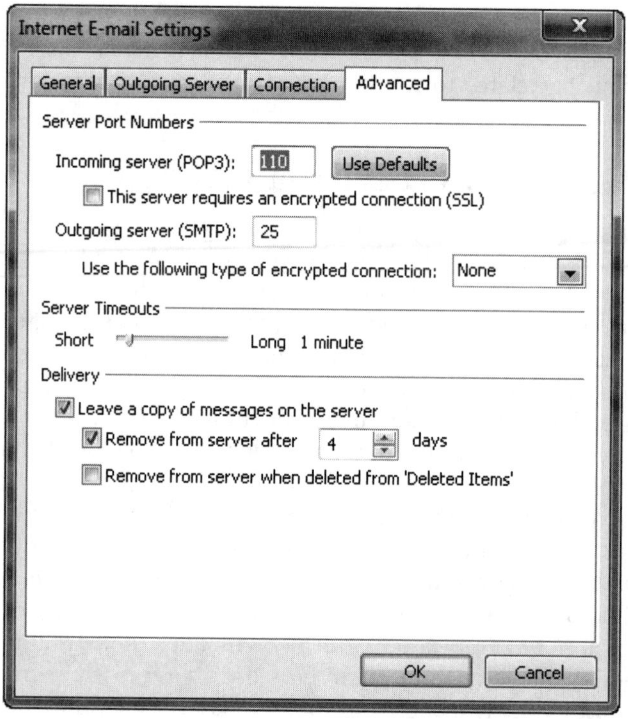

FIGURE 4-2 If you want to get email from a POP3 email account on your iPad, configure the settings required to leave a copy of the messages on your provider's email server.

Tip While you must opt to leave messages on your email provider's POP3 server, you are often limited to how much data you can keep there. If you go over that limit, you will no longer be able to get email until you delete some data stored there. Consider only leaving messages on the server for four days or less.

Once you're sure you've configured your computers correctly, you're ready to set up POP3 email accounts on your iPad. Luckily, the iPad and Mail know that you're using a handheld device, and the iPad is already configured to *automatically* leave a copy of your messages on the server for you. So, no worries; when you use your iPad to get your POP3 messages, they won't disappear from the provider's servers. This means that you can access your POP3 email messages (from Time Warner, Verizon, Comcast, and so on) on your iPad and retrieve them again when you log on to your account from your home or work PC.

The more difficult part comes in setting up your POP3 accounts. Not all accounts are supported at this time, and you may run into problems. Because of this we'll talk in detail here about how to set up POP3 accounts, and later you'll learn workarounds if a specific account doesn't work as you planned.

To create an email account in Mail for a POP3 email account:

1. On the Home screen, tap Settings.
2. Tap Mail, Contacts, Calendars.
3. Tap Add Account.
4. Tap Other.
5. Tap Add Mail Account.
6. Type your email name, email address, password, and description of the account.
7. Click Save.
8. If prompted, type any required information for the server names, host names, user names, and so on. You can get this information from your email provider. Click Save.
9. If you get all green check marks by each entry, the email account was properly set up. Send yourself a test email from this account to this account to be sure.
10. If you receive an error, you'll have to resolve it. See Figure 4-3.

To resolve errors:

1. Review the settings for incoming and outgoing servers. Make sure you've typed the names correctly. You can get the information you need from your email provider or the Internet if you're unsure.
2. If you're positive you've input all of this information correctly, click Save and go ahead and set up the email even if you receive a message that it may not work properly.
3. Then, in Settings, under Mail, Contacts, Calendars, click the problematic account.

FIGURE 4-3 Some errors appear easy to fix, such as changing authentication settings.

4. In the resulting window, scroll down to Advanced (as shown in the following illustration) and tap it.

..ıll AT&T 🛜		10:01 AM	
Settings	Cancel	**Time Warner**	Done

Host Name pop-server.tx.rr.com

User Name joli_ballew

Password ●●●●●●●●

Outgoing Mail Server

SMTP   smtp-server.tx.rr.com ›

Advanced   ›

Delete Account

(Settings list: Airplane Mode, Wi-Fi, Cellular Data, Brightness & Wallpaper, Picture Frame, General, Mail, Contacts, Calendar, Safari)

5. Review the settings. You may need to enable SSL (which is a security setting) or type in a different server port. It's best to call your email provider and ask what the settings should be. If you still can't get it to work, refer to Appendix B, or elect to apply one of the workarounds detailed later in this chapter.

6. With errors resolved, your email will arrive immediately. You can see how many unread emails you have in all of your accounts from the Home screen, as shown in this illustration.

How to... **Sync Mail with iTunes**

You can use iTunes to transfer information about your email accounts, but it won't transfer your passwords or your messages. It won't transfer the folders you've created. In fact, it won't sync web-based email accounts in Outlook (like Hotmail) either. And, because you'll probably have to configure special settings for POP3 accounts, it's best to avoid this as a setup option. We suggest you set up these accounts manually as detailed in this chapter and forgo syncing with iTunes. However, if you must sync your mail, here are the steps:

1. In iTunes on your computer, select your iPad in the left pane.
2. Click the Info tab.
3. Click Sync Mail Accounts from_____, and select your email program.
4. Select the accounts to sync.
5. Click Apply.

How to... Configure One Account as the Default

If you set up more than one email account on your iPad, the first account you set up will be the default account. The default account is the account your iPad will use to send mail when you want to share a photo, a contact, or any other data. The account you use most should be set as the default account, though, and that isn't necessarily the first account you configured. (You can always choose a different account before sending the data, but it's nice to have the correct account selected in most instances.) You should verify which account is the default and change it if you desire.

To configure an email account as your default account:

1. On the Home screen, tap Settings.
2. Tap Mail, Contacts, Calendars.
3. Tap Default Account.
4. Tap the account to use for the default account.
5. Tap Mail, Contacts, Calendars to return to the Settings page.

Tip　In this section we covered web-based email accounts and POP3 email accounts. The directions for setting up other accounts, such as IMAP or Microsoft Exchange, are similar.

Consider MobileMe

MobileMe is a service that "pushes" new email (and contacts, calendar events, and other data) over the air to all of your devices. The devices you can use include your iPad, iPhone, iPod Touch, Mac, and your PC. You can configure MobileMe on a single device and the rest will fall into place easily. Although you can get a free trial of MobileMe, it will only be free for 60 days. After that, it's $99 a year for you, or $149 for you and your family. If you're still interested, read on; if not, skip to the next section.

Tip　Once you have a MobileMe account, you configure it on your iPad the same way you input web-based or POP3 accounts.

Here are a few reasons to consider MobileMe:

- MobileMe keeps all data "in the cloud" (on Internet servers), and pushes the information to your devices.
- The MobileMe Inbox offers spam and virus protection.
- Contacts and addresses are synced automatically between compatible devices without docking.
- Calendars and events are synced automatically between compatible devices without docking.

- Photos are stored on Internet servers and you can allow friends and family to view them, upload their own, make comments, and more.
- iDisk offers a place to store, access, and share files online.
- Find My iPhone or iPad can help you find your iPad should it become lost or stolen.
- Me.com offers access to all of your data, from anywhere.

Verify Proper Configuration of All Accounts

If you haven't done so already, you should send a test email from your iPad for each account you've configured back to that account. So, if you created an account for Yahoo!, you'll want to send an email from that account back to that account. And if you've also created an account for Time Warner, you'll need to send an email from your Time Warner account back to that account too. This will allow you to see three things: first, whether the email accounts are properly configured on your new iPad; second, how long it takes to receive an email in your Inbox once it's been sent; and third, verification that the email also arrives at your home or work PC. There are instructions on how to do this in the section "Configure a Web-Based Email Account." For POP3 accounts, perform this test using a Wi-Fi network and a 3G network (if you have a Wi-Fi + 3G model and you've signed up for a data plan).

After that's complete, turn off your iPad and perform the same email test from each of your other devices that receive email from the accounts you configured on your iPad, including Macs, PCs, iPod Touch, and/or smartphone devices. Allow those emails to arrive at each of your devices, and then, turn on your iPad and verify that they come in there also. (If they don't, refer to the POP3 section earlier in this chapter to learn how to leave a copy of those email messages on the server for each device you own.)

It's important to do this testing because you may encounter odd bugs in the setup of your email accounts. For instance, at the time this book was written, you could send and receive email using a Time Warner email address while connected to 3G, but you could only receive (and not send) using a Time Warner email address while connected to Wi-Fi (without some serious hacking, which took us an entire day to figure out and likely won't work for other ISPs). In this particular scenario you can either turn off Wi-Fi to regain the ability to send email, or send email from a different account that does work with Wi-Fi. You'll have to continue to use a different account until Apple and/or your email provider resolve the problem.

In another scenario, if you're having trouble receiving mail, you can create a Gmail account with Google, for example, and set it up to receive email from any of your other accounts, and then set up the Gmail account on your iPad to receive your mail.

But there's one additional option: If you can't use Mail with your POP3 email address, you can always open Safari and navigate to the email provider's webmail page; you can send and receive email there while connected to Wi-Fi or 3G. For added convenience, create a web clip. You can then access the webmail page from your iPad's Home screen. For more information about web clips, refer to Chapter 3.

 We really like Gmail from Google because you can label emails at mail.google.com, and those labels will appear as folders within Mail on your iPad, allowing you to organize mail you want to keep.

Learn Mail Fundamentals

We're sure you know how to email. You can send and receive it, and you can probably even create folders on your computer and manage email you keep effectively. You can forward and reply, you can likely attach a picture, and you can browse folders like Sent and Deleted Items (or Trash). That said, in this section we won't bore you with anything too basic, but it is important to cover all of our bases to get every reader up to speed with emailing on the iPad. In this section you'll learn the following:

- How to find what you want and need by familiarizing yourself with Mail's interface
- How to send email and insert pictures and other data
- How to get the most from the available views
- How to view and respond to incoming email
- How to open and view an attachment

Explore Mail's Interface

Mail has some interface features you'll want to familiarize yourself with so that you can get the most from Mail. When you tap an email to read it, you'll see various arrows and buttons to help you navigate, as well as options to enable you to perform tasks, such as delete an email or reply to it. You'll also see information across the top of the page to let you know you are connected to the Internet, and options to access additional email accounts. The following illustration shows the accounts configured in Mail, in Landscape view. Here you can see the top of the Mail interface, again in Landscape view, while you're inside an account and reading an email.

![Mail interface top bar showing Time Warner, Inbox (46), Edit, Search Inbox, From: Bright Hub, Details]

Tip   It's really best to view Mail in Landscape view for now. In Landscape view you have easier access to all of the features. Portrait view does not offer the same amenities.

In Landscape view you can see that you're connected to a network across the very top of the screen, and in Mail the following options are included (from left to right):

- **Account Name**   The email account name if multiple email accounts exist. Click this name to return to the Inbox for the account, and click the Accounts button that appears in that pane to return to other accounts. Users with only one email account will not see an account name or an Accounts button. If you're unsure how juggling multiple email accounts works, refer to the next "Did You Know?" box.
- **Inbox (with a number)**   Lets you know what folder you're in, in this case Inbox, and how many unread messages you have there.

Mail Has Built-in Hierarchy of Folders

The icon that appears in the top-left corner of the Mail interface while you're in Landscape view is ultimately a "back" button. Mail is laid out such that Accounts is the starting place for Mail, or the "home" page, if you will. In Accounts, all email accounts are listed, and you tap to access them. Once you're in an account, you have access to the account's Inbox and Trash folders. To return to previous tiers, click this "back" button. The name of the button will change depending on where in the hierarchy you are.

- **Edit** Tap to delete or move selected emails.
- **Move** Tap to move an email.
- **Trash** Tap once to move the current email to the Trash folder.
- **Reply/Forward** Tap to have the option to reply to or forward the current email.
- **Compose** Tap to create a new email.
- **Details** Tap to view information about the sender and recipient(s) of the email. Tap Hide to hide details.

Compose an Email and Insert a Photo

You know how to compose an email if you've sent out test emails to verify your email accounts are working properly. You may have also noticed that the Compose icon appears across the top of the Mail screen no matter where you are in the app. While it may be easy to compose and send an email, there are a lot of hidden features you may not have uncovered. For instance, when composing a new mail message, you can

- Click the + sign to add contacts from your Contacts list.
- Tap the Cc/Bcc line to view the Cc and Bcc lines in the message.
- Tap the From line to change the account you want to send the message from.
- Tap and hold a word briefly to select it, select everything, or paste something you've already copied. (Once you select a word or Select All, you'll see options to cut, copy, paste, or replace.)

You might be surprised to learn that you can't attach a photo to an email from within the Mail app. You can copy and paste a photo, and you can send a photo from the Photos app, but there's no option to attach a photo in a new mail message as you're used to in Outlook, Apple Mail, or other computer email programs. However, you can copy and paste a photo, and the photo will appear in the body of the email.

To compose an email and insert a photo:

1. Open Mail.
2. Tap the Compose button.
3. Fill in the To: line using one of the following methods:
   a. Type an email address, or, begin typing and tap any result offered.
   b. Tap the + sign and select a contact from the resulting Contacts list (see the following illustration) by searching, scrolling, or tapping.

4. Tap and hold the Cc/Bcc line to view those lines and add additional recipients.
5. Tap the Subject line and type a subject.
6. Tap inside the body of the email and type a message.
7. To insert a picture:
   a. Press the Home button on the iPad to view the Home screen. (Don't worry, Mail will remember where you left off.)
   b. Tap Photos.
   c. Locate the photo to insert, and tap and hold it briefly until the Copy option appears. Tap Copy. Alternately, you can tap the button in the top-right corner (the one with the arrow on it) to see the options Email Photo, Assign to Contact, Use as Wallpaper, or Copy Photo.
   d. Click the Home button again to return to the Home screen.
   e. Tap Mail.
   f. Tap and hold briefly inside the message body, lift your finger, and tap Paste when it appears.
   g. To see the entire message without the keyboard, click the keyboard icon on the virtual keyboard to hide it (bottom-right corner).
   h. Repeat as desired, completing the message and adding more pictures. When finished, click Send.

Save an Email for Completion Later

To save an email for completing later, tap the Cancel button. Tap Save when prompted. (You have to have typed some words in the body of the email for this to work.) After you tap Save, the email will sit in the Drafts folder until you're ready to complete it. The Drafts folder will only be available when unfinished email is in there. Otherwise, it's hidden.

Email Multiple Photos

You can email multiple photos at once. This is quite a convenience, especially if you have a dozen or so pictures to send. You'll have to be in an album of photos to select multiple photos.

To select multiple photos to email:

1. In Photos, tap any album that contains multiple photos.
2. Tap the icon in the top-right corner, the one with the arrow on it.
3. Tap each photo to send. Each time you tap a photo, an arrow will appear on it.
4. When your photos are selected, tap Email in the top-left corner. (Note you can also tap Copy.) See Figure 4-4.

FIGURE 4-4 In an album, tap the icon in the top-right corner to select multiple photos to send.

Work with Cut, Copy, and Paste

In the last section you learned how to copy and paste a picture. You can use this same technique in other apps and for other uses. For instance, when composing an email, you can cut, copy, or paste text or other data in lieu of retyping information you already have. While this is a bit more complex than simply copying a picture, it's still pretty easy. The technique is to first make a selection by inserting a cursor in the appropriate area of the text. Then decide if you'd like to select the word, select everything, or select only a specific part of the data.

To cut or copy text and paste it into an email:

1. Compose an email as detailed earlier.
2. To copy text from another app, click the Home screen button and locate the data. (You can copy the data before composing the email, if you find that you can't access the data to copy easily during email composition. Text can be copied from apps such as Safari, Notes, Calendar, and Contacts, as well as from other emails.)
3. Touch and hold on the text you wish to copy until you see the magnifying glass.
4. Use the magnifying glass to drag the cursor to the position where you'd like to begin cutting or copying.
5. Release your finger to display the selection buttons.
6. Select the text:
   a. Tap Select to select the adjacent word.
   b. Tap Select All to select all of the text.
   c. Double-tap any word to select it.
   d. Drag the blue "grab points" to select more or less text.
7. With the text selected, tap Cut or Copy.
8. Tap and hold again where you'd like to paste the text. Release your finger and tap Paste to insert the text. Note that you can also replace text.

 Shake the iPad to undo the last edit. (We had to shake ours pretty hard, and you may not be comfortable with this.)

View Incoming Email and Respond to It

There's likely no need to rehash how to view email that's arrived; you simply drill into the email account you want to view, using the Accounts button and the Inbox. Once in the desired account's Inbox, you can preview any email in the Inbox list, and tap it to view it.

To reply to or forward an email:

1. With the email selected and open, click the arrow above the email. You can then opt to reply or forward. If you've selected an email that also contains images, you'll see the option to save those images too.

2. Tap Reply or Forward (see the following illustration).

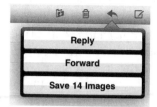

3. Complete the email as desired.

Open an Attachment

Attachments are add-ons to emails, and can be pictures, spreadsheets, videos, documents, or even presentations. You can open many types of attachments on your iPad, although not quite as many as you can on a Mac or a PC. As you'd expect, you'll notice a paper clip with an email that contains an attachment in the preview of the email; to open the attachment, open the email, scroll down to locate the attachment, and touch the attachment icon. You can view the attachment on your iPad, and if you have the iWork apps (see Chapter 7), you can edit many document types and save them.

Pictures behave a little differently than other attached data. You don't have to open pictures separately. Pictures will automatically appear in the body of an email, and a momentary tap and hold on the image gives you the option to save it or copy it.

This list includes some the types of email attachments you can view on your iPad:

- .jpg, .tiff, .gif, .png (images)
- .doc and .docx (Microsoft Word)
- .htm and .html (web pages)
- .key (Keynote)
- .numbers (Numbers)
- .pages (Pages)
- .pdf (Preview and Adobe Acrobat)
- .ppt and .pptx (Microsoft PowerPoint)
- .txt (text); .rtf (rich text format)
- .vcf (contact information)
- .xls and .xlsx (Microsoft Excel)

To view an attachment represented by a paper clip:

1. Open Mail and tap the email that contains the attachment.
2. In the body of the email, scroll down to locate the attachment icon.
3. Click the attachment to view it, noting that Mail only supports the attachment types listed here.
4. To stop viewing the attachment, if it's taking the entire screen, tap at the top of the document, presentation, or spreadsheet, and click Done.

To save an image in an email to your iPad:

1. Open an email that contains pictures.
2. Tap and hold briefly on the picture and then select one of the following options (see the following illustration):
   a. Save Image
   b. Save # Images (this option appears only if there are multiple images)

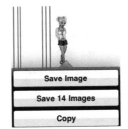

Manage Your Email

The best way to manage email is to read it and respond to it when it arrives, and then delete it. This keeps you up to date and keeps your Inbox from getting cluttered. Responding to an email can be as simple as reading and deleting it, sending a reply or forwarding the email to someone else, or it may be a bit more complex and involve saving the data in the email in the appropriate app (saving photos to the Photos app, for instance). Unfortunately, the world is not a perfect place. You'll have email you can't respond to right away, email you need to file so you can reference it later, email you're not sure what to do with, and other scenarios that don't allow you to deal with specific email as promptly as you'd like.

At the present time, there aren't many options for managing the email you acquire on your iPad. You can't create your own organizational folders just yet. So, the best way to stay organized is to delete items once you know you won't need them, or forward them to a different email account to store them, away from your default account's Inbox.

Beyond managing what you want to keep, you'll also use shortcuts for dealing with email, like using a flick to bring up the option to delete. You'll learn about that in this section too.

Remember, the email you receive on your iPad will also arrive at your home and/or work computer if you've configured them as detailed in this chapter. This means you can delete anything you don't actually need to deal with on your iPad, and deal with it when you're back at your home or work computer.

Use Gestures to Manage Email

When you manage your email on your home or work PC, or on a laptop, you can't generally touch the screen to perform tasks. You can on an iPad. Therefore, there are new ways to interact with email, including using gestures like swiping to delete email or flicking to scroll through a long email. As you already know, you can tap and hold to select data in an email, or tap to open an attachment. To perform these gestures and learn how to manage your email with them, try the following:

- **Delete a message** Tap the trash icon, or swipe left or right over the message title in the message list, then tap Delete.
- **Delete multiple messages** Tap Edit, select the messages you want to delete, then tap Delete.

How to...

Create Your Own Organizational System in Mail

If you want an organizational system complete with folders in Mail, you can do it with Gmail. It's not a perfect solution, but it might work for you. You'll have to create a new email account at Google (Gmail), create email labels at the Google web site that match how you'd like to organize your mail, and then, forward email you want to keep to it. Then, you can use that account's Inbox to store data you want to keep. Figure 4-5 shows an example.

FIGURE 4-5 With Gmail, you can create folders like Keep, Travel, and Work at Google's web site, and those folders will appear on your iPad.

FIGURE 4-6   Tap a contact to add them to your Contact list.

- **Move a message to a different mailbox or folder**   Tap the folder icon (Move icon) and then choose a mailbox or folder.
- **Move multiple messages**   Tap Edit, select the messages you want to move, and tap Move.
- **Zoom in on a message**   Pinch your fingers outward.
- **Follow a link**   Tap the link.
- **See all recipients of a message**   Tap Details.
- **Add a sender to your Contacts**   Tap Details, and then tap the contact to add. Click Create New Contact or Add to Existing Contact. See Figure 4-6.
- **Mark a message as unread**   Tap the blue dot next to the subject line in the preview pane.

Search Email Folders with Spotlight

Sometimes you need to locate an email but can't remember where it is or who it was from, but you do remember what the email was in reference to. Perhaps you need to locate an email that outlined the rules of the game bocce, for instance. You can use Spotlight Search to look through all of your emails for you, using a specific keyword (like bocce). Of course, the more unique the word, the more likely you'll find what you're looking for; performing a search for a less unique word would result in a longer list of search results.

To search for a specific email by keyword using Spotlight Search:

1. Open Mail and navigate to the desired account Inbox to search.
2. Type a keyword into the Spotlight Search window.
3. Review the results (see the following illustration).
4. To open any result, tap it.

Tip Remember, Mail on iPad is best navigated in Landscape view.

Explore Mail Settings

As you know, you can configure settings for Mail in the Settings app on the Home screen. You'll find the information under Mail, Contacts, Calendars. We've already discussed the Accounts section at length, but there are plenty of other options to explore, shown in Figure 4-7.

The first option under Accounts is Fetch New Data. As you can see in Figure 4-7, it's set to Push. Push is a technology that allows Internet servers to send information to your iPad as soon as the message is received by your email provider on their email servers. Some email servers will push email to you, while others won't. Supported email providers include MobileMe, Microsoft Exchange, and Yahoo!. Be aware that using Push will use battery power to obtain the updates and also because of the data it transfers, and can minimize battery life. Transfers while connected via 3G are counted towards your monthly data usage as well. This isn't a problem if you have unlimited access, but it can be if you have a limited plan.

Other email accounts such as POP, IMAP, AOL, and Gmail accounts aren't Push-compatible on the iPad. This means that no email will arrive at your Inbox in Mail until you open Mail and access the Inbox. At that time, Mail will check for email and obtain mail from your email servers. If this is inconvenient and you'd rather have Mail check for email automatically, even when you aren't using it, you can configure your iPad to fetch your email on a schedule, such as every 15, 30, or 60 minutes. You can also set Fetch settings to Manually so that no fetch occurs by default. As with Push, Fetch will drain your battery more quickly on than off. To maximize battery life, fetch less often or fetch manually. Fetch also kicks in for Push email accounts if Push is turned off, so if you're watching your data usage you may need to turn off Push and set Fetch to Manually.

FIGURE 4-7   The Settings app offers a Mail, Contacts, Calendars category.

Under Mail, you can configure various options for showing and previewing mail including:

- **Show**   To configure how many recent messages appear in your Inbox.
- **Preview**   To configure how many lines are available in an email.
- **Minimum font size**   To set how large or small text should appear in emails.
- **Show To/CC label**   To show or hide the To/CC label when composing a new email.
- **Ask before deleting**   To confirm or not confirm the deletion of emails.

- **Load remote images**   To load images at the same time you load an email, or not to.
- **Always Bcc myself**   To always send a copy of the email to yourself, or not to.
- **Signature**   To add and/or configure a signature for all outgoing emails. A signature appears at the bottom of the email. By default, the included signature is "Sent from my iPad."
- **Default account**   To set which account will be used by default when sending photos from the Photo app and when sending data from other apps.

Under Contacts, you can change:

- **Sort order**   To set if contacts are sorted by first name, last name or last name, first name.
- **Display order**   To set if contacts are displayed by first name, last name or last name, first name.

Under Calendars you can change:

- **New invitation alerts**   To set to on or off.
- **Time zone support**   To select a time zone.
- **Default calendar**   To set the default calendar if multiple calendars are available.

PART III

News and Entertainment

5

Go Digital with iBooks

HOW TO...

- Install iBooks and browse the iBooks library
- Read reviews and preview books
- Buy and download a book
- Open and read a book
- Create, locate, and delete a bookmark
- Adjust text size, font, and screen brightness
- Copy and paste text
- Search for and look up the meaning of a word
- Experiment with VoiceOver
- Sort and reposition books
- Delete a book

iBooks is a free app you can obtain from the App Store that enables you to browse, download, and read digital books you obtain from the iBookstore. It's an easy way to turn your iPad into a fully functional e-book reader. If you're already somewhat familiar with Amazon's Kindle, this is similar. iBooks offers some really innovative features too, including touch screen control, support for color images, and embedded videos within some books.

iBooks lets you do much more than download and read digital versions of books on your iPad, though. With iBooks you can personalize a book in a way you never thought imaginable with printed books, such as changing the font size and font type. You can purchase a book without ever setting foot into a physical store. You can even set an electronic bookmark so you don't lose your place. And if you're worried about not being able to preview the book before buying it, have no fear. You can view a sample of the book before you purchase it. Beyond all of that, though, you can search a book for a specific word or phrase, look up the definition of a word, locate a specific word in the book, and use iBook's available controls to navigate a book.

Tip iBooks is a free app, and there are lots of free books to choose from. Don't worry if money is tight; you can enjoy iBooks without spending a dime.

Get Started with iBooks

iBooks isn't installed by default; you have to get it from the App Store. It's free, though, and since you have the option of reading free books too, you don't have to lay out any money to enjoy iBooks. Figure 5-1 shows all of the books we've acquired, and they were all free.

iBooks has some pretty tight rules, though. You can't shop for books online at your computer; you have to go through the iBooks app on your iPad. iBooks aren't available in the iTunes Store either. So, if you want to purchase, download, and read iBooks, there's no way around installing the iBooks app and shopping at the iBookstore. The iBookstore does not offer audiobooks, magazines, or any other media. The iBookstore and the iBooks app are for obtaining and reading electronic books, and nothing else.

Tip If you're in the market for audiobooks, look to the iTunes Store. If you're looking for digital books from other sources, like Amazon, check out the App store.

The iBooks you acquire on your iPad can be synced to your computer. However, even though you can see their titles in iTunes, you can't read iBooks on your computer (at least not yet). You can only read iBooks on your iPad, iPhone, or iPod Touch. You can play audiobooks you acquire from iTunes on your computer, though, and you can play videos you acquire from the iTunes Store, but iBooks doesn't work that way.

FIGURE 5-1   The classics, from authors like Jane Austen, H. G. Wells, and Lewis Carroll, are all free at the iBookstore, along with many others.

Install iBooks

There are two ways to get the iBooks app. One way is to download the iBooks app from the iTunes Store at your computer (although you can download the app in iTunes, you can't get or read iBooks there). The next time you sync your iPad with your computer, the iBooks app will be transferred to it. If you're like most people, though, you'll opt to install iBooks from your iPad, which is what we'll outline here.

 At your computer, in iTunes under the Books tab, verify that books are configured to sync automatically.

To install iBooks using your iPad:

1. Click the App Store icon on the Home screen.
2. Tap the Featured button at the bottom of the screen.
3. Tap in the Spotlight Search window, and type **iBooks**.
4. Tap Free, next to the iBooks icon. When it changes to Install App, tap again.
5. Wait while the app installs.

 If iBooks is the first app you've installed, you'll notice that the app downloads to a secondary Home screen. To return to the Home screen with the Apple apps, flick right.

Browse for Books

The first step in browsing for books from the iBookstore is to get online. You have to be connected to the Internet to access the store. Once you're online, you'll need to locate the magic button in the iBooks app that transports you to it. That button is located in the top-left corner of the iBooks app and is labeled Store.

Once in the store you can browse to your heart's content. You can peruse the *New York Times* bestseller list, look through a list of Featured books (those chosen by the people at iBooks), view the Top Paid and Top Free books, and even preview books you think you'll enjoy. Of course, you can browse by category as you'd expect, such as History, Nonfiction, Romance, or Sports & Outdoors. You can also search for a specific title or author.

To browse books in the iBookstore:

1. Touch the iBooks app on the Home screen.
2. Locate the button labeled Store in the top-left corner of the screen and tap it. (That button will change to Library after you tap it, to enable you to return to your own personal iBooks library when you're finished browsing.)

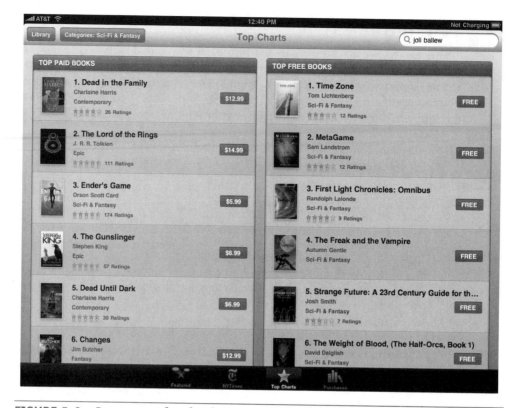

FIGURE 5-2 Some great free books are available from the iBookstore.

3. Once in the store, touch Featured at the bottom of the page to view Featured books, or to access Quick Links to things like Oprah's Book Club, Free Books, and $9.99 or Less.
4. Touch NYTimes at the bottom of the page to see the current top sellers for Fiction and Nonfiction books.
5. Touch Top Charts to see a list of Top Paid and Top Free books. See Figure 5-2.
6. Tap Purchases at the bottom of the page to see the items you've purchased, including books you've downloaded that were free.

Read Reviews of Books

Although you'll often go directly to the book you want buy in the iBookstore, sometimes you'll find an interesting-looking book while window shopping. Since you may not be familiar with the book or its author, you'll need a bit more information before you commit. That's where reader reviews come in. It's safe to say that most books will have reviews written for them by readers, but if not, at the very least, you'll be able to read a description of the book, find out a little about the author, and discover any special features included with the book.

Tip Watch for readers who post reviews that spoil the book's ending, or those labeled "spoiler alerts." You'll have to be careful to avoid reviews that may give away the ending of a book you're interested in.

To read the reviews for any book or to get more information about a book or its author:

1. Locate a book in the iBookstore.
2. Touch the book to go to the book's information page.
3. In the information page you'll see a description of the book, publisher, publication date, and more. You can tap to go to the Author Page, and you'll have access to price information and book ratings. If there are any customer reviews, you'll see those also. See Figure 5-3.
4. Tap outside the information window to close it.

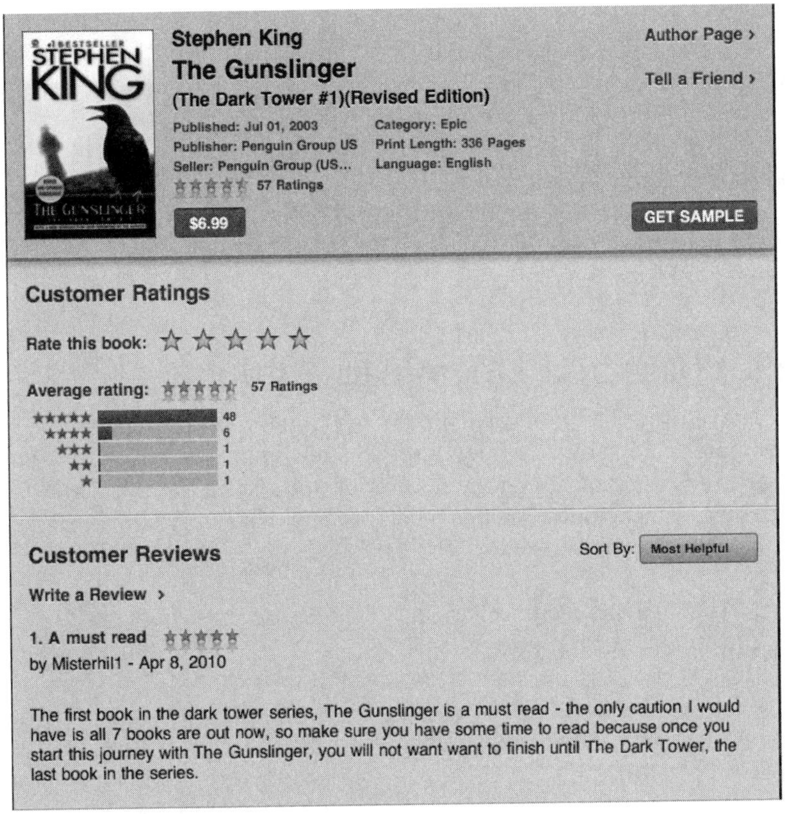

Stephen King
The Gunslinger
(The Dark Tower #1)(Revised Edition)

Published: Jul 01, 2003   Category: Epic
Publisher: Penguin Group US   Print Length: 336 Pages
Seller: Penguin Group (US...   Language: English
★★★★☆ 57 Ratings

$6.99

Author Page >

Tell a Friend >

GET SAMPLE

Customer Ratings

Rate this book: ☆ ☆ ☆ ☆ ☆

Average rating: ★★★★☆ 57 Ratings

★★★★★ 48
★★★★   6
★★★   1
★★   1
★   1

Customer Reviews   Sort By: Most Helpful

Write a Review >

1. A must read ★★★★★
by Misterhil1 - Apr 8, 2010

The first book in the dark tower series, The Gunslinger is a must read - the only caution I would have is all 7 books are out now, so make sure you have some time to read because once you start this journey with The Gunslinger, you will not want want to finish until The Dark Tower, the last book in the series.

FIGURE 5-3 A book's information page offers various information including the price and description.

After reading a book, come back here and write your own review.

Preview a Book

When you're in a "real" bookstore, you can open a book and flip through the pages. You can read the Table of Contents, front cover and back cover, and even the inside pages. Of course, you can sit down and read a chapter if the bookstore allows it. You can perform similar actions at the digital iBookstore, although you can only look at the parts of the book that iBooks wants you to see!

Some things you can preview include (as applicable to the book)

- Table of Contents
- Acknowledgments
- Foreword
- A sample chapter or part of a chapter

To preview a book, click the Get Sample button inside the information page. The information page with this button was shown earlier in Figure 5-3. A sample will download and will appear in your Library. It will have a "Sample" banner across it, as shown in this illustration.

While previewing the book, if you decide to purchase it, a Buy button is available. Just click Buy to purchase the book, shown in Figure 5-4.

Purchase and Download a Book

If you've ever used the App store on an iPhone or purchased music from your computer using iTunes, you will see lots of similarities between what you've seen there and what you see in the new iBookstore. Even the "Buy" and "Free" buttons look the same. Once you've located a book to buy, it's a very simple process to purchase and download the book:

1. Locate a book to purchase or download for free.
2. Tap Buy or Free, as applicable.

FIGURE 5-4   When you're sampling a book, the option to Buy is easily accessible.

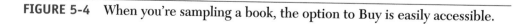

iTunes and Password Prompts

Just as with the iTunes or App Store apps, you'll be prompted for your password the first time you download something during a shopping session. Subsequent downloads will not require you to input your password, as long as you're still shopping in the same session. If you close out the app and launch it again, you'll need to enter your password again to make a download. It's a way to protect you in case someone else uses your iPad, while at the same time, remaining unobtrusive if you feel inspired to load up on books, apps, and music in one sitting.

3. Tap Buy Book or Get Book, as applicable, as shown here. iBooks may prompt you to enter your iTunes account password. When you buy a book, your iTunes account will be charged.

4. Wait while the book downloads to your Library, which should only take a minute or less.

Read a Digital Book

When you're ready to read a book, simply open iBooks and tap the book you'd like to read. All of the books you've downloaded are on the virtual bookshelf. You can view the books as thumbnails, the default view, or as a list.

To open and read a book:

1. Open iBooks.
2. Tap any book on your bookshelf to read it.
3. Hold the iPad in Portrait or Landscape orientation to view as a single page or facing pages.

With a book open, there are several ways to navigate through it:

- To turn a page, tap or flick near the right or left margin of a page to access the previous page and the next page. By default, tapping the left margin takes you to the previous page; however, in Settings under iBooks, you can change this behavior so that tapping the left margin takes you to the next page instead.

- To go to a specific page, tap near the center of the current page to show the slider at the bottom of the page (see the following illustration). Drag the slider to the desired page. Let go to jump to that page in the book.

"Don't you be."

other small businesses

7
Pages 338-339

288 of 492

289 of 492   1 page left in this chapter

- To return to or go to the Table of Contents of a book, tap the Contents button at the top of the page next to the Library button. If you can't see either button, tap in the center of a page to show them.
- To locate the start of a specific chapter, tap the Content button to access the Table of Contents, and then tap the desired chapter number to go there. To momentarily view the Table of Contents without losing your place, tap the Content button to view the Table of Contents, then tap the red Resume ribbon to return to the current page.
- Tap Library to return to the books in your Library to access a new book to read. If you can't see the Library button, tap in the middle of any page to access it.
- Tap the Home button to access another app or to stop reading. iBooks will remember the page you're on the next time you open the book.

Tip To read a book while lying down or to keep the iPad from switching views when you reposition yourself in a chair, enable the Screen Rotation lock. The Screen Rotation lock is located on the outside of your iPad above the Volume Rocker in Portrait view or to the right of it in Landscape view.

Highlight Text to Place a Bookmark

You can tap Library or click the Home button to leave your iBook, and when you return, iBooks will remember where you last left off reading. This is true even if you are reading multiple books at the same time. You simply don't have to create a bookmark when you leave a book. However, there are times when you *want* to create a bookmark, perhaps to make a note of a specific plot twist, clue, definition, or picture. You may also want to highlight a phrase so you can come back to it later. Once you've created bookmarks (which also work to highlight text), you can access the bookmarks by tapping the Contents button. The Contents button offers two tabs: Table of Contents and Bookmarks, and is located next to the Library button while you're in a book.

To create (or delete) a bookmark:

1. Tap and hold any word on the page. (You can also tap a picture.)
2. If you want to highlight (bookmark) more than the selected word, pull from the blue "grab" points until you've selected the text desired.

3. Tap Bookmark (shown right).
4. Tap any bookmarked word to choose a different color for the bookmark. You can choose Yellow, Green, Blue, Pink, or Purple.
5. Tap any bookmarked word to remove the bookmark. Tap and choose Unbookmark.

To access bookmarks you've set:

1. Tap the Contents button. If you can't see it, tap in the center of any page to show it.
2. Note the two tabs, Table of Contents and Bookmarks. Tap Bookmarks. See Figure 5-5.
3. Tap the bookmark to access that page.

Adjust Text Size and Font

You can adjust the text size and the font used in any book you get from the iBookstore. If you have to wear reading glasses to see the text on the page, consider making the font larger. If you have trouble reading the font used in the book, choose another one. And if you don't have any problems at all reading what's on the page and want to flip

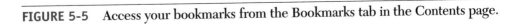

FIGURE 5-5   Access your bookmarks from the Bookmarks tab in the Contents page.

pages less often, consider a smaller font size. Everything you need is available on the top-right corner of iBooks. (If you don't see anything there, tap in the center of any page to show these controls.)

To increase or decrease the font size:

1. Tap the Fonts button. It consists of two capital letters, both A, one small and one large.
2. To increase the font size, tap the large A. Tap again to increase the font size more. Repeat as desired.
3. To decrease the font size, tap the small A. Tap again to decrease the font size more. Repeat as desired.

To change the font:

1. Tap the Fonts button. It consists of two capital letters, both A, one small and one large.
2. Tap Fonts.
3. Tap a font in the list.

 At the present time you cannot install your own fonts. You have to choose one of the fonts listed.

Adjust Brightness

By default, your iPad will adjust the screen's brightness automatically. There's a sensor in the iPad that ascertains how much light is available and uses that information to make the adjustments. You can disable Auto-Brightness in Settings, and Brightness & Wallpaper if you'd rather not have your iPad do this automatically. You can also change the brightness manually in iBooks while reading.

To change the brightness manually while reading a book in iBooks:

1. Tap the Brightness icon. It looks like a sun.
2. Drag to reposition the slider.

Explore Additional iBook Features

You're not finished yet! There are still more features to discover. You can copy text, look up a word in the dictionary (included with your iPad), and search for a specific word or phrase to locate it in the book or on Google or Wikipedia. The search results offer results for the entire book too, allowing you to easily find all instances of the word. There are options that enable you to reorder books on your Library's bookshelf, and delete books or samples of books you no longer want. There's an option to have a book read to you too, although what you hear won't sound anything like an audiobook.

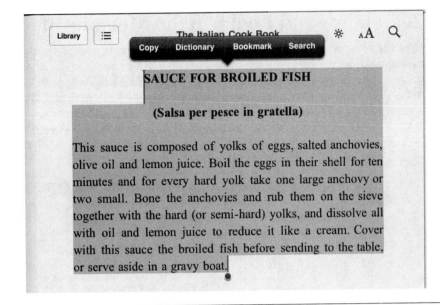

FIGURE 5-6   The Copy command allows you to copy text, even in many iBooks.

Copy Text

You can copy text in any free, public domain book and then paste that text in another app, such as an email in Mail or a note in Notes. You may have already seen the Copy option when creating a bookmark.

To access the Copy command:

1. Tap and hold briefly any word in the book. If the book is a free, public domain title (as most of the free books offered in the iBookstore are), the option to Copy appears along with Dictionary, Bookmark, and Search. If the book is a copyrighted work, you will not have the option to copy text.
2. As when copying in any other app, you can drag from the "grab" points to select additional text.
3. After you've selected the text, click Copy, as shown in Figure 5-6.
4. You can now open any Apple (or other compatible) app on your iPad and paste that text, as shown in this illustration.

Search For and Look Up the Meaning of a Word

If, while reading, you come across a word you don't recognize, a term you don't understand, medical terminology you'd like to learn more about, or a company name you've never heard of, highlight the word and click Dictionary or Search. The Dictionary option will look up the selected word using the iBooks' built-in dictionary. The Search option looks for additional references in the book itself, and if that doesn't lend a clue to the word's meaning (as shown in Figure 5-7), click Search Google or Search Wikipedia to learn more online. When you click either of these, iBooks closes and Safari opens.

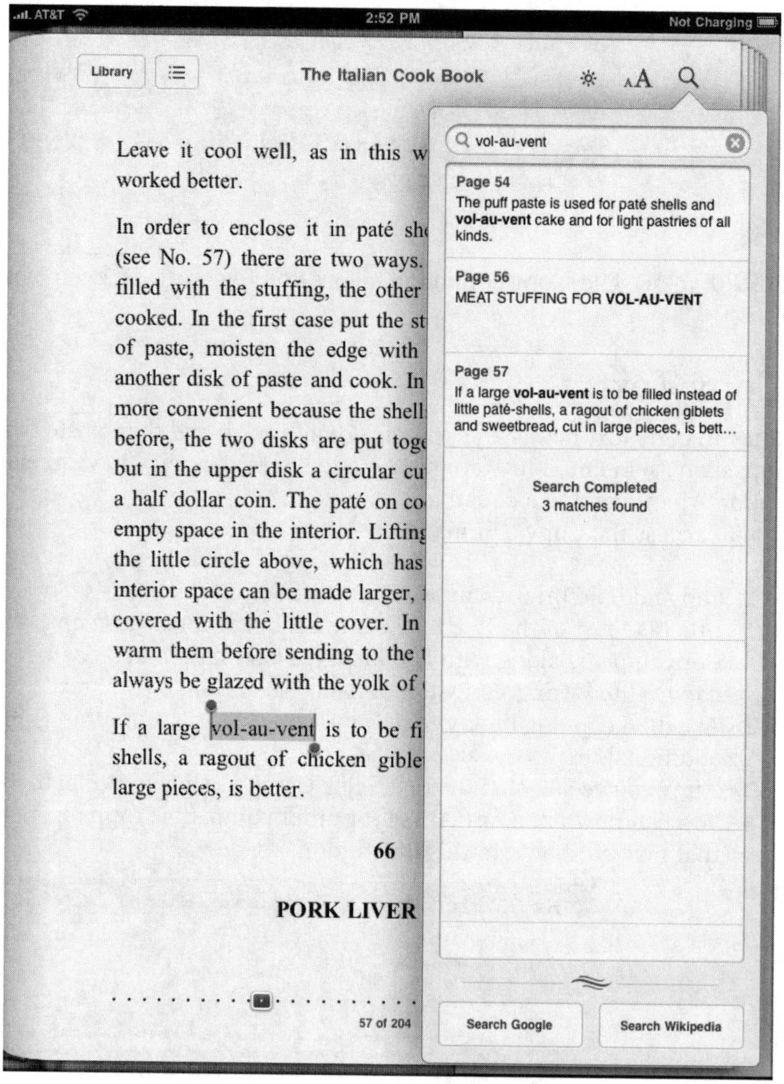

FIGURE 5-7   If you're not sure what a word means, search for a definition in the book or online.

To research a word in iBooks:

1. Tap to select the word and use the grab points if necessary to select words around it.
2. Tap Search.
3. Browse the other instances of the word in the book for a meaning, or click Search Google or Search Wikipedia.

 To select a word like the one shown in Figure 5-7, with hyphens, try to tap at the beginning of the word and then drag the grab points to select the rest of it.

To look up a word in the Dictionary:

1. Tap to select the word to look up in the Dictionary.
2. Tap Dictionary.
3. The definition will appear in a pop-up window on the screen.
4. Tap anywhere outside the box to make it disappear.

Experiment with VoiceOver

If you have a visual impairment, or if you simply don't like to read but don't want to spend the money required to purchase an audiobook, you can use VoiceOver to have your iPad read a book aloud. It's a little tricky to get started and to learn to navigate using VoiceOver, but once you get it down, it's a pretty nice feature.

There are a few steps to using VoiceOver with iBooks, first, enabling VoiceOver in Settings; second, accessing the iBooks app on the secondary Home screen; and third, setting VoiceOver to read the entire book, not just a single sentence. Before you start and while you're in iBooks, open a book you'd like to have read to you, and turn to the place in the book where you'd like to start. (This minimizes how many "gestures" you'll have to learn initially.)

To enable VoiceOver:

1. From the Home screen, tap Settings.
2. Tap General.
3. Tap Accessibility.
4. Tap VoiceOver and slide the switch from Off to On.
5. Double-tap OK in the prompt, and if desired, practice the available gestures in VoiceOver before continuing.
6. To exit Settings, tap the Home button.

To access iBooks (this is almost always located on a different Home screen):

1. Swipe left with three fingers to access a secondary Home screen.
2. Tap iBooks once to select it.
3. Tap iBooks twice to open it.

4. A book should already be open, if you followed the directions to open one prior to starting VoiceOver. If a book is not open, you can
   a. Tap a book to select it from your virtual bookshelf.
   b. Double-tap the book to open it.
   c. Use a three-finger swipe to locate the page to begin.
5. Tap the first sentence on the page. VoiceOver will read it.
6. To have VoiceOver read the entire page and the pages after it, double-tap on the first sentence of the paragraph.
7. To stop VoiceOver from reading, tap twice with three fingers. (We had to tap fairly hard.) Tap with three fingers again to start text again.

To disable VoiceOver:

1. Click the Home button to access the Home screen. If you are on a secondary Home screen, click the Home button again to return to the primary Home screen.
2. Tap Settings to select it.
3. Double-tap Settings to open it.
4. Tap General. Tap Accessibility. (If you can't access Accessibility, place the iPad in Portrait mode.)
5. Double-tap Accessibility to open it.
6. Tap VoiceOver.
7. Double-tap VoiceOver.
8. Tap the On/Off toggle for VoiceOver.
9. Double-tap the toggle to turn off VoiceOver.

Sort and Manage Books

After you've used iBooks for a while, you may discover that you have too many books on your bookshelf and in your Library, and they are getting hard to manage. You may have books you've read, books you started but didn't like, or samples of books from the iBookstore that you'd like to delete. You may have so many books that you need to sort your books by their titles, authors, or by their category. You may even want to reorder the books on your bookshelf, placing the books you want to read in the order you plan to read them. There are several options in the iBooks app that you can use to manage your books.

 If you're in a book now, tap Library.

To sort books by their titles, authors, or by their categories:

1. Tap the List icon in the Library. The list icon is to the left of the Edit button and consists of three horizontal lines.

2. At the bottom of the page, tap Titles, Authors, or Categories. Categories is shown here.

Note   You can tap Edit to delete books in this view and others.

To reposition the books on your bookshelf:

1. Tap the Thumbnail icon. The Thumbnail icon is to the left of the Edit button and consists of four small squares.
2. Tap Edit.
3. Drag and drop any book to a new position on the bookshelf.
4. Click the Done button when finished.

To delete a book:

1. In any view, tap Edit.
2. In Thumbnail view, tap the X beside the book to delete. In List view, tap the red minus button.
3. Tap Delete to verify.
4. Repeat as desired, and then click Done.

Note Deleted books remain in your iTunes library on your computer provided you've previously opted to sync books (and have actually synced them). If you delete a book you purchased, you can also download it again from the Purchases tab in iBookstore.

6

Read News and Commentary, and Use Social Networks

HOW TO...

- Find and read your local newspaper
- View an RSS feed
- Read the *New York Times*
- Explore free news apps
- Read an online magazine
- Follow friends on social networking sites
- Explore free social networking apps
- Send an SMS text
- Instant message with AIM
- Locate and read a blog
- Locate and listen to a podcast

With an iPad, you can stay up to date with everyone and everything. You can read newspapers, magazines, and blogs, and you can listen to and watch podcasts to stay in touch with the world. You can use social networking to stay in touch with friends. And with the right third-party apps, you can even exchange texts with friends who have cell phones, a feature not supported out of the box from Apple. You can even exchange instant messages through familiar instant messaging applications, like AIM. If you're looking for a way to stay in touch, this is the chapter for you.

Read Newspapers and Magazines

There are lots of printed newspapers that offer online versions for web users. Reading a newspaper online and on your iPad is generally a much more convenient experience than reading its printed counterpart. When reading a newspaper on an iPad, you'll never again elbow the person next to you on a bus when trying to turn a page. You won't have to fold up that paper when you arrive at your destination, and then look for a place to recycle it. And, if you see something interesting, you can email the article to a friend (versus clipping it and putting it in the mail, ugh)!

More and more magazines are available online too. You can find out if a magazine you like is available by searching for it on the Internet. Many magazines are available free too, whereas you'd otherwise have to pay for them at the newsstand. A few magazine publishers have created an app version of their publications that is designed specifically for the iPad. Check out the iPad versions of the magazines *Popular Science*, *GQ*, and *Time*. Open Safari and type **app.time.com** for a quick preview. You can also browse the App Store for magazine apps.

Find and Read Your Local Newspaper

If you have a favorite local newspaper (or a hometown newspaper), you may be able to find an online version of that paper, and read it on your iPad. At the present time, many online newspapers are free, even though their printed versions have to be purchased, so there's good reason to check it out. Some larger newspapers require you to create a user account to view the paper online, and a few require you to subscribe and pay a fee to access them online. If you already subscribe to the print version of a paper, the online version will likely be free too, provided you create an account and sign in.

To locate the online version of your favorite newspaper:

1. Tap Safari and tap the Search window.
2. Type the name of your local paper.
3. Review the results and tap the official newspaper page.
4. You can almost always view the front page of a newspaper, so tap any link on that page to see if access is available to the rest of the site. See Figure 6-1.

 Just because you can access your newspaper's front page doesn't mean you have full access to the paper. You may be able to read some articles but not have access to the classified ads, or you may be able to view only a few pages before being asked to create a user account.

5. If required, create a user name and password and/or set up a subscription to access the paper online. If you already know you want to subscribe, look for an icon for eEdition, Online Edition, or something similar.

FIGURE 6-1 Your local newspaper may be available online, for free.

Newspapers and RSS

Most newspapers, magazines, blogs, and such also offer an RSS option. RSS stands for Really Simple Syndication, which is a way for you to get the latest information and news in a list, also called a "feed," and forgo scanning the paper for the headlines you want. Each time you visit the RSS feed (or page), the information on it is updated. If you see an orange RSS button on your newspaper's online front page, tap it to see the results. If you like the results, bookmark the page so you can access it again later.

 If you really get into RSS, consider downloading an RSS reader to manage the feeds you like. You can find RSS readers at the App Store.

To access a newspaper's RSS feed:

1. Navigate to the newspaper, blog, or other entity that offers the RSS feed you wish to view.
2. Tap the RSS button. **RSS**

3. Read the RSS feed and bookmark it if desired. A partial RSS feed is shown here.

There are also apps at the App Store that offer RSS news and information. Try NewsRack ($4.99) or search for the latest in RSS by typing **News RSS** into the App Store's Spotlight Search window.

Read the *New York Times*

The *New York Times* seems to be the defining newspaper for many Americans, so a chapter on newspapers, magazines, blogs, and such wouldn't be complete without a trip to the *New York Times* online newspaper's front page! Once on the page, you can zoom in on any article to increase readability or tap any link to access the full article.

To access the *New York Times*:

1. Tap Safari to open it.
2. Tap inside the address window and type **nytimes.com**. (Your iPad knows you want an http:// in front of that, so there's no need to type it.)
3. Explore both Portrait and Landscape view. Portrait view is shown in Figure 6-2.

While exploring the paper, tap each tab: Home, Today's Paper, Video, Most Popular, Times Topics, and Most Recent. From the Videos page, tap any video to play it. To access controls while watching a video, tap the video once.

Explore Free News Apps

If you like news, you'll be amazed at the variety of free news apps you have access to from the App Store. There are apps from Reuters, BBC, AP, and *USA Today*. There are apps for NPR, Bloomberg, and other popular agencies.

To see the most popular news apps:

1. If Safari is open, tap the Home button to access the Home screen.
2. Tap App Store.
3. Tap Categories.
4. Tap News.
5. Browse the available apps. Try BBC News, Reuters News Pro for iPad, and others.

FIGURE 6-2   The *New York Times* is available to everyone.

Read an Online Magazine

If you subscribe to a lot of magazines, you know what a pile you can acquire in only a few months. It's difficult to read them all and even more difficult to throw them away. Moving from the printed version of a magazine to the online version can resolve these issues, by making your magazines available on your iPad. You can also take all of your magazines with you wherever you go, without all the weight and inconvenience.

There are several ways to locate an online magazine:

- Visit the home page for the magazine, for instance, *Time* magazine can be found at www.Time.com and *Newsweek* is located at www.newsweek.com.
- Search for "online magazines," and visit a web site that offers access to them. For example, www.onlinenewspapers.com/magazines offers magazines from around the world. You'll be amazed at what you find. Even expensive magazines like *Scientific American* can be accessed online, for free.
- Visit the App Store and look for your favorite magazine there, or search for "magazines." Although there aren't too many there at the present time, there may be more later.

FIGURE 6-3 Zinio, a free app from the App Store, lets you easily subscribe to just about any digital magazine.

- If you know you want to subscribe to a particular magazine, get the Zinio Magazine Newsstand app from the App Store. From there you can access just about any magazine imaginable, and subscribe to it or purchase the current issue. See Figure 6-3.

Facebook, Tweet, and Text

There are many ways to build and maintain your social contacts using your iPad. You can post to Facebook and other social networking sites, you can tweet on Twitter, and you can even text your friends on their cellular phones or hold instant messaging conversations via familiar instant messaging applications, like AIM. None of these things are available out of the box, though; the Facebook app isn't preinstalled, nor is a Twitter app, and by default, you can't text or send instant messages on an iPad. However, there are lots of free apps to help you do all of these things and more, and they're all available from the App Store.

Follow Friends on Social Networking Sites

You may use Facebook, or you may use another social networking medium like MySpace to connect with friends online. You may belong to online groups. You may also host a personal blog with WordPress, or share your thoughts using other networking options. Whatever you do, you can likely find a way to do it on your iPad. Because Facebook seems to be the most popular social networking site at this time, we'll focus on Facebook here.

No matter what social networking option you use, open Safari and navigate to its home page. For Facebook, type **facebook.com**. When prompted, log in. You should be able to use the site in the same manner you're used to on your computer at home. You can

- Post status updates and view your friends' updates
- View videos friends have posted
- Join groups
- Post your own pictures via email
- Edit your personal information
- Invite people to join you or any group you create
- And lots more!

If you have a Facebook account (and if you don't, you can create one), search Groups for HTDE: iPad. Our group is open to everyone, and you can easily post your own pictures and videos, write on our wall, and "talk" to other iPad fans online. Figure 6-4 shows our group. Once on the group's page, tap Add Bookmark (+) and tap Add to Home Screen, and you'll have one-tap access to the group! See Figure 6-4.

Explore Free Social Networking Apps

There are free social networking apps at the App Store, just as there were free news apps. There are apps you can purchase too. To find a social network app related to your social networking site, at the App Store search by the network name, like Facebook, or perform a more general search with a phrase like *Social Networking*. You'll find all kinds of related apps including those that allow you to chat with others, send and receive instant messages, and upload and share photos. Photobucket for iPad, for instance, allows you to upload media from your iPad directly to your Photobucket albums. You can share these albums with anyone you like.

To get started:

1. Tap the App Store icon on your Home screen.
2. Tap the Categories tab, and select Social Networking.
3. Browse the available apps or search for a specific term, like Facebook or MySpace.

Tweet with Twitter

If you tweet or if you want to, visit www.twitter.com on your iPad via Safari. Sign up or sign in to get started. As shown here, you can easily type your thoughts in the "What's happening?" box, tap Tweet, and be done. You can also view the tweets of

FIGURE 6-4 Log in to Facebook and search for HTDE: iPad to join our group.

those you follow, just as you would on your computer. (There are also lots of Twitter apps from the App Store you might enjoy.)

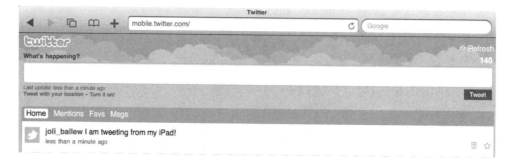

To access Twitter quickly, add a web clip to Twitter on your Home screen (click +
and click Add to Home Screen).

Send an SMS Text

An *SMS text* is a short text message that's generally sent from a cell phone to another
cell phone, and generally, the recipient of the text sends one back. This exchange
of words via cell phones is called *texting* and is achieved over a cellular network like
AT&T. You can send a text from your iPad to a cell phone, even if you don't have a
cellular data plan, though, using a third-party app called Textfree. Currently there are
two versions of this, one called Textfree and one called Textfree Lite. The latter is free;
the former you have to pay for. There are other texting apps, though, so don't assume
you have to use this one. We're only discussing this one because it was the first one
we tried and the texting app with the most reviews (implying it's quite popular).

  At the time this book was written, there were not many texting apps available for
the iPad. By the time you read this, though, there may be many more. Try a search
for SMS Text and see what you find in the App Store.

To get Textfree Lite and send your first text:

1. Tap the App Store icon on your Home screen.
2. Search Textfree.
3. Locate the Textfree Lite app.
4. Tap Free, and tap Install App.
5. Tap the icon for Textfree. You'll notice that the app only takes up half the screen,
   because it was originally designed for the iPhone and iPod Touch.
6. Create an account when prompted.
7. Tap the New Message icon.
8. Type the cell phone number to send the text to, tap Start Text, and type your
   message.
9. Tap Send.

Instant Message with AIM

Instant messaging is quite different from texting. Texting is done between two cell phones; instant messaging is done between two computers. Instant messaging is often called *chatting*. There are lots of ways to exchange instant messages, including Windows Live Messenger, AIM, Facebook Chat, Google Talk, Skype Chat, and Jabber, to name a few. If you currently exchange instant messages on your computer, you may be able to continue to exchange instant messages in the same manner on your iPad.

One of the instant messaging options is AIM, created by AOL. With it, you can chat directly with Facebook friends; get updates from Facebook, MySpace, Twitter, and others; add a location to your status; and more.

Explore Blogs, Podcasts, and Newsgroups

You can keep up with social commentary via the web from your iPad. You can read blogs, listen to podcasts, and join newsgroups, for instance, and have easy access to a wide range of opinions from just about every segment of the population. Often, these types of Internet communications and updates consist of personal views on politics and social issues, like health care, immigration, and a host of other hot (and sometimes volatile) topics, but can also encompass things like technology, breaking news, and simple personal observations.

Locate and Read a Blog

A blog is a "web log," and is often updated daily, sometimes hourly, and occasionally more often than that. A blog is written and posted to a web site, and the entries are listed most-recent-first. More often than not, a blog consists of observations made by a person about a specific thing, like their take on a new technology or what is going on in their business or company, but blogs also offer descriptions of events that allow others to access minute-by-minute details. (Some news correspondents offer blogs about a war or specific battle, for instance, or how quickly flood waters are rising during a dangerous storm.) More often than not, though, blogs are simply social commentary and include how the person feels about specific things, sometimes on volatile issues like healthcare, war, immigration, and the like.

You can search for blogs the same way you search for anything on the Internet, using keywords. If you know or have heard about a specific blog you want to read, perform a search for the person and his or her blog. You can search for "iPad Blog" and you'll see plenty of results. Here's the Apple blog.

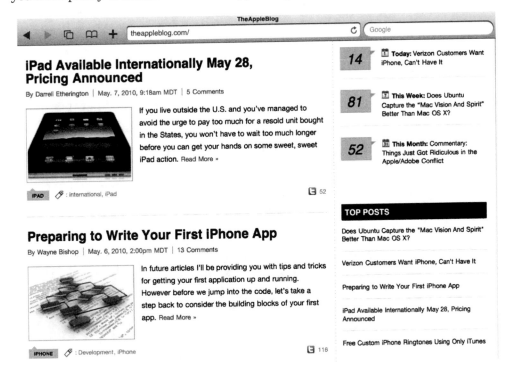

Locate and Listen to a Podcast

A *podcast* is a form of audio and video broadcasting over the Internet. It's kind of like a radio show on demand, if you can imagine that. Since we've talked quite a bit about news in this chapter, we'll take a look at podcasts available from news outlets.

One way to access podcasts is to open Safari on your iPad and navigate to a web site you know offers podcasts. If you like CNN, try cnn.com/services/podcasting. The following illustration shows an example, and we've zoomed in on it so that you can see the three buttons available (Subscribe, Listen, and iTunes).

Subscribe lets you subscribe to the podcast series, Listen lets you access the podcast immediately, and iTunes opens the podcast series in iTunes so you can download this podcast or any other that's available from the series, as shown in Figure 6-5. CNN offers podcasts for Larry King Live, CNN News Update, CNN Student News, In Case You Missed It, and more.

Podcasts can help you keep in touch with the latest news, sports, entertainment, technology, and more, without having to actually "tune in" to a show or suffer through the show's commercials.

You can also access podcasts from the iTunes Store, right from your iPad's Home screen. Just tap the Podcasts tab. From there you can view a list of featured podcasts, or tap the Categories button in the upper-left corner to further sort by category. iTunes features the largest selection of audio and video podcasts on the web. The iTunes interface makes it easy to find what you're looking for. All podcasts are free and can be downloaded on demand. You'll learn all about iTunes in Chapter 9.

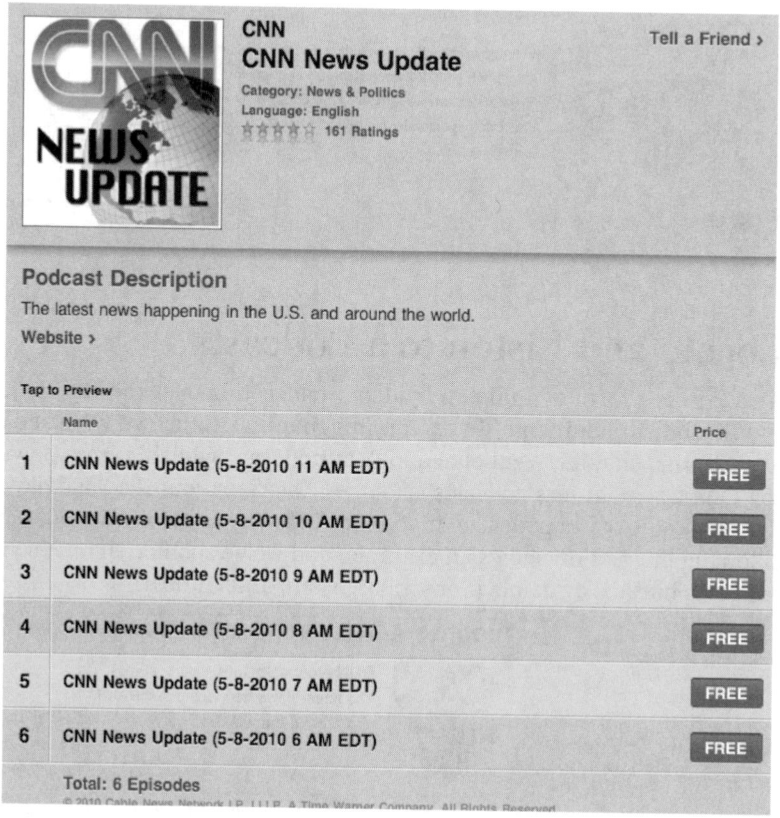

FIGURE 6-5 When you tap iTunes in the CNN options, iTunes opens on your iPad where you can acquire the podcast and previous ones.

7

Get and Use Apps from the App Store

HOW TO...

- Open and explore the App Store
- Use the Search box to find an app
- Read reviews of apps before you buy them
- Purchase and download an app
- Download and install a free app
- Get app updates
- Start and use an app
- Find apps created specifically for the iPad
- Delete apps you don't use
- Consider iWork
- Back up apps to your computer

The App Store is available via an Internet connection and the App Store icon on the Home screen. The App Store is where you get "apps." *Apps* are programs you can run on your iPad (or iPhone or iPod Touch), and they run the gamut with regard to what they offer. If you can imagine doing it, there's probably an app for that!

For example, there are apps that let you keep track of your workouts, apps that tell you how many calories are in the food you're eating, apps that help you choose or follow your fantasy football team, apps that are games, and even apps that enable you to play a virtual instrument, like a guitar or piano. You can get apps for Solitaire or Tetris, apps that help you learn a new language, and apps that enable you to communicate via social networking, right from your iPad. The App Store offers them all, upwards of 150,000 with more and more coming every week.

Once you're in the App Store, it's simple to browse listings of apps like "What's Hot" or "Top Charts." You can also browse by category, including Social Networking, Education, or Games. You can even filter apps by which ones are free, which is a perfect place to start if you're unsure about what apps are or what they offer. Let's start off simple—let's browse the App Store for the most popular apps first.

Explore the App Store

To use the App Store, you must be connected to the Internet. You'll also need an iTunes Store account, something you set up when you registered your iPad. To enter the store, simply tap the App Store icon on the Home screen. You can download and install any of the apps in the store, including apps designed for the iPhone and iPod Touch. When searching for apps, try to stick to apps created specifically for the iPad, at least for now. You know these apps will take advantage of the iPad's larger screen and Multi-Touch features, and will have been tested on an iPad. (Some apps created for the iPhone look distorted when you position them to take up the entire iPad screen, even though they work as they should.) You can also sync apps you have already purchased for your iPhone or iPod Touch using iTunes, if you want to try those apps on your iPad.

Open the App Store and Explore

The easiest way to get started with the App Store is to simply try it out. Touch the App Store icon while connected to the Internet and start browsing. Most of the time, that's all there is to it. On occasion you may find that you aren't connected to the Internet (when you thought you were), but there's really not much that can go wrong here.

To open the App Store and explore the apps:

1. Position yourself within range of a free wireless network and connect to it, or use your provider's 3G network to connect to the Internet.

Note   To learn more about how to connect to the Internet, see Chapter 2.

2. Touch the App Store icon on your iPad. If you are within range of and connected to a Wi-Fi network or connected through 3G via AT&T paid services, you'll see the store and be connected. If you aren't connected to the Internet, you'll receive a message stating that you can't access the store until you are.
3. Note the four options across the bottom of the App Store: Featured, Top Charts, Categories, and Updates. Tap to switch views.

Find the Most Popular Apps

If you want to browse the most popular apps in the App Store, you can do so easily. There's an option at the top of the Featured page entitled What's Hot. What's Hot shows what's "trending" at the moment. This doesn't mean the apps in this list have outsold all others or are more popular in the long term; it just means that at this moment, they're hot.

To browse What's Hot:

1. Touch the App Store icon on the Home screen.
2. Touch Featured at the bottom of the App Store interface.
3. Touch What's Hot at the top of the App Store interface. See Figure 7-1. There are lots of browsing options:
   a. Flick left and right on the thumbnails on In the Spotlight.
   b. Scroll up and down to see additional categories (The Newsstand and Quick Links).
   c. Tap the left and right arrows in a category to view more.
   d. Tap See All to see everything in a category.

FIGURE 7-1   Find out what's trending by looking at What's Hot.

There are free apps too, and the fact that they're free often makes them popular. There are free versions of games like Solitaire, free practical apps like calculators, and apps that let you play air guitar or a virtual piano. There are media apps from companies like Netflix and ABC, and free newspapers, including *USA Today*.

To find popular and free apps for your iPad:

1. Touch the App Store icon on the Home screen.
2. Tap Top Charts at the bottom of the page.
3. In the right pane, scroll to browse the Top Free iPad apps.

 Tip Although we'll discuss purchasing apps later in this chapter, if you find a free app you want, click Free, and click Install App.

Find Apps by Category or Search

You may not care about what's hot, and you may not even care if the app you're looking for is free or if you have to buy it. What you care about is finding an app that will do a specific thing, such as enable you to play Tetris on your iPad, have a specific keyword in its description such as Facebook or Netflix, or keep track of certain data such as calories eaten or miles driven. In these instances you need to browse apps by their category, or search for them by their name.

There are lots of categories of apps, and you can browse them from the App Store. Just click the Categories button at the bottom of the page. Here are some descriptions of a few of the available categories and what you can expect to find in them:

- **Games** As you'd expect, you'll find games here. There are all kinds of games to choose from including action, adventure, arcade, board, card, casino, dice, and so on.
- **Entertainment** Generally apps under the Entertainment category are meant to "entertain." These apps don't usually have anything to do with entertainers, although they can. For the most part, you'll find jokes, quizzes, aquariums, and games like Truth or Dare.

Tip Touch the Back button to return to the Categories screen.

- **Utilities** For the most part, apps in the Utilities category are things like alarm clocks, battery boosters, levels, messaging programs, web browsers, spell checkers, system activity monitors. They're "utile."
- **Social Networking** This is where you'll find programs for communicating with others via Facebook, AIM, GPS tracking, and instant messaging. Look for Facebook, Skype, Yahoo! Messenger, and Google Chat, to name a few.
- **Music** You won't find songs here; instead look for apps that teach you how to learn to play the guitar; apps that let you listen to radio stations, play finger pianos and drum kits; and apps that offer the lyrics to your favorite songs.
- **Productivity** These apps are meant to help you be productive, in terms of getting things done. There are PDF readers, apps that help you find the lowest

gas prices in your area, apps that convert measures and money, and even apps to help you redecorate your house.

- **Lifestyle**   Lifestyle apps help you cook, mix drinks, give a toast, or spout a great quotation. You'll find diary apps, find-a-restaurant apps, and even apps to help you grill the perfect steak or find the perfect bottle of wine. Not all of the lifestyle apps are Rated G, though—but the titles usually give that away!
- **Reference**   This category contains dictionaries, grammar guides, math apps, and similar reference materials.
- **Travel**   Here you'll find apps for tracking flights, sharing trip information, keeping travel journals, and even apps to help you pack.
- **Sports**   Sports apps offer just what you'd expect. Keep track of your favorite teams and players here. Learn the rules of the game, where to fish, and how to hit the perfect golf shot.

There are more categories, but we're sure you're getting the idea. App makers put their apps in the category that best relates to what they offer. Other categories include Navigation, Healthcare and Fitness, Photography, Finance, Business, Education, Weather, Books, and Medical.

To browse apps by category:

1. Touch the App Store icon to enter the store.
2. At the bottom of the page, touch Categories, as shown in the following illustration.
3. Touch any category to view the available apps.

If you've searched for an app by What's Hot or What's Free, and you've looked for an app in the appropriate category but still haven't found what you want, consider searching for it by keyword. There's a Spotlight Search box in each of the App Store's windows, and all you have to do is touch and type. Search the App Store using keywords that describe what you're looking for, and try to only use one or two unique keywords for best results.

Here's an example. Say you want to locate an app that can help you decide what plants would be best for your climate, when to plant them, and how to take care of them. Touch Search and type plants. You'll get lots of results and can browse them and read the reviews to find one you want. Later, if you decide on roses, for example, you can search for an app that tells you about growing roses. This time, you'll look for an app that tells you where and when to plant roses, how much to water, how to fertilize, how to trim, and so on. Although a search for "roses" will produce results that don't include what you're looking for, there's a good chance you'll find a gardening app that just deals with the rose.

To use the Search box to find an app:

1. Touch the App Store icon on the Home screen.
2. Touch inside the Search window. If you've searched before, you may see the keyword you typed last time. If this is the case, use the X to erase what's there.
3. Use the keyboard to type in a keyword. It's best to search using one keyword first, and if there are too many results, try typing two.
4. Touch Search on the keyboard to show the results. See Figure 7-2.
5. If you see iPad apps and iPhone apps, see if one of the iPad apps will work for you before opting for an app made for the iPhone.
6. Tap the icon for the app to learn more about it.

FIGURE 7-2   You'll see apps for the iPad and the iPhone. If given a choice, see if an iPad app suits your needs.

Read Reviews of Apps

You should always read the reviews of app before you purchase them. While an app may look good on an iPhone and have many excellent reviews, it may lose its luster on an iPad. Additionally, app reviews can reveal bugs with an app, problems contacting the manufacturer, or information regarding the value of the app in comparison to its price. Finally, reviews can help uncover any problems with the app, such as it being too violent or sexual (like a game), or not including information required to make it useful (which is often the case with reference apps).

Just about every app has a few reviews. Some have a ton. To find and read reviews for apps:

1. In the App Store, locate an app that you would like to learn more about.
2. Touch the app. You won't have to buy the app right now; touching the app here takes you to the app's information page.
3. Scroll down to the bottom of the information page, as shown in the following illustration.
4. Read any app review on the page, and if there are more than will fit on one page, touch More.

Customer Ratings

Rate this app: ☆ ☆ ☆ ☆ ☆

Average rating for the current version: ☆☆☆   266 Ratings

★★★★★ ▮▮▮▮▮▮ 78
★★★★ ▮▮▮ 23
★★★ ▮▮▮▮ 42
★★ ▮▮▮▮ 36
★ ▮▮▮▮▮▮▮ 87

Customer Reviews

Write a Review ›

30 Reviews For The Current Version

5. Click the Back button to return to the app's information page.

Purchase, Download, and Install an App

We'll assume that you've found an app you like, and you're ready to purchase, download, and install it. Since we want to be thorough here, we'll detail each of these: how to purchase an app from the iTunes Store, download, and install it; how to download and install a free app from the iTunes store; and how to keep your apps up to date by downloading and installing updates.

Tip On the fence about apps? Try a free app. You can always delete it if you don't like it. No harm, no foul.

Purchase and Download an App

If you've read the reviews and are ready to purchase an app, you're in the right place. Get your iTunes password handy; you'll be asked for it. Remember that you'll have to be connected to the Internet too.

To purchase and download an app:

1. Locate the app you want to purchase in the App Store.
2. Touch the app to go to its information page, if desired.
3. Touch the price of the app.
4. Touch Buy App.
5. Type your iTunes password, if prompted. (If you've already made a purchase during this App Store session, you won't be asked for your password again.)

Note iTunes passwords are case-sensitive.

6. Watch the download process on your Home screen. Once the download is complete, tap the app to start it.

Download and Install a Free App

If you're on the fence about apps, or simply aren't ready to shell out any money for one, try a free app. If you're a fan of Facebook, try the Facebook app. It's got to be good if over 20,000 people have downloaded it! Not into social networking? Look for Pocket Pond HD, Jumbo Calculator, or The Weather Channel Max for iPad. If you want to really step out, try the ABC Player. With it you can watch the latest episodes of many of your favorite ABC shows from *Desperate Housewives* to *Castle* to *Private Practice*.

To download and install a free app:

1. Locate the free app you want in the App Store.
2. Touch the app to go to its information page, if desired.

Agree to Terms of Service

The first time you use the App Store, you may be prompted to agree to Terms of Service. If so, click OK to continue. Read and review the terms, and click Agree. Note that you may have to touch Agree again. If prompted to "try your purchase again," start over with Step 1. Agreeing to the Terms of Service is a one-time inconvenience, and you should not be prompted again unless the terms change.

3. Touch Free.
4. Touch Install App.
5. Type your iTunes password, if prompted.
6. Watch the download process on your Home screen. Once the download is complete, tap the app to start it.

Install App Updates

Manufacturers often offer updates to their apps to enhance their quality, offer more features, or add more data. You'll know when these updates are available because a number will appear on the App Store icon, and you'll see a number on the Updates tab of the App Store once it's opened. It's up to you whether or not to install updates. If it's an app you use and the update is free, you have nothing to lose. If it's an app you never use, it's probably better to delete the app altogether and get it off your iPad (why waste the space?). And if it's an app you use but the update costs money—well, you'll have to decide if you want to pay for the update or not. Thus, you should always read the information offered about the update before installing it. To check for update information, review it, and install app updates from your iPad:

1. Touch the App Store icon.
2. Touch the Updates tab. It will have a number on it if updates are available.
3. If more than one update is available, don't immediately click Update All. You should go through each update individually to verify that you really want to download and install the update. That said, touch any item in the list to view update information.
4. Decide if you want to install this update or not.
   a. To install a single item, click the Free button on the app update information page (or the price icon) and click Install.
   b. If prompted, enter your iTunes password.
   c. To install all updates, click Update All.

You can also check for updates any time and install them, using your computer:

1. Connect your iPad to your computer.
2. Under Library in the source pane, click Apps.
3. Check the bottom-right corner to see if updates are available.
4. If updates are available, click the arrow button next to the description of how many updates are available.
5. You can view updates, or opt to download all free updates at once.
6. When all desired updates are installed, scroll to the bottom of the page and click Done.

 To make sure you have the most recent version of iTunes, click Help, and click Check for Updates. To make sure you've downloaded everything you've paid for, click Store and click Check for Downloads.

Use Apps

You're probably surprised that we've dedicated this many pages to apps and we haven't even shown you how to use an app yet! The wait is over. To start any app, simply touch it on the Home screen to which it was downloaded.

The first time you start an app, you'll probably see an introductory screen that either tells you how to use the app or offers a button for getting directions. After bypassing that, you may then see a menu screen that offers options for the app, like entering data, inputting a zip code or city, adding a player, or continuing where you left off the last time you used it. Because all apps are different, the best we can do is generalize the options you'll see when you start an app, and what you'll need to do to use it.

To start an app and use it:

1. Locate the icon for the app on the Home screen.
2. Touch the icon to start the app.
3. Read the introductory statements, and read any directions supplied.
4. Click Start, Play, Begin, or another option. Once you've started an app, you may be prompted with instructions for play or use, as shown in the following illustration.

Note If you like an app and want to move it to another Home screen for easier access, tap and hold the icon for a second until all icons start to "wiggle," and then drag the app to its new location. Press the Home button to apply.

Find the Perfect App

By now you know that there are a ton of apps! And if you've downloaded your fair share, you've likely seen the good, the bad, and the ugly. You probably also know that good reviews don't always mean great apps. Even apps with excellent reviews can be less than optimal on the larger iPad if created for the iPhone, fail to offer what you're looking for or do what they're supposed to do, or don't entertain the way you expected. And by now, you know that just because an app is "hot" doesn't guarantee it's a great app, and free apps won't always meet your expectations.

There are apps that have been specifically designed for, or redesigned for, the iPad. These apps are optimized for the iPad's larger screen, compared to the iPhone or iPod Touch. You'll find these apps in a special section of the App Store, as detailed here:

1. Enter the App Store on your iPad.
2. Tap Top Charts at the bottom of the page.
3. View the top apps for iPad. If the screen also shows apps for the iPhone, scroll down to the bottom of the page and tap Show iPad Apps.

Delete Apps You Don't Use

We don't know what model iPad you purchased—if it was the 16GB, 32GB, or 64GB model—but no matter, you don't want to keep apps you don't use on your iPad. You only have so much space, and there's no need to fill up that space with apps you'll never use. Therefore, you should delete apps you know you don't like.

Depending on how the app arrived on your iPad (either directly or via your computer), permanently deleting an app from your iPad may take up to two steps. If you've downloaded an app directly to your iPad through the App Store and haven't synced the iPad back to your computer since, you can delete the app from the iPad immediately and permanently. When you delete an app from your iPad, it's not there any more, and it isn't taking up any space.

If the app arrived on your iPad via your computer or has been synced back to iTunes, a copy of the app will remain on your computer even after you've deleted it from the iPad. So, if you really want to delete all traces of an app, you'll have to delete it from your iTunes library on your computer too. If you like, though, you can leave the app on your computer, and if you ever change your mind about it, you'll have the option to sync it back to your iPad.

To remove an app from your iPad:

1. Locate the app to delete on the iPad.
2. Touch and hold the icon for the app until all of the icons start to "wiggle."
3. Click the X that appears on the app, as shown in Figure 7-3.
4. Click Delete to verify you want to delete the app.
5. Click No Thanks or Rate if prompted to rate the app before deleting it.
6. Press the Home button to stop the icons from "wiggling."

To remove the app from your computer:

1. Connect your iPad to your computer.
2. Under Library, click Apps.

FIGURE 7-3   To delete an app from your iPad, tap the X.

3. Right-click the app to delete. In the drop-down list that appears, click Delete.
4. Click Remove, as shown in Figure 7-4. Note that the app will be removed from your iTunes library on your computer and will also be removed from your iPad and other devices, if you have not removed them manually.

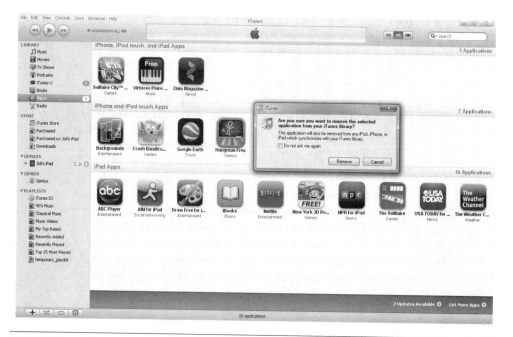

FIGURE 7-4   To completely delete an app, you must also remove it from your iTunes library on your computer.

Consider iWork

The iWork suite of applications includes Keynote, Pages, and Numbers. You can use the apps to be productive while away from your home or work computer. Unlike other productivity apps you may have encountered, the iWork apps are extensive, and you can do much more than just open and lightly edit documents, presentations, and spreadsheets. Unlike many apps designed for the BlackBerry or iPhone, these apps actually enable you to create things; you can create a slideshow presentation; a newsletter, brochure, or report; and even a spreadsheet, all from scratch or using the templates provided. Every app in the iWork suite of apps is surprisingly substantial, and offers much more than you probably expect.

There are three apps available in the iWork app suite: Keynote, Pages, and Numbers, and each app costs $9.99. Each app has a specific function, and you can use an app to edit existing documents, presentations, and spreadsheets, or create new ones. You may not need every app in the iWork suite, though, so before you buy, make sure you know what you want and need. As an aside, the iWork apps are compatible with Microsoft Office file formats.

Understand Keynote

Keynote is a presentation app. It's the iPad's version of the larger Keynote application originally designed for Apple computers. If you're familiar with Microsoft Office products, it's Apple's answer to PowerPoint. With Keynote, you can create stunning presentations that include pictures, animated charts, transitions between slides, playback of presentations you create, and more. You can use the Media Browser to easily add your own images too. You can even add shadows, reflections, and picture frames with a simple touch. As with other iWork apps, you can add tables and charts.

There are lots of great things about Keynote:

- A dozen themes to help you easily build your presentation
- The ability to drag objects like pictures and text to move them around on a slide
- Options for animating slides and transitioning between them
- A media browser for locating pictures, tables, charts, and other data quickly
- A navigator to help you reorder slides and add new ones

Changes are saved each time you make a change, automatically, and you can always "undo" your work even after you've left the app and returned to it later.

Did You Know?   You Can Present with Your iPad

When you're ready to share your presentation, you can connect your iPad to a projector, TV, or monitor using an optional adapter. You can also email your presentation or use iTunes to copy the presentation to your computer if you need additional options.

Understand Pages

Pages is a word processing app. It's the iPad's version of the larger Pages application originally designed for Apple computers. If you're familiar with Microsoft Office products, it's Apple's answer to Word. With Pages, you can create just about any type of document you can imagine, from newsletters to reports to flyers. As with Keynote and Numbers, you can use the included templates to create documents quickly. Pages also offers spelling and punctuation tools, and options for adding bulleted and numbered lists. You can even set margins and tabs! As with other iWork apps, you can drag the data around in the document to move it. This makes placing text and images a breeze.

Here are a few other reasons to consider Pages:

- Sixteen templates for easy document creation
- A page navigator that lets you access parts of your document quickly
- The option to type with a dock and wireless keyboard for more efficient document creation
- Formatting tools to make any document pop
- Easy photo-editing options like twisting photos, rotating them, or resizing them, with a touch of your finger
- Various options for sharing files including via email and iTunes, but also by exporting as a PDF or a Microsoft Word file

 If you need to print your flyer, brochure, or document, email it to someone who can print it for you, or email it to yourself and print it at home. Keep your eyes open for third-party printing apps too; someone is bound to create a way to print from the iPad!

Understand Numbers

Numbers is a spreadsheet app. It's the iPad's version of the larger Numbers application originally designed for Apple computers. If you're familiar with Microsoft Office products, it's Apple's answer to Excel. With Numbers, you can enter and edit data and create tables and charts from it. You can add almost anything, from the miles you drive to the money you spend. You can manage your household budget or keep track of soccer team members, goals, and assists. As with the other iWork apps, you can drag and drop data anywhere you want. It's much more flexible than other spreadsheet apps, and was redesigned from the ground up just for the iPad.

Numbers includes lots of features you wouldn't expect in a portable spreadsheet app:

- Sixteen predesigned templates for easy spreadsheet creation
- Drag-and-drop technology for moving and calculating data in tables
- Forms that look like recipe cards for keeping data organized
- The ability to create stunning and useful charts of data you've entered

- An intelligent keyboard for entering data and a full calculation engine for calculating data
- The ability to import and edit files from Microsoft Excel and export them as a Numbers document or PDF

If you think you can benefit from any of these apps, they're all available from the app store.

Back Up Apps on Your Computer

When you sync your iPad to your computer, your apps will automatically be backed up. You should sync and verify that a backup is taking place, though, especially if you've recently purchased an expensive app.

To back up your apps on to your computer:

1. Connect your iPad to your computer.
2. Click your iPad in the source pane of iTunes.
3. Click the Apps tab.
4. Tick Sync Apps, if it is not ticked already.
5. Verify that your new apps are selected in the list.
6. Click Sync.
7. Do not disconnect your iPad from your computer until the backup and sync process is complete.

8

Use Your iPod App

HOW TO...

- Learn sync options and supported file formats
- Sync music from your computer to your iPad
- Browse your iPad's music collection
- Play a song and adjust the volume
- Pause and restart a song or skip to the next song
- View album art or the track list
- Create, save, and manage a Genius playlist
- Create a Standard playlist
- Shuffle songs in any list
- Use the Search box to find a song
- Explore audiobooks, podcasts, music videos, and iPod settings

The iPod icon is positioned at the bottom of your iPad, and when touched, allows you to access the music on your iPad, play it, and view album art and track information. While playing music, you'll have access to familiar controls, like pause, skip, and repeat, and some that you may not be so familiar with, like shuffle and Genius. You can use the iPod app to create playlists, sort your music, and search for specific music by its attributes too. The iPod app is just about the only app that can run in the background while you do other things on your iPad; most other apps have to be closed before you can open another one. You can even use the volume controls on the outside of your iPad when your iPad is locked and the screen is dark.

Note For the most part, in this chapter we'll focus on music. However, you can listen to and control audiobooks, podcasts, and music videos in the same manner and using the same controls.

Get Music onto Your iPad

There are two main ways to get music onto your iPad. You can use iTunes and your computer to copy (sync) music you already own to your iPad, or you can purchase music directly from the iTunes store to your iPad. When syncing with your computer, you can opt to sync your entire Music library or just specific playlists, artists, and/or genres. Each time you acquire music, either from your iPad or your computer, it can be synced too, so your music libraries will always be up to date.

 Currently, you can't drag and drop music from your computer to your iPad, but if that's something you'd like to do, watch for upcoming third-party apps. This feature would come in handy if you were at a friend's house and wanted to copy some of their music, but didn't want to use iTunes.

Copy Options

If you haven't synced any music yet, it's time! You need to get some music onto your iPad. As you know, there are a few ways to do this, and you'll probably apply a combination of these techniques to populate your iPad with music. Here are the most common copy options, spelled out in more detail:

- You can connect your iPad to your computer and use iTunes to transfer your music. You should choose this option *using the computer you used to set up your iPad*. With this option you can
  - Use iTunes on your computer to manage your Music library.
  - Tell iTunes to look for shared music in other libraries on your home network.
  - Tell iTunes to share your Music library with other computers on your home network.
  - Transfer previously purchased music to your iPad.
  - Keep your Music library automatically synced between the computer and your iPad.
  - Keep only specific music that you hand-select in your library automatically synced between your computer and your iPad.
  - Disable automatic syncing with iTunes, if desired.
- You can get music "over the air" and without connecting to any computer. You should choose this option if
  - You don't have any music on any computer, and thus, nothing to transfer.
  - You plan to get all of your music from the integrated iTunes store on the iPad and do not want to sync that music with your computer because you don't have access to a computer.
  - You do not have your own computer (and you set up your iPad on a friend's or family member's computer).

iTunes is covered in Chapter 9.

Your iPad only supports the following audio formats:

- **AAC (16 to 320 Kbps)**   Advanced Audio Coding, a common audio format. You may have AAC music files on your computer already as it is the default standard for ripping CDs into iTunes.
- **Protected AAC from the iTunes Store**   Advanced Audio Coding, again, but purchased from the iTunes store and protected by Apple usage policies. To play Protected AAC songs on your iPad, you'll need to sign in to iTunes using the same account you purchased the songs with.
- **MP3 (16 to 320 Kbps)**   MPEG-1 Audio Layer 3 is a common audio format for consumer audio storage, and is the de facto standard for digital music players (also called MP3 players). You probably have MP3 files on your computer, and those files can be played (as can the others in this list) on your iPad (and iPod, and iPod Touch, and almost any other digital music player).
- **MP3 VBR**   This is an MP3 file with a Variable Bit Rate allowing for alternate types of encoding. You may have these file types on your computer.
- **Audible (Formats 2, 3, and 4)**   Audible.com is an online audiobook seller. The file format they use is Audible. Formats 2, 3, and 4 are compatible formats for the iPad, iPod, and iPhone. Format 2 creates the smallest file size and the quality of the audio is the poorest of the formats. Format 4 creates the largest file size and offers the best quality of these formats. (The larger the file size, the more space it takes up on your iPad.)
- **Apple Lossless**   An audio codec developed by Apple for lossless compression of digital music. The data is stored as an MP4 file. You may have these types of files on your Mac, and these files do not utilize any "rights management" schemes like the Protected AAC files you may have from iTunes.
- **AIFF**   Audio Interchange File Format. The AIFF file is most commonly used on Apple computers and is a format for storing audio files. AIFF files are compatible on Windows PCs and Linux machines too, and of course, compatible with the iPad.
- **WAV**   Waveform Audio file. WAV files have been around a long time, and were used way back when on Windows 3.1. Like AIFF files, they are compatible with Apple, Linux, and Windows, in addition to the iPad.

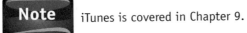 If you don't have any music on your PC or Mac, you may want to skip over to Chapter 9, and purchase some music from iTunes. Then, come back to this chapter when you're ready.

Find Out the Format of a File

You can find out what format any audio file is by right-clicking the file on your computer and choosing Properties. For the most part, we'll bet that the audio files you have are compatible. You probably have some Protected AAC files from an older iPhone or iPod Touch, MP3 or MP4 files from CDs you've ripped from your own CD collection, and maybe even a few books from Audible. Don't worry too much about compatibility though; iTunes will inform you of any problems.

Sync with iPad

If you want to copy music from your main computer to your iPad, you can do so using iTunes. The very best scenario is to put all of your music on one computer (the computer you used to activate your iPad), and use that computer to copy, manage, and ultimately sync music between the two. The main advantage to using iTunes to copy music from your computer to your iPad is that once it's copied, any changes made to either music library (iPad or computer) can be automatically synced each time you connect the two devices.

If you plan to set up syncing, it's important to note that you should choose one computer, put your music on it, and then use that computer each time you want to back up, update, or sync your iPad. You should not use multiple computers when syncing your iPad. You can use your iTunes account and play your iTunes music on multiple computers, though; that's not the issue. The issue is picking one computer, and using that one computer to sync your iPad, every time.

To sync music from your PC to your iPad using iTunes (performing this on a Mac is similar):

1. On your PC, connect your iPad. iTunes will open automatically.
2. The backup and sync process will likely start, but you can continue with the tasks here, even while the sync is in progress.
3. In the source pane in iTunes, on your computer, click the icon for your iPad.
4. Click the Music tab. See Figure 8-1.
5. As shown in Figure 8-1, you can opt to sync music (or not), sync your entire Music library, or sync only specific playlists, artists, and genres. You can also include music videos and voice notes. Make that selection now. You might opt not to sync your entire library if
   a. Your library is larger than the space available on your iPad, or you do not want to take up the space you have with only music.
   b. You don't want all of the music in your library on your iPad because you don't like it all.
   c. Some of your music is protected by another music program and can't be played on your iPad.

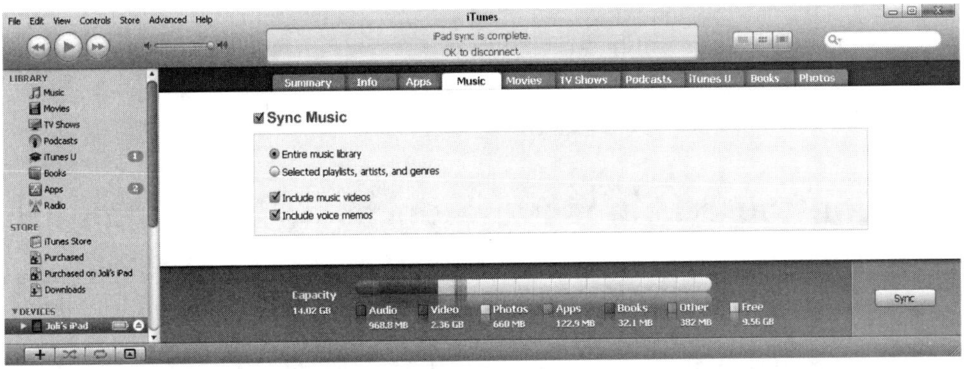

FIGURE 8-1   In iTunes, on your computer, and with your iPad connected, click the Music tab to see your syncing options.

6. If you opt to sync your entire Music library, you're finished, and can click Sync if you like. If you opt to sync only specific playlists, artists, or genres:

   a. Select the desired options, shown in Figure 8-2.

   b. If you like, tick Automatically Fill Free Space with Songs.

   c. Click Sync.

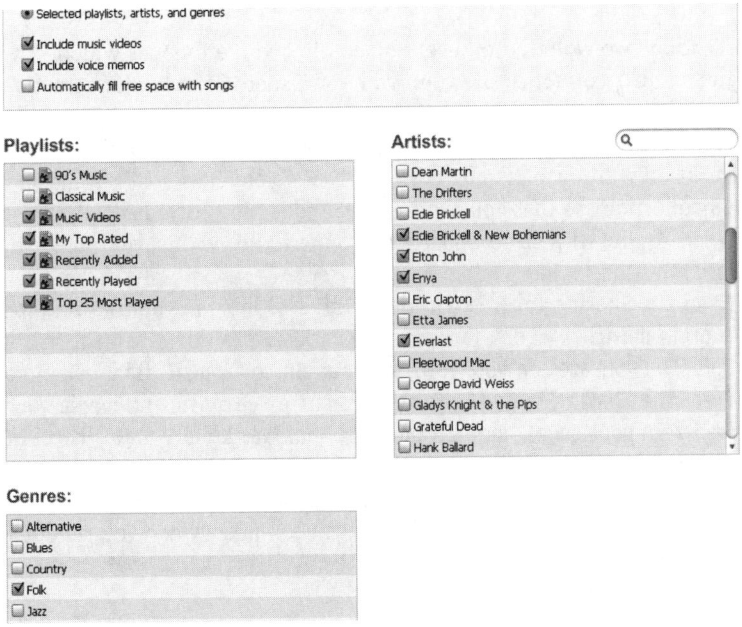

FIGURE 8-2   You can easily select specific playlists, artists, and/or genres.

Once syncing is set up, syncing will occur automatically each time you connect your iPad to your computer.

Configure iTunes Preferences on Your Computer

There are several preferences you can set in iTunes on your computer to help you get more out of iTunes, and thus more from your iPad. To view the Preferences options, click Edit, and click Preferences, as shown here.

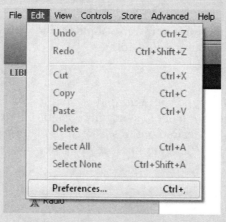

Although we won't detail every option in the Preferences window, here are a few that might interest you (click OK when you're finished making your selections):

- **From the General tab**   On this tab, there are options regarding what happens when you insert a CD into your computer's CD drive. If you know you're going to be ripping an entire CD collection (so that you can sync that collection to your iPad), change the setting for When You Insert a CD to *Import CD and Eject*. This will make ripping your large CD collection less time-consuming.
- **From the Sharing tab**   If you want iTunes to look on your network for shared libraries that contain music, tick Look for Shared Libraries. Note that when this is selected, you could end up with duplicates on your iPad, so clean up your music libraries before you do this.
- **From the Sharing tab**   If you want to share the music and media you've acquired on your iPad with your own home network, tick Share My Library on My Local Network. Note that you can share the entire library or only specific playlists.
- **From the Store tab**   Tick Automatically Download Missing Artwork, and iTunes will look to the Internet for album artwork for songs you import when you rip CDs in your CD collection.

Locate and Play a Song on Your iPad

Now that you have some music on your iPad, it's time to play a song. That's the most basic thing of course, playing some music! If you copied single songs, entire albums, or even playlists from your computer to your iPad, you'll see those once you open the iPod app. You'll be able to tap a playlist you've transferred, and you'll see that playlist in the source pane. See Figure 8-3.

Note Because everyone's music collection is different from everyone else's, what you see in the images here will differ from what you see on your device when you browse it for music.

In this section you'll learn how to browse for a song by its title, and browse music by artist, album, genre, or composer. You will also learn how to play an existing playlist and what's in the default Libraries, like Music, Podcasts, Audiobooks, and more. You'll learn to play a song and adjust the volume, and how to switch from Album Art view to Track view. Of course, you'll use the controls, including pause, repeat, skip, and others.

Browse Your Music Collection

Whatever music you copied from your computer will appear in your iPod app. Playlists, if you have them, will appear in the source pane along with the default categories. If you don't have any playlists, you'll see just the libraries that are already in place. Here are a few of the libraries you'll see:

- **Music**   This is just music. All of your music is stored in this library. The default view is Songs, and the songs are listed alphabetically. See Figure 8-4. Note the other available views across the bottom: Artists, Albums, Genres, and Composers; there will be more on that later.
- **Podcasts**   This library only holds media deemed by the iPod app to be podcasts. You may not have anything in here yet.
- **Audiobooks**   This library only holds media deemed by the iPod app to be audiobooks. You may not have anything in here yet.

FIGURE 8-3   After you've synced, music and playlists will be transferred. "Happy Songs" is a playlist transferred from your computer.

FIGURE 8-4   The Music library contains all of your music, and is sorted alphabetically by song title.

You'll probably see a few default Smart playlists under your library selections, including Recently Added, My Top Rated, Top 25 Most Played, and others. Across the bottom of the iPod screen, you'll see the following categories. Tap any category title to change the results:

- **Songs**   Click Songs to view all of the songs in your iPod app by title. Tap any letter on the right side of the page to go to the songs that start with that letter.
- **Artists**   Click Artists to view your music by artist. If you have multiple albums by the same artist, tap the artist's name to view the albums, as shown here.

- **Albums**   Click Albums to view your albums in alphabetical order. If you know what album you want to listen to, this is the best way to find it.

- **Genres**   iTunes classifies your music automatically by genre. Genres include Folk, Rock, Alternative, and Soundtrack, among others, as shown in the following illustration. If you know you want to listen to a specific genre (say Folk, when your mom stops by), this is the place to go.

| Alternative | Folk | Jazz | New Age | R&B/Soul |
| 5 Albums, 28 Songs | 3 Albums, 4 Songs | 1 Song | 2 Albums, 17 Songs | 1 Song |

| Reggae | Rock | Singer/Songwriter | Soundtrack | Vocal |
| 2 Songs | 31 Albums, 83 Songs | 3 Albums, 4 Songs | 3 Albums, 3 Songs | 1 Song |

- **Composers**   Click Composers to view your music by the composer of that music.

Tip   Drill into any artist, album, or other folder to locate a song. Tap any song to play it.

Play a Song

Playing a song is one of the simplest things you can do with the iPod app. As you are aware, though, you have to find a song first. If you just want to experiment, touch Music in the iPod app, and tap the first song to play it. If you're feeling a little more adventurous, try tapping the various titles within the Library pane to locate media (like Recently Added, Audiobooks, or Podcasts).

Once a song is playing, there are a few things you'll want to do right away, including changing the volume.

To adjust the volume:

1. Locate the Volume Rocker on the outside of the iPad.
2. Click the top of the Volume Rocker to make the music louder; click the bottom part to make the music softer.
3. Click and hold the bottom part of the rocker to mute the music. (Basically, doing this just reduces the volume to zero extremely quickly.)

Note   While a song is playing, tap the screen to access the iPod controls. You can then move the volume slider on the screen to adjust the volume without using the Volume Rocker.

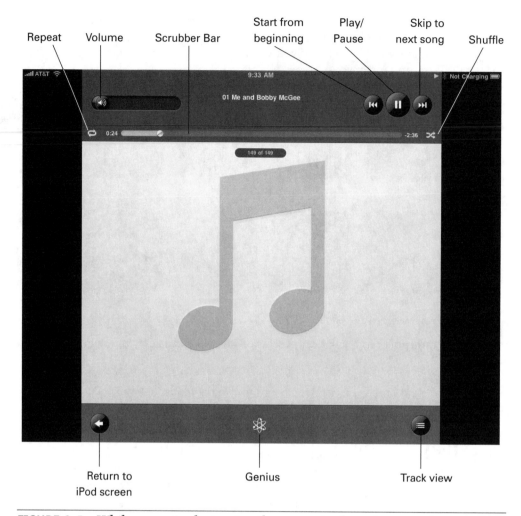

Repeat   Volume   Scrubber Bar   Start from beginning   Play/ Pause   Skip to next song   Shuffle

Return to iPod screen   Genius   Track view

FIGURE 8-5   While a song is playing, tap the screen to show the controls.

To pause and restart a song:

1. While a song is playing, tap the screen. The iPod controls will appear. See Figure 8-5. (We've intentionally selected a song with no associated album art to make the controls easier to see.)
2. Touch the Pause button to pause the song (the Pause button consists of two horizontal lines). The icon will change to a Play button, which is a right-facing arrow. Click it again to play the song from the point where it was paused.
3. Click the square Stop button to stop playing a song. Click the Play button to restart the song.

Connect Wired or Wireless Headphones

You won't always want to play your music for all the world to hear; in fact, most of the time you'll probably opt for headphones. There are two kinds of headphones you can install, wired and wireless (Bluetooth).

To install wired headphones, simply plug them into the headphone jack on the outside of the iPad. To install wireless stereo Bluetooth headphones, activate Bluetooth under Settings | General | Bluetooth and follow the manufacturer's instructions.

To restart a song or move to the next song:

1. Tap the left-pointing arrow, located to the left of the Play/Pause button, to restart the song.
2. Tap the right-pointing arrow, located to the right of the Play/Pause button, to skip to the next song.
3. You can also move the slider on the Scrubber Bar to quickly move to a particular place in a song.

View Album Art or the Track List

When you play a song, you have the option to view the iPod screen, album art, or information about the album or tracks on the playlist. Album art is just that—it's the album cover. The Track view shows the list of songs in an album, among other things. Track view allows you to move among songs in an album or playlist, and is shown in Figure 8-6. You know about the iPod view already, which offers easy access to the libraries and playlists on your iPad.

To see these additional views:

1. Tap any item in the Library pane that has multiple songs in it. If you're unsure, tap Music.
2. Tap a song to play it.
3. Tap the album or song in Now Playing, at the bottom left of your iPod screen, to access Album Art view, which is shown in this illustration.

Now Playing:

Bob Acri
Sleep Away
Bob Acri

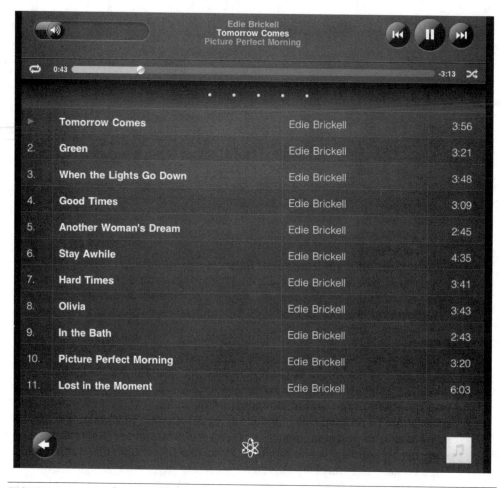

FIGURE 8-6 Track view offers information about what's next, how long each song is, and the song title and artist, among other things.

4. While in Album Art view, tap the screen to access the controls. Tap the icon located in the bottom-right corner to switch views, as shown in the following illustration. (Alternately, double-tap the screen.)

5. To return to Album Art, double-tap the screen or tap the Album Art icon, now located at the bottom-right corner of the screen. To return to the iPod screen, tap the left-pointing arrow located in the bottom-left corner of the screen.

Tip   Any time you want to open or close a window or switch views in the iPod app, try a tap or a double-tap.

Incorporate Playlists

The list of songs on an album is technically a playlist; it's a list of songs to be played. The songs listed in this kind of playlist don't change. Some playlists do change, though. The Most Played list is an ever-changing playlist (Smart playlist), composed of songs you listen to the most. The songs in the Recently Added playlist will change too, as you add music.

You can create your own playlists, though, and add any songs you like to personalize your music experience. And, you can let Genius create playlists for you, using information it has obtained by keeping tabs on what you listen to the most, how songs are categorized, and more. Genius is a cool feature that analyzes your Music library and what you listen to the most, and draws conclusions about what type of list you'll like, based on a song you pick. For instance, if you ask Genius to create a playlist based on your favorite Simon and Garfunkel song, you can be sure that the list Genius creates will contain similar music, both in genre and mood. Since a Genius playlist is the easiest type of playlist to create, let's start there.

Note Genius is part of iTunes 8 and 9, and thus, you must sync your iPad with a computer that has iTunes to get Genius on the iPod app.

Create a Genius Playlist

Genius is part of iTunes installed on your computer. You have to have Genius enabled in iTunes on the computer you sync with your iPad for Genius to work. Once enabled, Genius will compile information about your Music library and use that information to create playlists it thinks you'll like based on the music you listen to most and the music you've purchased from iTunes. Follow the steps here to see if you can create a Genius playlist, and if you can't, follow the instructions for enabling Genius in iTunes.

To have Genius create a playlist for you:

1. In the iPod app, locate the Genius button and tap it. The Genius button is to the left of the Add Playlist (+) button on the bottom-left corner of the iPod interface.
2. Touch the song you want to be the basis for this playlist. iTunes will create a playlist for you. If you get a message that says Genius is not enabled, refer to the next "How To" sidebar, "Enable Genius."
3. The playlist will appear in the iPod Library list, under Genius, and the playlist will begin to play immediately.
4. To create a different playlist, stop playing the current Genius playlist and repeat these steps. You can also click New in the top-right corner. Alternately, click Refresh to have Genius reconsider the songs included and create a new list with new songs.

Tip When you enable Genius in iTunes, Genius Mixes will be automatically created based on what you listen to most in your iTunes library.

You can also create a Genius playlist based on a song that's currently playing:

1. With a song playing, tap Now Playing in the bottom-left corner of the iPod interface.
2. Tap the album cover to show the controls.
3. Tap the Genius icon.
4. Tap the right-facing arrow to return to the iPod Library list, not the new Genius playlist under Library.

How to... **Enable Genius**

If you received a message in Step 2 that Genius playlists are not enabled, follow these steps at the computer you use to sync your iPad:

1. Connect your iPad to your computer.
2. Click Genius from the source pane in iTunes, and then click Turn on Genius.
3. Type your password.
4. Read and agree to the Terms of Service.
5. Wait while Genius compiles the required information.
6. Click your iPad icon in the source pane.
7. Click Sync.

Manage Genius Playlists

After you've created a Genius playlist, you have the option to save it, and once you save it, you have the option to refresh or delete it. When you refresh a Genius playlist, a new list of songs is created based on the song you selected. Saved Genius playlists will be synced to your computer automatically. Once a Genius playlist is synced with your computer, though, you'll have to use iTunes to delete it from your iPad; you will no longer have the option to delete from inside the iPod app.

To save and then delete a playlist:

1. While the playlist is playing and on the screen, tap Save.
2. Once the playlist has been saved, tap Delete to delete.
3. To delete a Genius playlist you've created and saved, and synced:
   a. In iTunes on your computer, locate the Genius playlist to delete. It's under Genius in the source pane.
   b. Right-click the playlist and click Delete to remove it, as shown in the following illustration.
   c. Sync your iPad.

Create a Standard Playlist

A Standard playlist is a playlist you create by hand-picking the songs you want to include in it. You can create playlists for any type of scenario you can imagine, for instance, jogging or working out at the gym, going to bed at night, waking up in the morning, dinner music, and more. If you wanted to, you could turn your iPad into a portable D.J., by creating playlists for parties, weddings, and similar events.

To create a Standard playlist on your iPad's iPod app:

1. Tap the + sign at the bottom of the iPod interface. This is the Add Playlist button.
2. Type a name for the playlist and tap Save.
3. Select songs for the playlist by tapping them. After you select a song, it'll turn gray in the list.
4. When you are finished, tap Done.

 You can also make playlists from other categories in your iPod library, such as podcasts or audiobooks.

5. You can now edit the playlist. Tap the red minus sign and then tap Delete to remove a song, or tap Add Songs and repeat the previous steps to add more. See Figure 8-7.
6. Tap Done.

The next time you sync your iPad with your computer, the new playlist will be copied.

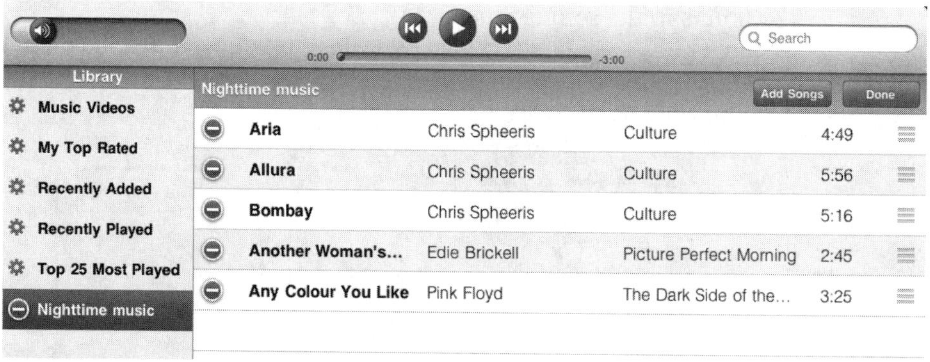

FIGURE 8-7 You can easily edit a playlist.

To edit a playlist:

1. Tap the playlist to edit and then tap Edit.
2. To move a song up or down in the list, drag it to the desired location. You must drag from the far-right end of the song, to the right of the information regarding the song's duration.
3. To delete any song, tap it and tap Delete. (Deleting a song from a playlist doesn't delete it from your iPad.)
4. To add more songs, tap Add Songs, tap the songs to add, then tap Done.

Shuffle Songs in Any List

Songs always appear in some sort of list. The list may only include tracks from a specific album, or it can contain myriad songs or titles in a list for Genre, Composer, and other categories. It can be a list that Genius created for you, or a Standard playlist you created yourself. When you play songs in any list, they play from top to bottom, or from start to finish, no matter what the source of the list. You may want to shuffle those songs so they play in random order (especially if this list is in alphabetical order, or if the songs in the list are grouped by artist or album).

Note You can tap Shuffle at the top of the Music library to set the iPod app to automatically shuffle all songs.

To shuffle songs in any list of music and thus play them in random order:

1. In the iPod app, locate any list of songs. Consider a Genius playlist, Standard playlist, or simply the songs in the Music library.
2. Start the playlist.
3. Tap the Now Playing icon in the left corner of the iPod screen.
4. Tap the Album Art to view the controls.
5. Click the Shuffle button. The Shuffle button is located to the right of the "time remaining" information on the Scrubber Bar, as shown in the following illustration:
   a. If the Shuffle button is blue, Shuffle is enabled.
   b. If the Shuffle button is gray, Shuffle is not enabled.

Repeat   Shuffle

The icon to the left of the Scrubber Bar and to the left of the amount of time the song has been playing is the Repeat button. Tap it to repeat the song once it's finished playing (a "1" will appear by it). You can also tap to repeat the song over and over.

Search for Media

You may have discovered by now that there are lots of ways to view your music, including by song title, artist, genre, and composer, to name a few. While this may work for a while, you'll probably tire of all of the scrolling and tapping involved in finding that perfect song. In this section you'll learn how to search your media for a song, artist, or genre quickly, using the Spotlight Search box in the iPod interface.

The iPod app contains a Search box that you can use to search for just about anything. If you're looking for a song, audiobook, podcast, or any other item that is in any of your iPod libraries, you can search for it here. When you type something in the Spotlight Search box, the results will appear as you type. The more you type, the fewer the number of matching results, and thus, the shorter the list of results. The more precise you can be regarding what you want to find, the better results you'll have. So, try to type unique words, not common ones. For instance, if you're looking for a song that mentions the word "sunshine" in it (like "The Age of Aquarius," or "Ain't No Sunshine When She's Gone"), type **Sunshine** in the Search box. The results will appear in a list underneath. Likewise, typing Bobby brings up songs about "Bobby," such as "Me and Bobby McGee," along with a list of Bobby Darin songs.

To use the Search function of the iPad:

1. In the iPad app, click inside the Spotlight Search window.
2. Type a word or two into the Search window.
3. Review the results, as shown in the following illustration. Click any result to play the song.

Explore Other Types of Media

We've focused on music in this chapter, but there are many other kinds of media you can listen to using the iPod app on your iPad. These include audiobooks, podcasts, and music videos.

Explore Audiobooks

You can get audiobooks from the iTunes Store, and this is detailed in Chapter 9. If you have an audiobook already, either one you've purchased or one you've synced from your computer, you can find it and listen to it using the iPod app on the iPad. For more information on purchasing and downloading audiobooks from iTunes, refer to Chapter 9.

Your iPad also supports Audible files, and Audible is one of the largest audiobook companies in the world. In addition to audiobooks, Audible.com offers magazines, radio shows, podcasts, stand-up comedy, and speeches from people who shape culture, politics, and business.

Tip Audiobooks are perfect for commuters, those who don't have time to read, or those who have difficulty reading due to a vision problem.

If you're interested in Audible, from your home computer navigate to www.audible .com. Browse the library to see what they have to offer, which currently stands at over 75,000 titles. If you see something you like, set up an account, purchase the book, and download it. With the plan you choose, whether it's simply one credit a month or 24 credits for an entire year, you'll also get access to the audio version of the *New York Times* or the *Wall Street Journal* (you choose). (For the most part, a credit equals one book.)

When you listen to an audiobook with the iPod app, the controls you're familiar with already are available, but they perform different things now. You'll still tap the audiobook in the Audiobooks library to get started, and you'll still click the book's icon in Now Playing to access the controls; however:

- There's now a speed control icon to the right of the Scrubber Bar. You can choose from ½×, 1×, and 2×. The ½× speed is the slowest and 2× is the fastest. See Figure 8-8.
- You can use the slider to move to a new position in the book.
- There's a 30-second repeat button at the bottom that lets you rewind 30 seconds, in case you miss something.
- When you click to see the Track view, you have access to the chapters in the book.

Explore Podcasts

Podcasts are digital media files, similar to audiobooks, which are released to the public and often downloaded through web syndication. They are recorded and then made available for download. They aren't live, although some are recorded live and uploaded later. All podcasts offered through iTunes are free, although you can sign up for services that offer podcasts for a price. You can listen to a podcast of the latest news at www.cnn.com/services/podcasting using Safari, or you can download podcasts to your iPad and listen to them in your iPod app.

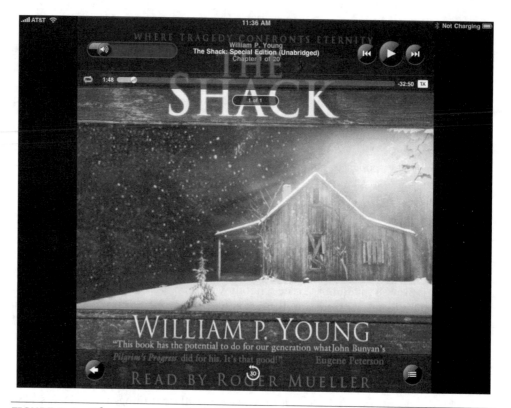

FIGURE 8-8   There are controls for listening to audiobooks that include increasing or decreasing the speed at which it is read.

 Tip   You can find a long list of podcasts at a podcast directory site such as www.podcastdirectory.com.

To listen to a podcast in Safari:

1. Open Safari on your iPad and navigate to www.cnn.com/services/podcasting.
2. Click the link for any podcast to listen to it.

To listen to podcasts using your iPod app, open iTunes, tap Podcasts, and download a podcast. Once it's downloaded, open the iPod app, tap Podcasts, and tap the name of the podcast to listen to, as shown here.

Explore Music Videos

Music videos are just that, music and videos mixed together. From the time of MTV's introduction way back in the '80s, music videos have been all the rage. You can watch music videos on your iPad and save them to your Music library. You can get free music videos on the Web, from places like Download.com and of course, from iTunes and the iTunes Store.

To explore music videos:

1. Purchase or acquire a music video. iTunes sells music videos, and we acquired Michael Jackson's "Bad" for only $1.99.
2. Once you've purchased and downloaded the video, open the iPod app.
3. Tap Music Videos.
4. Tap the video to play it, as shown here.

Library	▶ Bad	Michael Jackson	4:19
⚙ **90's Music**			
⚙ **Classical Music**			
≡ **Happy Songs**			
⚙ **Music Videos**			

5. As with other media, you can tap the video to show the controls.

Configure iPod Settings

As with other iPad features, you can configure settings for your iPod app. Just tap Settings on the Home screen. You can turn on or off the following:

- **Sound Check**   To set your iPod app to play all songs at the same level. Sometimes sound from different sources can be louder or softer than the other songs in your library.
- **EQ**   To choose a specific equalizer sound, like Acoustic, Hip Hop, Latin, Spoken Word, and Treble Booster or Treble Reducer.
- **Volume Limit**   To set a maximum volume limit and lock it.
- **Lyrics and Podcast Info**   To enable retrieval of lyrics and podcast information, when available.

9

Shop the iTunes Store

HOW TO...

- Explore the iTunes interface
- Browse and buy music
- Browse, rent, buy, and preorder movies
- Browse and watch TV shows
- Browse and listen to podcasts
- Browse and listen to audiobooks
- Browse and listen to media from iTunes U
- Explore art, classical music, museums, cultural exhibits
- Explore Genius

The iTunes Store is a one-stop shop for music, TV shows, movies, podcasts, audiobooks, and even college lectures from universities all over the country. You can preview and buy just about any kind of media imaginable. And, as with other iPad media, it's easy to sync your newly acquired media to your desktop computer.

The iTunes app, which is what you use to access the iTunes Store, is already on your iPad and ready to use. There's no need to download and install it, or do anything special at all. And, because you created an account when you set up your iPad, you already have an account configured too. All you need to do is click the iTunes icon to get started.

Once you've acquired media from the iTunes Store, you'll use other apps to view it or listen to it. You listen to music, podcasts, and audiobooks with the iPod. You can watch movies and TV shows with the Videos app. You can watch music videos and listen to media from iTunes U from both the iPod and the Videos apps.

Note For more information on watching, listening to, and managing media on your iPad, refer to Chapter 8 for more information about the iPod app and Chapter 11 for more information about the Videos app. Here, we're really just concerned with the iTunes Store.

Get Started with the iTunes Store

The iTunes Store is a media outlet complete with music, movies, TV, videos, and more. To get started, simply click the iTunes app on the Home screen. The iTunes Store is shown in Figure 9-1, with Music selected.

The iTunes Store looks pretty similar to the App Store you learned about in Chapter 7. There are seven buttons that run across the bottom and four buttons and a Spotlight Search window across the top. In order to effectively navigate the iTunes Store, you need to familiarize yourself with these buttons and features as quickly as possible. You'll use the buttons across the bottom to navigate iTunes by media type, by tapping the button that matches the media you'd like to browse. Once you're in the proper category, the items across the top will help you find exactly what you want.

The seven buttons that run across the bottom of the iTunes Store are

- **Music**   Touch to go to the music part of the store. You'll find music from just about every artist imaginable, and have easy access to music videos and what's free on iTunes.

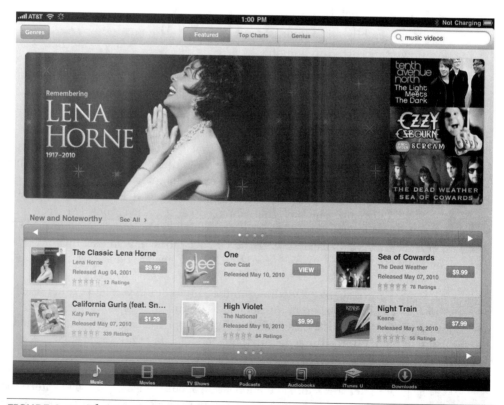

FIGURE 9-1   The Music part of the iTunes Store is only a small part of what's available. There are other categories including Movies, TV Shows, and Audiobooks.

- **Movies**   Touch the Movies icon to go to the Movies part of the store. Here you can buy or rent movies, see recent arrivals, and access free movie previews.
- **TV Shows**   Touch TV Shows to view everything related to TV. You can purchase entire seasons of shows or simply a single show. Once purchased, those shows belong to you and are stored on your iPad. You can watch them on your iPad anytime you want. As with other media, you can copy them to your computer too. So if you want to watch one of these shows on a larger screen, you can.
- **Podcasts**   Touch Podcasts to browse podcasts that are available from the iTunes Store. You will find free items here, and you can browse both audio and video podcasts.
- **Audiobooks**   Touch Audiobooks to see what the iTunes Store offers in the way of audiobooks. As you know from the last chapter, though, you can also purchase and sync audiobooks from Audible.com, and in this chapter you'll learn how to get free audiobooks with iTunes U.
- **iTunes U**   Touch iTunes U to visit the intellectual side of iTunes. Browse college lectures from Yale or Berkeley, browse K-12 offerings, and even watch videos taken in museums and television stations. You can even access free audiobooks.
- **Downloads**   Touch Downloads to see items related to media you're currently downloading. Once the media has been downloaded, the list will be empty, and data will be available in its associated app (music in iPod, movies in Videos, and so on).

Note   To access any category, simply touch the related button.

Once you're in the proper category, explore the media in it using the four buttons that run across the top of the iTunes Store, or use the Spotlight Search window to search for something specific:

- **Genres**   Tap this button to show the available genres at the iTunes Store. The genres listed change depending on what you've selected across the bottom of the screen. For instance, if you're browsing TV Shows, then the Genres button produces Home, Animation, Classic, Comedy, Drama, Kids, Nonfiction, Reality TV, Sci-Fi & Fantasy, and Sports. If you're in Movies, Genres include some of those and others like Thriller and Documentary. (Tap Genres again to hide the list.)
- **Featured**   Tap Featured to view media that Apple thinks is noteworthy. The media listed here are handpicked by Apple. Depending on the category you're in (TV Shows, Movies, Music, and the like), you'll see options under Featured including New to Rent or Own (Movies), What's Hot (Music), Latest TV Episodes (TV Shows), New in Fiction (Audiobooks), and the like. You'll see arrows that allow you to move left and right among the listings, and a button with a price for each one you see. There's also an option to "See All."
- **Top Charts**   Tap Top Charts to see the most popular media at the moment for a specific category. This list will change often as the top sellers change. What's hot today may not be hot tomorrow!

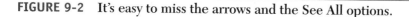

FIGURE 9-2 It's easy to miss the arrows and the See All options.

- **Genius** Tap Genius to see if iTunes has any Genius suggestions for you. Genius will compile information about your preferences as you download media, and then offer recommendations for other media you might like. Genius bases its recommendations on what you've previously purchased or sampled. If you purchase a specific genre from the Top Charts listings in the music category, Genius will suggest similar songs in that genre as they are released. If you prefer show tunes, Genius may well suggest movie soundtracks and Broadway releases.

Browse Music

The best way to become familiar with the iTunes Store is to browse music. Touch Music to access music available from the iTunes Store. You'll see several panes, boxes, and lists, most of which were detailed previously. Notice the arrows by New and Noteworthy under Featured, and note the See All option (see Figure 9-2). Tap these to explore more.

Now, scroll to the bottom of the music's Featured page to see Quick Links, where you can access Music Videos, Movies, and more. Remember to tap Featured, Top Charts, and Genius at the top of that page too.

In any music-related page, tap Genres to cull down the media to a specific type for that page. For instance, if you're in the Top Charts category of music and you only want to see songs that are considered "country," click Genres and choose Country, as shown in Figure 9-3. The list will change and only supply the top songs in that category. Continue to experiment with Featured, New and Noteworthy, and other categories, and sort by Rock, Pop, or Reggae, for instance.

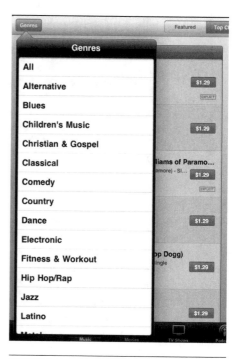

FIGURE 9-3 You can sort any music page by genre. Sorting by Genre is available in other categories too, including Movies and TV Shows.

Sometimes you know exactly what you want. You can use Spotlight Search inside the iTunes Store to search for a specific song or album:

1. Tap inside the Spotlight Search box in the top-right corner.
2. Type the artist's name, a song name, or other identifying information.
3. Tap Search on the keyboard or, if the result appears in the list (shown in the following illustration), tap that to locate the song.

As you browse for music, note that you can tap the album artwork to open a window that details the media, just as you can obtain information about an app by tapping its icon in the App Store. From the information page you'll find related information such as a list of tracks on an album, user reviews and ratings, the option to view the Artist page or tell a friend (via email), and more. To close the information window, tap anywhere outside of it.

Buy Music

Once you've found a song you like, you can purchase it. You'll see the price in a button beside the song. Tap once to start the purchasing process. It will be an easy process, even the first time through, because you already set up an account with the store when you activated your iPad. You'll be prompted to input your password and to verify you want to make the purchase, but it doesn't take more than a few seconds to get what you want.

To purchase a song:

1. Locate the song to purchase and locate the price button beside it. Note that you can also purchase albums, music videos, movies, and podcasts, if available.
2. Touch the price button.
3. Tap Buy Song, Buy Album (shown here), or other prompt.

4. Input your password.
5. Wait while the song downloads. If you want to watch the download process, tap the Downloads button on the bottom of the page.
6. You'll find the song, music video, or album in the iPod app.

Explore Movies, TV Shows, Podcasts, and Audiobooks

You may not be aware of all of the media that's available to you. You know you can buy movies from the iTunes Store, but you may not know that you can also rent them. You can purchase entire seasons of your favorite TV shows, or you can purchase a single show. You can even purchase the latest episode of a show you missed, if the production company makes it available. There are podcasts and audiobooks too; there's so much media that you could never watch or hear it all! As you know, you access the media options from the bottom of the screen. Let's continue to look at each of these in more depth, starting with Movies.

Browse and Obtain Movies

Your new iPad can play HD movies as well as Standard Definition movies, and you can rent or buy them from the iTunes Store. New movies are a little pricey, though, and can run you $20.00 or so apiece, which is about what you'd pay to buy them on DVD. Renting is a little steep too; a new movie often rents for about $5.00, about the same as what it would cost at Blockbuster or a similar store, or using an "on demand" service from your cable company.. However, if you want to be the first on the block to watch a movie after it's been released to the public, and you want to watch it on your iPad, this is the way to go.

The great thing about the iTunes Store with regard to movies is that it is possible to watch a newly released movie anytime and anywhere, right from your iPad.

You browse for, purchase (or rent), and download movies the same way you located and purchased music earlier, and you have the same access to ratings and reviews. Use the tabs across the top to locate the movie you want, and tap the appropriate icon to view and purchase the movie.

Here's an example if you'd like to walk through the process here:

1. In the iTunes Store, tap Movies.
2. In the Spotlight Search window, type the name of any movie (we'll search for *The Princess and the Frog*).
3. Tap Search.
4. In the results, scroll through the page to locate the Movies results. You may see Albums, TV Episodes, or Songs, for instance.
5. Tap View when you locate the movie. The movie's information page will open, shown in Figure 9-4.
6. Read any reviews, view ratings, read the movie summary, watch a preview, and use other tools to help you decide if this movie is the one you're looking for.
7. Tap Rent to rent the movie, or Buy to buy it. Note that both of these options may not be available; for instance, you may only be able to rent a movie, and not buy it. (Keep reading to learn more about buying versus renting.)
8. Wait while the movie downloads, and then open Videos to view it. For more information about the Videos app, refer to Chapter 11.

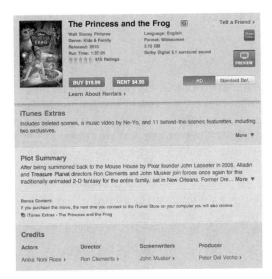

FIGURE 9-4   Most of the time you can rent or buy the movie.

To Rent or To Buy?

You may already know you want to buy a movie, because you love it and want to have access to it all the time. You may be equally sure you want to rent it. However, if you're on the fence, here's a little more information about renting and buying from iTunes.

If you buy a movie, you own it, and can watch it as often as you like and on up to five authorized devices. "Authorized" devices can be PCs and Macs, and Apple devices such as the iPad and the iPhone. You can authorize and unauthorize computers in iTunes from the Advanced tab.

 To learn more about authorized devices, visit http://support.apple.com and search for "authorize." Then, on the right side, click Learn More about iTunes or something similar.

Renting a movie is much different from owning one. When you rent a movie, you only get to keep it for a short period of time. Here are the rules:

- When you rent a movie, you have 30 days to watch it.
- When you start a movie you've rented, you have 24 hours to finish watching it.

The rental expires when one or the other of these conditions has been met. So, if you think you're going to want to watch the movie more than once, it may be in your best interest to buy. (Before you commit to anything, read the section on Netflix later in this chapter. You may find Netflix to be a good alternative to iTunes, and less expensive.)

Preorder Movies

When new movies are soon to be released, you can preorder them from the iTunes Store. You'll see a small orange "preorder" button on movies that have yet to be released. Tap this button to see when the movie is expected to be released, and what the preorder price is. You can also read customer reviews of the movies, as you can on other Movie pages in the iTunes Store. You can also view the trailer, see a list of cast members, and more.

1. Locate the movie you'd like to preorder and click the orange preorder button.
2. On the next page, click Preorder.
3. Type your password.
4. If prompted to verify your purchase, do so.

 To close a pop-up window that contains information about a movie, song, podcast, or some other media, tap outside of it.

Did You Know?

Netflix Offers Another Media Option

If your movie-watching ritual is relegated to new movies and you don't mind paying to buy or rent them individually, the iTunes Store may be all you need to satisfy your movie needs. If you enjoy watching older movies, and you watch a lot of them, you have additional options. One of the options is Netflix. For under $10 a month you can have a DVD or two at home and watch all you want on your iPad from the Netflix Instant Queue. The movies you have access to watch instantly aren't new, though, but if you enjoy older movies, this may be the best way to go. Unlimited on-demand movies, right from your iPad, for under $10 a month is a great deal.

To explore Netflix:

1. Open the App Store and browse for the free Netflix app.
2. Download and install it.
3. Browse the available free movies, sign up for a free trial, or just sign up!

Browse and Watch TV Shows

What we love most about the TV Shows portion of the iTunes Store is the Free TV Shows section. That's right; you can watch TV shows for free right from your iPad! Some are simply trailers or sneak peeks, but others are entire episodes. To access free TV episodes, from the Featured tab, scroll down and tap Free TV Episodes. The Free TV Episodes page is shown in Figure 9-5.

Tip   Once you've downloaded a TV show, to watch it, open the Videos app and tap the show to start it.

Beyond the free episodes, which may be just what the doctor ordered when you're waiting for a plane or commuting on a bus to work, there are episodes you can purchase. Did you miss the first season of *Modern Family*? You can buy the entire season for about $55.00, or single episodes for about $3.00. The same is true for popular shows like *House*, *Desperate Housewives*, and *Lost*, although prices can differ. All you have to do is browse to locate the TV show you want, and click the price button to get it.

When browsing TV, note that there are various ways to browse. As with music and movies, you can tap Featured and Top Charts, and if you've previously purchased TV shows, tap Genius to get recommendations. There are other options to explore at the bottom of the Featured page:

- **HD TV**   Some television shows are broadcast in HD as well as standard format. If you want an HD episode, look here.

FIGURE 9-5 You can get free TV episodes at the iTunes Store.

- **Free TV episodes**   Check out what's free, as previously detailed in this section.
- **Shows Just Added**   To view TV shows that were recently added to the iTunes Store.
- **Networks and Studios**   To select a network or studio and see what is available from them. There are lots to choose from, including ABC, BBC America, Cartoon Network, Disney XD, FOX, HBO, and more.
- **iTunes Picks**   To view iTunes picks for Best TV Comedies, Best TV Dramas, Best Kids Shows, and more.
- **Latest TV Episodes**   To access the latest TV shows added to the iTunes Store. This is where you'll find last night's *Desperate Housewives* or last weekend's episode of *Saturday Night Live*.

As an alternative to purchasing an episode of *Desperate Housewives* or any other show aired on ABC, download and install the ABC Player from the App Store. You can watch quite a few of ABC's TV shows for free, including your favorites like *Desperate Housewives, Dancing with the Stars, Castle, Brothers and Sisters*, and more.

Browse and Watch Podcasts

As you know by now, a podcast is an audio or video recording that has been made available to the public. Often podcasts are created by smaller entities than TV shows and movies makers. In the Podcasts section you may find "Indie" type subjects, offerings from NPR, newspapers, and news broadcasts, and even podcasts from ordinary people, stating opinions on sports, health, or other subjects. The best way to get a feel for podcasts is to click the Podcasts button, look for a free podcast, and play it. Podcasts, once downloaded, play in the iPod app.

Browse and Listen to Audiobooks

Audiobooks require quite a bit of input from actors, producers, directors, and writers. Because of this, audiobooks tend to be rather expensive, and you don't usually find too many free ones. In our opinion, though, the price of the audiobook isn't generally an issue, especially for those who don't have time to read but want to keep up with the latest fiction, non-fiction, biographical, and top sellers in books, or for those who are sight-impaired.

 Before you purchase a book from anyone, check out the iTunes Store's iTunes U. The Audiobooks section has some audiobooks you can listen to, without putting out any money at all!

If you have never listed to an audiobook, you really should give it a try. Audiobooks are perfect for commuters, great on airplanes, and ideal for those who have difficulty reading due to a vision problem (or too much sunlight on their iPads). To get started, click the Audiobooks button in the iTunes Store interface.

As with other categories, you can access quick links to various subcategories in the Audiobooks section. Tap Audiobooks, tap Features, and then scroll to the bottom of the Featured page to view the following categories:

- **New in Fiction**   To browse the newest audiobooks in the Fiction category.
- **Staff Favorites**   To browse favorites picked by the people at Apple and iTunes.
- **New in Non Fiction**   To browse the newest audiobooks in the Nonfiction category.
- **Top Fiction**   To browse the audiobooks in the Top Fiction category. These aren't what's new, necessarily, but what's the most popular overall.
- **Audiobook of the month**   To access audiobooks chosen for the "of the month" category. Often the Audiobook of the month is a bestseller and extremely popular.
- **Books made into films**   To access audiobooks for books that have been made into films, like *Precious*, *Angels & Demons*, *Twilight*, and *Frost/Nixon*.

If you aren't looking for something newly released, though, you can always search the store for a title or author. A search will produce results that are categorized, and in this case, you'll look at the audiobooks results. Tap any book to learn more about it, including how many hours of entertainment you'll be getting if you purchase it.

To purchase, download, and begin listening to an audiobook:

1. In the iTunes Store app, click Audiobooks.
2. Locate the audiobook to purchase.
3. Click Buy Book.
4. Input your password and wait while the download completes.
5. Once the download is complete, close the iTunes Store and open the iPod. You'll find the book there, as shown in the following illustration.

Get Smart with iTunes U

iTunes U, presumably short for iTunes University, offers audio and video related to learning and higher education. Here you can obtain media to help you learn a new language or a new skill, or even listen to lectures given previously at Yale, Stanford, Berkeley and other universities. You can browse museums without ever setting foot in them, listen and watch experts detail and describe an artifact in a museum, and explore information stored in the Library of Congress, among other things.

Browse and Listen to iTunes U

iTunes U offers a host of information, and it's all free. Open the iTunes Store and touch the iTunes U button to get started. Check out the following categories and features, listed next. Here are a few things to watch for, noting that media available here changes often:

- Tap Universities and Colleges on the Featured page to access media from colleges ranging from Aberdeen College to Yeshiva University. Tap any college name to see what's available from that college, as shown in the following illustration.

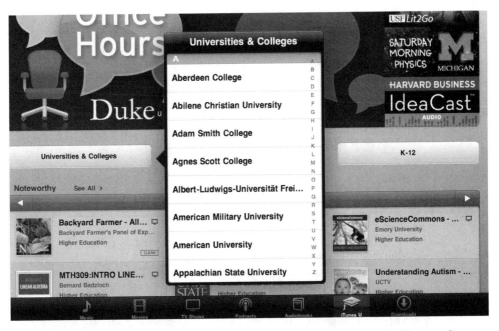

- Tap Beyond Campus on the Featured page to access educational offerings from off-campus institutions like museums and opera houses.
- Tap K-12 on the Featured page to access media from various K-12 institutions.
- Tap See All next to Noteworthy from the Featured page to see what Apple deems noteworthy. You might find offers from the Library of Congress, Stanford, and other highly notable institutions.

After you've browsed these common categories, perform a search in the Spotlight Search window for these:

- **Open Yale Courses**   These are entire semester-long courses on topics ranging from the Civil War to understanding Dante.
- **Music Highlights**   In the results, scroll down to iTunes U to see Yale Music, Jazz Insights, Indian Raga Music, and more.
- **Technology Highlights**   In the results, scroll down to iTunes U. Here you'll find educational media on things related to technology including music technology, criminal justice, computing, science, and more.
- **Lit2Go**   In the results, scroll down to iTunes U. Here you'll find audiobook classics like *Moby Dick*, *Peter Pan*, *Treasure Island*, *Oliver Twist*, and *A Tale of Two Cities*. They are free, and are read by volunteers. However, these books are audiobooks and allow you to listen to books on the go, right from your iPad. For the purpose of reading a book for a class or for pleasure, this is certainly a way to do it on a budget.

To listen to free media you find in iTunes U:

1. Browse to locate the media to obtain.
2. Click Free and click Download.
3. Wait while the media downloads. You can follow the progress in the Download link on the right side of the iTunes Store interface.
4. Once the download is complete, close iTunes and open your iPod. If the media is an audiobook or podcast, you can listen to it here. If you don't see it, look in the Videos app, under iTunes U.

Explore Art, Classical Music, Museums, and Cultural Exhibits

There's a Quick Link for Beyond Campus on the right side of the iTunes U interface. That's where you'll go to obtain educational media outside of college campuses, such as museums, opera houses, the Smithsonian, and others. Check out the following (noting that this list can change as time passes):

- **Library of Congress**   Explore films and webcasts, podcasts, and classes for librarians, including entire classes on cataloging.
- **Higher Education Channel Television**   Explore movies and shows related to higher education categorized into topics including I Love Jazz, Impact, Global Thinking, and Leaders and Legends.
- **Metropolitan Museum of Art**   Browse the museum by subject, from African Art to Medieval Art to Photographs. You can also explore featured exhibits, and learn more about the museum itself.
- **Washington National Opera**   Listen to opera from the latest opera seasons as well as archived media. Some of the archived media include *A Streetcar Named Desire*, *Das Rheingold*, *Madama Butterfly*, and *Tosca*.

To listen to any item in these categories:

1. Browse to locate the media to obtain.
2. Tap Free, and then Download.
3. Wait while the media downloads. You can follow the progress in the Download link on the right side of the iTunes Store interface.
4. As with other downloaded media, you'll find it in the Videos app or the iPod app. Figure 9-6 shows a video from the Brooklyn Museum.

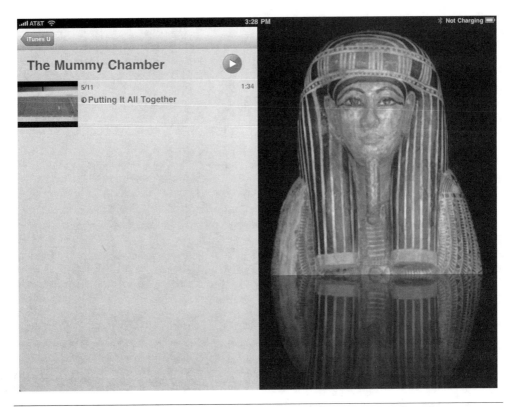

FIGURE 9-6 You can watch educational museum videos, among other things.

Let the iTunes Store Lead the Way

You can let iTunes help you decide what media to browse and/or buy. In any category (Music, Movies, TV Shows, and so on), just click Genius, and let the recommendations begin. iTunes will analyze what you've purchased and/or downloaded and then offer suggestions regarding what other media you might enjoy. For instance, if you like the Red Hot Chili Peppers and you purchased their latest album on iTunes, Genius may suggest that you may also like the Dave Matthews Band.

 Genius has to be enabled in iTunes on your computer (the one you sync your iPad to) before you can use it on your iPad. See Chapter 8 for more information on enabling Genius.

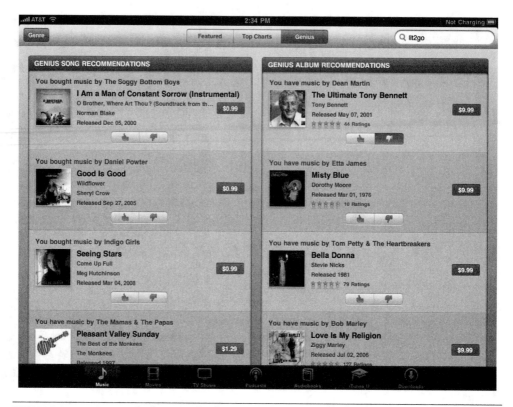

FIGURE 9-7 Genius helps you find new media you may like by making suggestions based on your previous purchases.

To use Genius:

1. Tap any category button across the bottom of iTunes, making sure to tap a button for a category you've previously made purchases or downloaded media from.
2. Tap the Genius button at the top of the page.
3. Review the recommendations, and if you wish, tap the thumbs-up or thumbs-down icon to improve your recommendations next time. See Figure 9-7.

Note The songs and media you obtain while using your iPad can be synced to your computer via iTunes. You can choose what to sync and when. Syncing is detailed in Chapter 1.

PART IV

Photos and Video

10

View, Manage, and Share Photos

HOW TO...

- Open the Photo app and explore its interface
- Sync photo folders using iTunes
- Explore views and use gestures
- Copy or delete a photo
- Share photos in an email
- Send a photo to Facebook
- Assign a photo to a contact
- Set a photo as wallpaper
- Create a slideshow of pictures with transitions
- Use Picture Frame
- Add music to a slideshow
- Import photos with the optional Camera Connection Kit

Photos is an app that comes on your iPad that enables you to view and share photos with others easily. Because of the size of the iPad, you no longer have to have others crowd around a tiny screen to view the photos you want them to see. The pictures are brilliant and bright, and are positioned to fill the entire screen, making sharing fun and effective. You can flick from left to right to change photos, flip the entire device to share a photo with someone sitting across from you, and tap and pinch to open an image in full screen or zoom in on one. You can easily change views from Portrait to Landscape by simply turning the device 90 degrees left or right. You can even use your iPad as a digital photo frame and create your own slideshows of pictures with music!

There are multiple ways to get photos onto your iPad, including syncing with iTunes on a PC or Mac, sending photos to yourself in an email, or using the optional Camera Connection Kit from Apple. If you don't yet have any photos on your iPad or have been too nervous to fully sync your iPad with your computer for fear of how much you'll actually put on it, don't worry—we'll show you how to add only what you want here. You'll also learn how to use the optional components you can purchase to import pictures from a camera or media card.

The Photos app offers features that allow you to share a photo too, including the ability to send any photo in an email (or send multiple photos), assign a photo to a contact, or use a photo as wallpaper. It's a pretty powerful app, and you'll find you use it often.

 Tip iPad supports several common image formats including JPEG, TIFF, GIF, and PNG.

Explore the Photos Interface

To open the Photos app, just click Photos on the Home screen. Photos will open, and you'll immediately notice at least two tabs across the top of the page: Photos and Albums. You may also see tabs for Events, Faces, and Places if your photos have been synced from programs such as iPhoto or Aperture on a Mac, or perhaps embedded with relevant information from a camera phone. If it isn't already selected, tap Photos. Here you can see all of your photos shown singly, and you can scroll through them by "flicking" your finger up or down the screen.

Tip Don't see any photos? Read and work through the next section to copy photos to your iPad from your computer.

Note what's available in the Photos interface. Specifically, note which of the five tabs are available to you:

- **Photos** You'll have this tab. Use this tab to view thumbnails of all of your photos individually and to scroll through those thumbnails by flicking. Tap any photo to view it in full screen.
- **Albums** You'll have this tab too. Use this tab to view your photos by albums. Some albums are created by default by Photos, like Saved Photos. But an album can also be something you create on your computer to organize your own photos. When you sync the pictures you have in folders from your computer, you sync their respective folders to your iPad too. Figure 10-1 shows Albums.

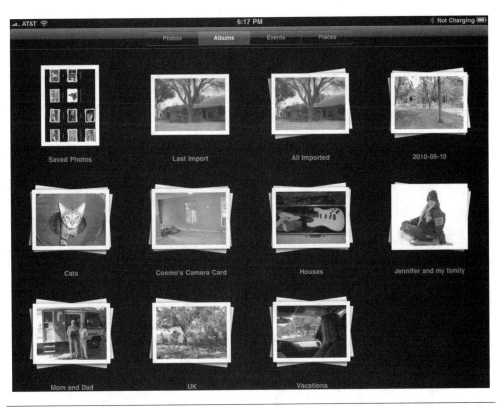

FIGURE 10-1　You create folders on your computer, move pictures into them, and then sync your iPad and computer to transfer the folders and their contents to your iPad.

- **Events**　If you use a Mac and iPhoto or Aperture to organize and manage your photos, you'll see an Events tab. Events are photos you organize by their dates and event names when you import them to your Mac. You may also see an Events tab even if you don't sync your iPad with a Mac, provided you've somehow acquired photos on your iPad that it can classify as an event.
- **Faces**　If you use a Mac and iPhoto or Aperture to organize and manage your photos using the built-in face-recognition feature, you'll see a Faces tab. If you don't use a Mac, you won't. Faces lets you mark a person's face with a name, and then Photos can sort photos by a person, based on the information about their face.
- **Places**　When you acquire photos on your iPad, they may be categorized into "Places" if the iPad can figure out where they were taken. If you've uploaded or

synced photos taken with a GPS-enabled camera or iPhone, you may see results in the Places tab, as shown in the following illustration.

You'll see additional options when you view a photo. To view any photo and these additional options, tap it. It will open in full-screen mode, and the additional options will appear at the top of the page. You can use the Share icon to share the photo with others via email, send the picture to a social networking site like Facebook, or assign to a contact or as wallpaper. You can also copy the photo. If you subscribe to MobileMe, you can also opt to send the picture via MobileMe to ultimately sync at your computer (without actually connecting to it). Tap the Share icon to view the options (that's the icon with the right-facing arrow). There's also an option to create a slideshow, as shown in the following illustration.

Copy Photos from Your Computer Using iTunes

We covered syncing in Chapter 1, but you may not have been ready to commit at that time to putting data on your iPad. You can refer to that chapter for the full explanation, but here's what you'll need to do if you just want to copy a folder or for the purpose of working through this chapter:

1. Connect your iPad to your computer. iTunes will open.
2. In iTunes, click your iPad in the source pane.
3. Click the Photos tab.
4. Click Sync Photos From.
5. Note the default picture folder. In Windows, it's the Pictures folder, but you can select a different folder using the arrows if your pictures are located in another folder.

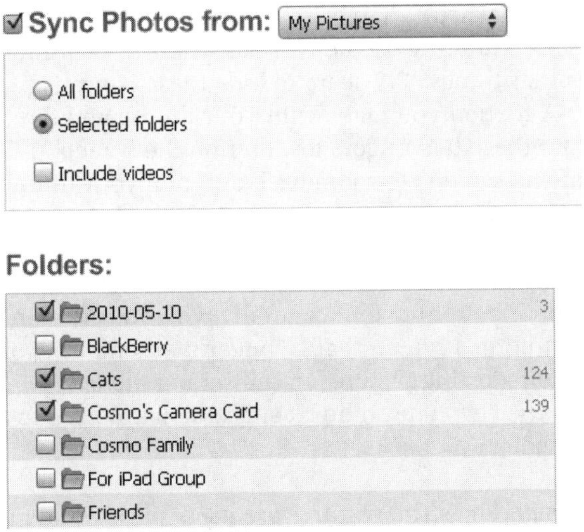

FIGURE 10-2   You don't have to commit to syncing all of your photos; just pick a couple of folders for now, if you want.

6. To select only certain picture folders, tick Selected Folders. You'll see something similar to what's shown in Figure 10-2.
7. Select the folders to sync (copy) to your iPad.
8. Click Apply. A sync will occur immediately and you'll have photos on your iPad when it's complete.

View Photos

Now that you know a little about the interface and have some photos on your iPad, you're ready to view some photos. As you are aware by now, you can view photos in lots of ways by clicking the tabs at the top of the Photos interface. For now, we'll focus on the Photos and Albums tabs.

View All Your Photos

To view all of your photos in a list, with each photo shown one at a time (versus categorized in Albums), click the Photos tab. You can use various gestures to view them, including using a tap, flick, or pinch, and by physically repositioning the iPad. If you're not sure what some of those words mean, here's all you need to know:

- **Tap (on a thumbnail)**   A single, light touch on the screen, on any thumbnail for a photo. When you tap a thumbnail of a photo in the Photos tab, the photo will open in full screen.

- **Tap (on a picture)**   Tap briefly anywhere on the screen when in full-screen mode. This will bring up the title bar where you can return to the previous page, among other things. Tap again to hide these controls.
- **Pinch**   A motion you make with your thumb and forefinger. To zoom in on a photo, put these two fingers together on the screen and pull them apart while touching the screen. To zoom back out, pull your thumb and forefinger back together while touching the screen. You can also reverse-pinch on a thumbnail to see it in full screen.
- **Flick**   A quick motion you make across the screen, right to left, left to right, top to bottom, or bottom to top, generally with your forefinger. You can use a flick to move around in a screen that is longer than one page or to move from photo to photo when viewing pictures in full-screen mode.
- **Double-tap**   Two taps in quick succession are used to zoom in on and then zoom out of a photo.

To understand how the gestures are used, perform the following steps. You can use these motions in Photos and while viewing photos from the Photos tab:

1. In Photos, click the Photos tab.
2. Tap the thumbnail for any photo to view it in full-screen mode.
   a. Once in full-screen mode, pinch the photo to zoom in and out.
   b. Flick the photo to the left to see the next photo in the list. Flick right to return to the previous photo.
   c. Pinch inward on any photo to return to the Photos page.
3. Tap another thumbnail to open the picture in full-screen mode. Then you can
   a. Turn the iPad left or right 90 degrees to change view modes.
   b. Flip the iPad as you would to show a photo to someone sitting across from you. Flip again to return.
   c. Tap and hold your finger briefly anywhere on the photo and then tap All Photos when it appears, as shown in the following illustration.

4. At the Photos tab:
   a. Flick to scroll through thumbnails of photos if there are more than can be shown in a single screen.
   b. Rotate the iPad 90 degrees left or right to change from Portrait to Landscape.
   c. Tap any photo in the Photos tab. Drag your finger across the bar that appears at the bottom of the page to skim through all of your photos quickly. If you don't see this bar, which is shown in the following illustration, tap the bottom of the page to view the controls.

View Photo Albums

In the preceding section, we focused mostly on how to navigate and view photos from the Photos tab in the Photos app. In this section, you'll explore the Albums tab. As you know, a physical photo album is a collection of photos that you put together yourself, for the purpose of easily accessing them when you wish. Like a physical photo album, albums in the Photos app also have multiple photos. But accessing the photos in these albums is much more convenient than accessing a physical album, especially since all of the albums fit nicely in a single unit—your iPad!

Note You can't create an album on your iPad. You have to create the album on a PC or Mac and sync the iPad to copy it.

The first thing you'll notice when you explore Albums is that each album has multiple images, and those images appear as a stack of photos, which represents the album itself. You can tap any album to view the photos in it, and tap Albums to return to the Albums page. Additionally, you can use the same techniques you already know, like tap, pinch, and flick, to navigate the photos in your albums, although these movements will often produce different results. (Pinching outward on a stack of photos will allow you to "peek" at the photos, for instance, and if you continue pinching outward, the album will open.)

To see how gestures work in Albums, perform the following steps:

1. Click the Albums tab. Note the stacks that designate the albums.
2. Tap any album to open it, and then browse the items in the album using tap, pinch, and flick in the manner described in the previous section.
3. When in full-screen mode, tap once to view the controls and tap the name of the album in the left corner to return to the albums. Then, click Albums in the top-left corner to return to the album page.
4. Back at the Albums tab, pinch an album by dragging your thumb and forefinger outward. Note this allows you to peek at the album. Continue pinching outward to open it.

Delete Photos

You may have photos on your iPad you don't want. You can delete photos that you've imported using a camera card, saved from the Internet, or obtained via email. You can't delete photos you synced from your computer; you have to use iTunes for that.

Create a Photo Album

Since you can't create a photo album on your iPad, you will have to create it on your computer. On a Mac, you'll probably use iPhoto to create albums, and on a PC, you'll create a new folder. For both, once the folders are created, you'll move or copy photos into it.

If you use iPhoto on a Mac, click File, and click New Album to get started. Name your album, and then drag the photos you'd like to appear in the album from your library to the new album. If you use a PC, create a folder in the Pictures folder and copy or move pictures into it as follows:

1. On your PC, click Start, and click Pictures.
2. In the Pictures folder, right-click an empty area of that folder (in any white area in the right-side pane).
3. From the resulting menu, click New, and then Folder.
4. Name the folder.
5. Move pictures into this folder. You can cut and paste, or position this window with another window side by side, so that you can drag photos to it from other folders on your computer.

Once the album is created on your Mac, or a folder is created on your PC, you'll need to sync your iPad to the computer to get the new "album" on it.

To delete photos from your iPad that you've imported and not synced from your computer:

1. In the Photos app, use the Photos tab to locate the thumbnail of pictures to delete that were imported (not synced from your computer).
2. Click the right-facing arrow next to Slideshow.
3. Tap the photos to delete.
4. Tap Delete.
5. Tap Delete Selected Photos. See Figure 10-3.

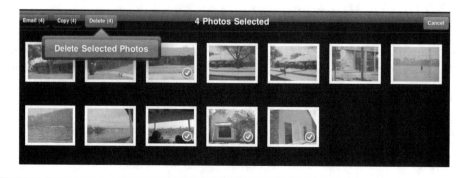

FIGURE 10-3 If you have duplicate photos, you can easily delete them.

Share Photos

It's easy to share photos with the people around you. The iPad has a large enough screen that people can view photos easily, and those photos can be viewed in Portrait view or in Landscape view. You can flip the iPad 180 degrees toward you or away from you to show a photo to a person sitting across from you. You can even pass the iPad around the room if you trust people not to drop it! And you may have even experimented with the dock or carrying case (optional components) for positioning your iPad as a digital photo frame and perhaps even placed it on your fireplace mantle for all to see.

The people you want to share your photos with aren't always in the same room with you, though. You may want to share your photos with a grandparent in another state or a son who's in college. You may want to share your photos with people you've never even met. You can share photos with others via email, MobileMe, Facebook, and various other ways.

You can also share photos by assigning a photo to a contact or setting it as wallpaper. You can copy photos too, with a tap and a quick hold or by accessing the Copy command from the Photos interface. You can then paste any image you've copied into an email or other app.

Share a Photo in an Email

You'll have to have an email account set up on your iPad before you can email a photo, and setting up email is detailed in Chapter 4. If you haven't worked through that chapter yet, just come back to this section after you have. You don't have to ever email a photo if you don't want to; it's just one of the options for sharing.

To email a photo:

1. In Photos, locate the photo to email.
2. Tap it to open it in full-screen mode.

Did You Know?

You Can View Videos Too!

If you have compatible videos in the Photos folder on your computer and you sync that folder to your iPad, those videos will appear in the Photos app on your iPad, alongside your still photos. (The same applies to photos you copy from the Camera Connection Kit, detailed later in this chapter.) Just tap any video to view it. Unlike other videos you watch on your iPad (which open in Videos), these videos will open in Photos.

3. Position your finger in the top-right corner of the screen and look for the Share icon. It's the icon with the right-facing arrow, as shown in the following illustration. Tap it.

4. Tap Email Photo.
5. Complete the email as desired.
6. When ready, click Send.

To select multiple photos to email:

1. From any album or list of photos, tap the Share button. That's the right-facing arrow in the top-right corner.
2. Tap up to five photos to select them.
3. Tap Email.
4. Complete the email as desired.

Send a Photo Using MobileMe

MobileMe is an add-on feature you have to subscribe to and pay for. MobileMe is the updated version of .Mac and iTools, if you're familiar with those, but includes many more features. MobileMe offers a free, 30-day subscription, but the yearly rate is $99 and you'll be enrolled when the trial runs out unless you intervene. There's also a free MobileMe Gallery App that's a must-have to MobileMe users.

You can use MobileMe to send photos to your own personal MobileMe Gallery, an area on the web (or in the cloud, if you prefer) that you can use to store your photos and share them with others. People you allow access to can view pictures, download their favorites, and/or contribute their own pictures. Viewers can also skim albums to see what's inside, select an album, and choose viewing options such as Mosaic, Carousel, or Slideshow. MobileMe offers automatic resizing, so your photos adjust instantly to fit the viewer's browser window too, thus making it perfect for those with larger displays.

Note   MobileMe is a service that pushes email, contacts, and calendar events over the air to all your devices. This means that you can keep your iPhone, iPad, Mac, and PC in perfect sync. No docking required.

To send a photo to your personal MobileMe Gallery:

1. In Photos, locate the photo to share. Tap it. (Note you can select multiple photos, as detailed previously.)
2. Position your finger in the top-right corner of the screen and look for the Share icon.
3. Click the Share icon and click Send to MobileMe.
4. Complete any additional information as prompted.

Tip   To learn more about MobileMe and to subscribe, visit www.apple.com/mobileme/.

Send a Photo to Facebook

There are so many Facebook users that we'd be lax if we left out how to send a photo to Facebook. If you're a Facebook user, read on. If not, feel free to skip this section! Before you can share a photo on Facebook from your iPad, you have to perform a few setup tasks:

- You have to get a personalized upload email address from Facebook. You'll use this email address to post pictures to your Facebook page.
- You have to have email set up on your iPad. You have to be able to send email in order to send a photo via email to Facebook.
- You have to be connected to the Internet when sending the photo.
- You have to send the photo to the personalized email address to post it to your Facebook page.

To get a personalized upload email address from Facebook:

1. From your Facebook home page, click Photos.
2. Click Upload Photos.
3. Click Mobile Photos.
4. Click Send My Upload Email to Me now.
5. Add this email address as a contact and name it Facebook Photos. (See Chapter 13 for information on adding a contact.)

Now you're ready to send a photo from your iPad to your Facebook home page:

1. In Photos, locate the photo to send to Facebook. Tap it. If you like, select multiple photos, as detailed earlier.
2. Locate the Share button, and click Email.

3. Select the Facebook Photos contact you added in Step 5 earlier.
4. Type a subject in the subject line, and click the Mail icon to send it.

Currently when emailing photos to Facebook, what you write in the subject line is included with the picture. Anything you write in the body is not.

Assign a Photo to a Contact

With the iPhone, you'd generally snap a photo and assign it to a contact on the fly. Just because your iPad doesn't have a camera to take pictures (or a phone feature, for that matter), doesn't exclude the option to use a photo you have for a contact, nor the need to. You still do a lot with contacts, including emailing, Skype-ing, and messaging with third-party apps, so assigning a photo for a contact is still useful.

With the iPad, you'll have to get a picture by importing it from a digital camera, media card, or by syncing to a computer. You can get it via email too. Once that picture is on your iPad, though, it's a simple process to assign it to a contact.

To assign a photo to a contact:

1. In Photos, locate the picture to assign to a contact. For best results, choose a headshot. Tap it to open it in full-screen mode.
2. Click the Share button, and click Assign to a Contact.
3. Choose the contact from the Contacts list.
4. If you wish, move and scale the image (see the following illustration).
5. Tap Use.

Set a Photo as Wallpaper

Wallpaper is what you see when your iPad is locked and the slider is available to unlock it, as well as the picture you see on the Home screen. You can set any photo as wallpaper, using the same techniques detailed earlier.

To set a photo as wallpaper:

1. In Photos, locate the picture to set as wallpaper. Tap it to view it in full-screen mode.
2. Click the Share button, and click Use as Wallpaper.
3. Tap Set Lock Screen, Set Home Screen, or Set Both, as shown in the following illustration.

Copy a Photo

There are many reasons why you would want to copy a photo, but you'll probably want to paste it into the body of an email. You may have apps that allow you to paste into them as well, like iWork apps including Pages, Numbers, and Keynote. Whatever you need to copy a photo for, it's easy to do.

To copy a photo:

1. In Photos, locate the picture to copy. Tap the photo to view it in full-screen.
2. Click the Share button, and click Copy.
3. Open an app that supports the Paste command and can accept photos (Notes can't). For example, you can open a new Mail message.
4. Tap and hold, and tap Paste when applicable.

Create a Slideshow

One of the best investments you can make to accessorize your iPad is the dock. The *dock* is a small white stand that you can use to display your iPad on a coffee table, mantle, or desk. You can then do lots of things with it, like present a slideshow of pictures (or use a keyboard or watch a movie without having to hold your iPad in your hands or lap). If you intend to use your iPad as a digital photo frame in the long term, you can even connect the power cable and plug it in so it'll stay charged.

Save a Photo from a Web Page

To save a picture from a web page, touch and hold the photo, then tap Save Image. The same sequence works in an email.

FIGURE 10-4 Easily create a slideshow with music and transitions from the Slideshow button.

It's easy to create a slideshow of pictures anytime you want, and view it anywhere you want. To create a slideshow:

1. Open the Photos app and select an album you'd like to display in a slideshow. (You can tap the Photos tab to use all of your photos.) Tap a photo in the album to view it in full-screen mode.
2. Optional: Place the iPad on its dock. If you wish, connect the iPad to a power source to keep the battery from draining if you plan to show the slideshow for a while.
3. Tap Slideshow.
4. To play music with your slideshow:
   a. Move the Play Music slide to On.
   b. Tap Music and select a song.
5. Choose a transition.
6. Tap Start Slideshow. See Figure 10-4.

To change how long you'd like to play each slide for, or to repeat or shuffle photos, tap Settings on the Home screen, tap Photos, and make your changes as desired. You can opt to change slides every 2, 3, 5, 10, or 20 seconds.

Tip To stop playing the slideshow, tap the screen.

Use Picture Frame

Picture Frame is a feature kind of along the same lines as Slideshow. With Picture Frame, though, when your iPad is locked, you can display an album of photos. This is a great way to enjoy your iPad while at the same time, charging it in an iPad dock.

You configure settings for Picture Frame in the Settings app; just tap Settings and Picture Frame. You can choose a transition, opt to zoom in on faces, or shuffle the pictures, to name a few. You can also opt to show all photos, only albums, or only events. With that done, it's easy to start or stop Picture Frame:

1. Press the Sleep/Wake button to lock the iPad.
2. Tap the Sleep/Wake button again or Home button to view the Lock screen.
3. Tap the Picture Frame icon next to the slider to start the show.
4. Tap anywhere on the iPad to access the Lock screen again, where you can tap the Picture Frame icon to stop the show.

Import Photos with Optional Components

You know you have several options for getting pictures onto your iPad. You could connect your iPad to your computer and transfer photos by syncing them with iTunes, for one. You could email yourself the photos you'd like to have on your iPad, and save them as they arrive in Mail. You can also save photos you find using the iPad's Safari web browser. No matter which of these you choose, though, there's nothing simpler than using a $29 optional component to transfer photos, specifically, the Camera Connection Kit, which includes the Media Card Reader.

With the Camera Connection Kit, you can import pictures and videos directly from your digital camera. With the Media Card Reader included with the kit, you can import pictures and videos directly from a media card. This makes importing your latest pictures a breeze; instead of having to transfer the pictures from your camera to your computer and *then* to your iPad, you simply import them directly to the iPad, with no intermediate steps.

Tip To order these components, visit www.store.apple.com, and click Shop iPad. Scroll to the bottom of the page to view the available accessories.

Import Photos with the Optional Camera Connection Kit

To use the USB adapter from the Camera Connection Kit, simply connect one end to your iPad and the other to the USB cable you connect to your digital camera. The adapter connects to the iPad via the 30-pin port at the bottom. Turn on your digital camera and position any settings for playback on that camera, as warranted.

Once the camera has been connected:

1. Wait while the iPad reads the picture information on the card or camera.
2. Green check marks on photos denote that they've already been uploaded to your iPad. You may or may not see this.

FIGURE 10-5 Select the photos to import by tapping them.

3. Tap once on each photo to copy to your iPad and click Import. Tap Import Selected. Alternately, you can click Import All. See Figure 10-5.
4. After the import process has finished, click Delete to remove the files from your media card or click Keep to keep them.

Import Photos with the Optional Media Card Reader

Using the Media Card Reader is even easier than using the USB adapter. Just insert the Media Card Reader into the proper port on your iPad, remove the media card from your digital camera, and insert it into the Media Card Adapter.

Once the camera has been connected:

1. Wait while the iPad reads the picture information on the card.
2. Green check marks on photos denote that they've already been uploaded to your iPad. You may or may not see this.
3. Tap once on each photo to copy to your iPad and click Import. Tap Import Selected. Alternately, you can click Import All.
4. After the import process has finished, click Delete to remove the files from your media card or click Keep to keep them.

11

View, Manage, and Share Videos

HOW TO...

- Open and navigate the Videos app
- Sync videos on your computer to your iPad
- Play a video and explore video controls
- Watch media you've purchased from iTunes
- Show closed captioning
- Delete a video
- Open and navigate the YouTube app
- Search for, bookmark, rate, comment, and share a video
- Install the ABC Player for the iPad
- Watch a TV show from ABC
- Search for additional Internet TV programming
- Sign up for a free trial to Netflix

The Videos app, which comes preinstalled on all new iPads, allows you to watch music videos, movies, and TV shows you purchase or rent from iTunes, and videos you've synced from your computer. You can also watch video you've downloaded from iTunes U here too, as video podcasts. The Videos app supports high definition and standard definition videos and movies, supports closed captioning, and can be viewed in wide-screen mode, among other things. You can also view personal videos here, provided you've synced them to your iPad.

The YouTube app, also included, enables you to easily browse YouTube videos. If you have a YouTube account (it's free), you can sign in and access videos you've uploaded yourself from your computer, rate and comment on videos, view your subscriptions, and more. You can even email a link to a video to someone to share it.

Of course, there are myriad third-party apps that are related to video; these are apps that you'll need to download and install yourself, because these apps aren't included by default on your iPad. One seriously worth considering is the Netflix app. This app (along with a monthly membership fee) enables you to watch movies and recorded TV shows right from your iPad, and there are literally thousands to choose from. If you want to avoid another monthly charge, though, try the ABC Player for the iPad. This free app enables you to watch recorded TV shows, such as *Lost* and *Grey's Anatomy* (for no cost). Of course, new apps appear every day, so you'll need to keep your eyes open for upcoming apps like those that are expected from Hulu, NBC, and various other TV-related entities, as you can be sure new apps will be arriving regularly!

Explore the Videos App

When you're ready to sit down with your favorite movie, you'll sit down with the Videos app. You can watch almost any type of video, including those filmed in high definition (HD). You can watch complete movies, podcasts, music videos, and TV shows, as well as media you download from iTunes U. Because there are no buttons or controls that remain on the screen all the time, you can watch media using the entire iPad's screen too, giving you a more "at-the-movies" feel. Figure 11-1 shows how the Videos app looks on your iPad.

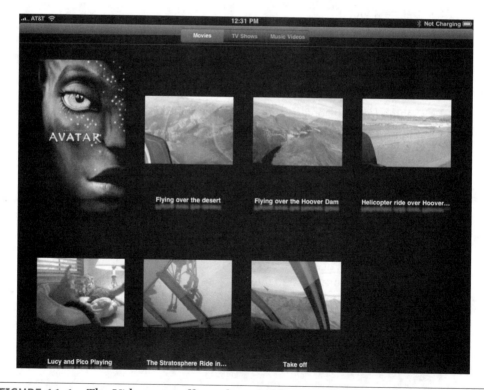

FIGURE 11-1 The Videos app offers tabs to hold various kinds of video. Tabs appear when you've acquired media that fits in the category.

Open and Navigate the Videos App

To open the Videos app, you simply tap it. Once the app is open, you will see tabs that apply to the type of video you've acquired. Here are some of the tabs you'll see. Note that tabs will appear as media becomes available that belongs in these categories and tabs disappear when that media is no longer available:

- **Movies**   The Movies tab holds movies you've purchased or rented. Tap the Movies tab to see what's there. Other video will appear here too, including anything classified as a "movie" during the syncing process.
- **TV Shows**   The TV Shows tab holds TV shows you've acquired. You won't see this tab if you don't have any TV shows.
- **Podcasts**   The Podcasts tab holds video podcasts you've acquired. You won't see this tab if you haven't downloaded any video podcasts.
- **Music Videos**   The Music Videos tab holds music videos you've purchased from iTunes. You won't see this tab if you don't have any music videos.
- **iTunes U**   The iTunes U tab holds media obtained from iTunes U. You won't see this tab if you don't have any iTunes U media.

Get Movies or Videos on Your iPad

Computers have specific folders to hold videos. On a PC, that's the Videos or My Videos folder. Unfortunately, iTunes doesn't automatically sync videos from the Videos folder.

If you know that you have videos and movies on your PC but you don't see any on your iPad, then you'll need to sync the Videos folder or tell iTunes where to find those movies and videos so it can sync them, or move the media to the folder where you store your pictures (and allow the Pictures folder to sync). The first option is by far, the best. The latter, while an option, is not the best solution, and here's why.

If you are considering simply moving videos to your Pictures folder, you'll have to view the videos you move using the Photos app on your iPad, not the Videos app. If this is okay with you, first check to make sure your video files are in a format compatible with the iPad, such as MP4, M4V, or MOV. Then, after you've moved the videos, and, while your iPad is connected, tell iTunes from the Photos tab to also

Did You Know?   **You Can Upload Videos with the Camera Connection Kit**

If you record video with a digital camera and upload that video to your iPad with the optional Camera Connection Kit or Media Card Reader, iPad-compatible videos will appear in the Photos app, not the Videos app.

sync videos from that folder, as shown in the following illustration. (If you only sync specific folders, make sure to put the video in one of the folders you opt to sync.)

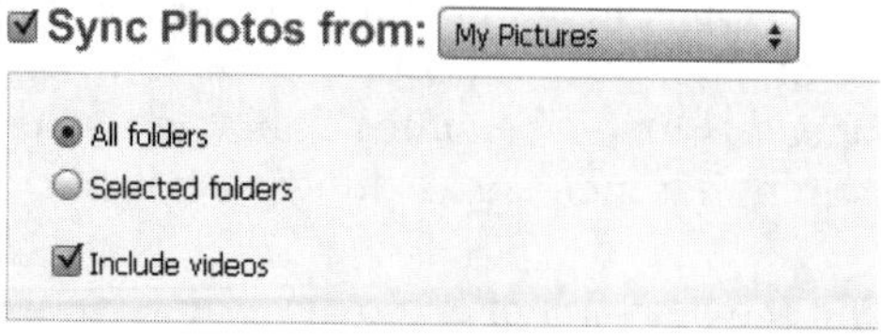

☑ **Sync Photos from:** [My Pictures   ⬍]

◉ All folders
○ Selected folders

☑ Include videos

If you'd like to view your video in the Videos app, you'll need to point iTunes to the folder where you store those videos and movies on your PC:

1. Connect your iPad to your PC.
2. In iTunes, under Library, click Movies.
3. Click File, and click Add Folder to Library.
4. Browse to the location on your computer where you save the videos you'd like to sync. This may be a Public Videos folder, shown in Figure 11-2, or your personal Videos or My Videos folder. Click Select Folder, or something similar.
5. In iTunes, click your iPad in the navigation pane.
6. Under Movies, tick Sync Movies.
7. Configure syncing as desired. Figure 11-3 shows an example.
8. Click Apply.

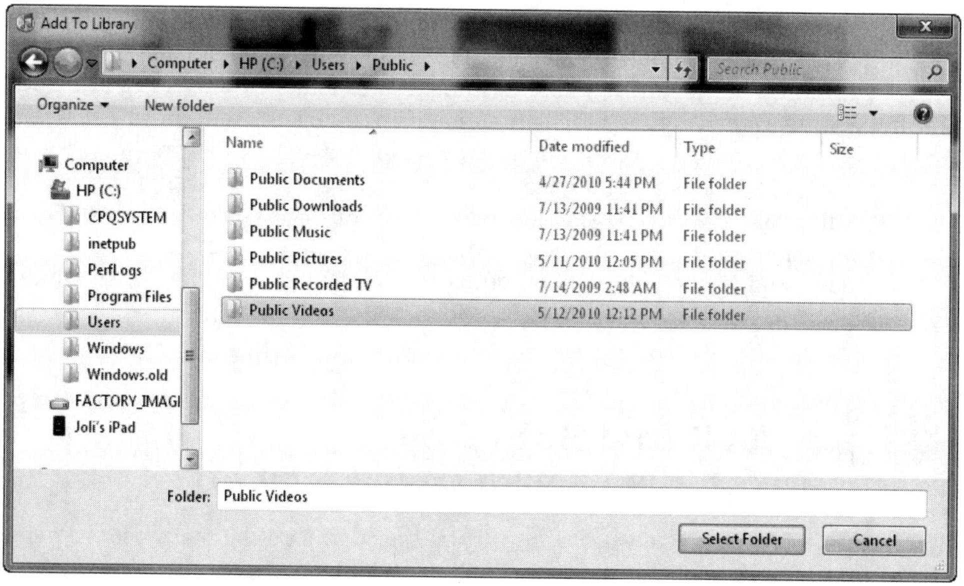

FIGURE 11-2   You can add folders for iTunes to sync to your iPad, if they aren't included in the sync process by default.

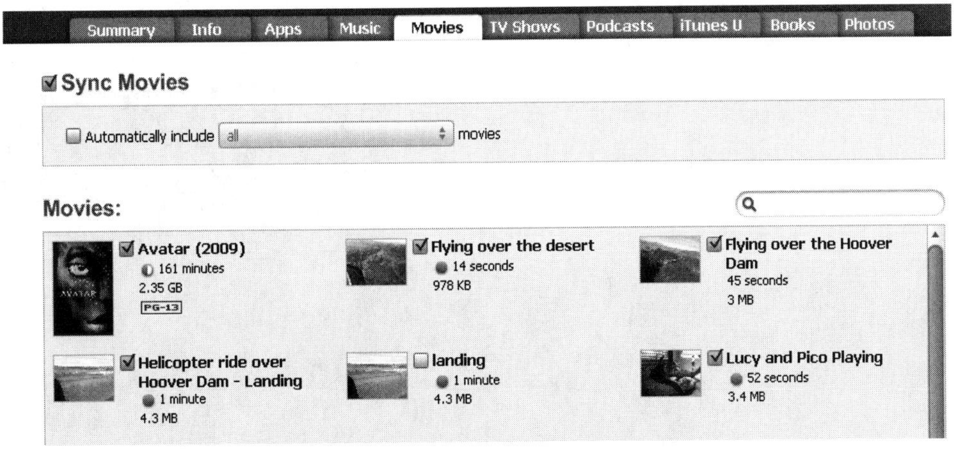

| Summary | Info | Apps | Music | **Movies** | TV Shows | Podcasts | iTunes U | Books | Photos |

☑ Sync Movies

☐ Automatically include all ⇕ movies

Movies: (🔍   )

☑ **Avatar (2009)**
    ⏱ 161 minutes
    2.35 GB
    [PG-13]

☑ **Flying over the desert**
    ● 14 seconds
    978 KB

☑ **Flying over the Hoover Dam**
    45 seconds
    3 MB

☑ **Helicopter ride over Hoover Dam - Landing**
    ● 1 minute
    4.3 MB

☐ **landing**
    ● 1 minute
    4.3 MB

☑ **Lucy and Pico Playing**
    ● 52 seconds
    3.4 MB

FIGURE 11-3 Select the movies to sync, or opt to sync all of them.

If you don't have any videos or movies to put on your iPad, but you'd like to work through this chapter, you can get a free video podcast from iTunes:

1. Tap iTunes from the iPad's Home screen.
2. Tap the Podcasts tab.
3. Locate a free video podcast.
4. Tap it to view the Information page.
5. Tap free, and then tap Get Episode.
6. When the download completes, open the Videos app and tap the Podcasts tab.

If you haven't set up iTunes to automatically sync all podcasts, the podcasts you download directly will disappear when you sync your iPad to your computer.

Play a Video

Hopefully you now have some video, or at the very least, you have downloaded a free video podcast from iTunes. Now you're ready to find and play your video using the Videos app.

To find and play a video using the Videos app:

1. Tap the Videos app on the Home screen.
2. Tap the tab that contains the media to view.
3. Tap any video to see more information.

4. Turn the iPad so you're in Landscape view.
5. Tap the Play button, shown here.

To use the video controls while watching a movie:

1. Tap the screen one time.
2. Tap the Rewind button to start the video again or skip to the previous scene in a movie. Tap and hold the button to skim backward through the video.
3. Tap the Fast Forward button to skip to the next video in the playlist (such as a multi-episode TV series) or skip scenes within a movie. Tap and hold the button to fast forward through the video.
4. Tap the Pause button to pause the video; tap it again to resume playing.
5. Use the slider to adjust the volume.
6. Tap the button in the top right of the page to switch to wide-screen view, and back. See Figure 11-4. You can also accomplish this by double-tapping anywhere on the screen.
7. Drag across the Scrubber Bar at the top of the video to pinpoint a new location.

Watch Media You've Acquired from iTunes

In Chapter 9, you learned all about browsing the iTunes Store for movies, TV shows, music videos, and even college lectures. In that chapter you also learned how to rent and buy movies and TV shows, how to preorder movies that have yet to be released, and how to browse the hottest movies of the day. If you made any purchases at the iTunes Store in that chapter that are video-related (movies, TV, podcasts), you'll find that video in the Videos app. Just tap it once to play it.

If you have not yet purchased anything from iTunes, consider doing it, at least once, so that you can get the full iPad–iTunes experience. (If you're on the fence about

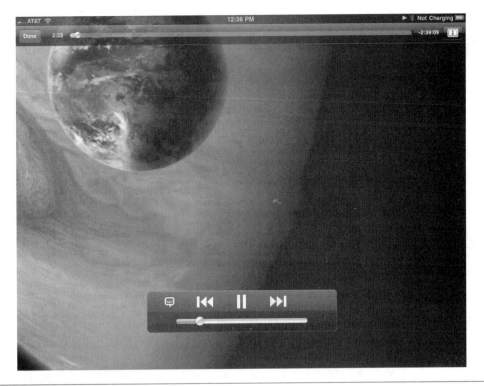

FIGURE 11-4   Tap to view the video controls.

a movie, you can preview it before buying, or rent it.) You can even purchase a single TV show if you like.

To watch media you've purchased from iTunes:

1. Open the Videos app.
2. Tap the appropriate tab to locate the media in it.
3. Tap the thumbnail for the media, as shown in the following illustration.

4. Tap Play.

Note If you buy a movie or TV show, it's yours (unlike renting). The next time you open the Videos app on your iPad, it'll still be there.

Show Closed Captioning

Closed captioning is the text version of a show or movie, and the text appears across the top or bottom of the movie while you watch it. Closed captions are embedded in a video or TV show and can be enabled when needed. Closed captioning was originally created for people who are hearing-impaired, but it can also be quite useful when you can't hear the movie dialog because of a noisy environment or don't have headphones available. Along with the text, closed captions can also include descriptions of sounds played in the background, like a song playing, a person singing, or a door creaking.

Caution You have to be careful to purchase or download media that includes closed captions to have access to it.

You can enable closed captioning for the videos you watch on your iPad. Here's how:

1. On the Home screen, tap Settings.
2. Tap Video.
3. Move the slider for Closed Captioning from Off to On.
4. Make a note of the other settings here, including where to start playing the video by default. You can choose Where Left Off or From Beginning.
5. If closed captions are available for a movie, TV show, podcast, or the like, you'll see them when you play the video in the Videos app.

Delete a Video

You can delete videos from the iPad to save space. Videos can consume quite a bit of free space. When you delete a video on your iPad that you've synced from your computer, it is removed from your iPad, but it is not removed from your computer. To delete a video from your computer, delete it from the Movies or Videos folder manually, or delete it in iTunes.

To delete a video on your iPad:

1. Open the Videos app.
2. Tap and hold a video until an X appears on it.
3. Tap the X to remove the video.
4. Tap Delete to confirm.

If you delete a rented movie from your iPad, it's deleted permanently.

Explore the YouTube App

YouTube is a video-sharing web site where users can upload and share videos they take or movies they create. Companies and artists also use YouTube to share clips of movies they produce, commercials they create for their products, TV show teasers, and music videos. Most of the video on YouTube is created and uploaded by individuals, though, and runs the gamut from funny to serious to downright filthy.

You can access YouTube videos from the YouTube app on your iPad. You'll need to be connected to the Internet, either using free Wi-Fi or an unlimited 3G data plan. (If you have a limited plan, make sure you're connected to a free network before continuing.) While you can browse all you want on YouTube without creating a user account, if you want to rate videos, post comments, or perform similar tasks, you'll have to create one. (You'll also need a user account to upload videos from your computer to YouTube.) For now, go ahead and browse without an account, and if you decide later that you need one, you can create one.

As with other apps, there are familiar buttons across the bottom:

- **Featured**   These are apps that are featured by YouTube because they're unique, meaningful, funny, or exhibit some other reason for featured status.
- **Top Rated**   When viewers view videos, they also often rate them. The videos in this category are the highest rated videos of the day, week, and all time.
- **Most Viewed**   YouTube keeps track of how often viewers watch a video, and the videos in this category have more views than the others.
- **Favorites**   The videos here are ones you bookmark as videos you like. (The bookmark icon is the same icon you have access to in Safari.) You can then access your favorite videos anytime you want to watch them again or show them to a friend.
- **Subscriptions**   If you like a particular YouTube user, you can subscribe to them. You can then view all videos posted by that person easily, as well as any new videos they post.
- **My Videos**   If you've uploaded any of your own video to YouTube, you'll have easy access to it here. You can also see how many people have viewed your videos,

and read any comments that have been posted, as shown in the following illustration.

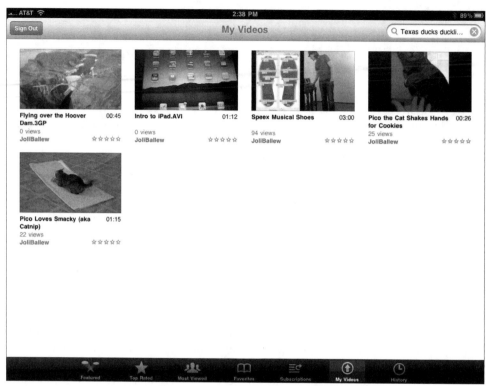

- **History** The videos you've viewed on YouTube are listed here. This offers an easy way to access a video again, should you desire.

How to... ## Create a YouTube Account

Here's how to create your own YouTube account:

1. Open Safari and navigate to www.youtube.com.
2. At the bottom of the page, tap Sign In.
3. If you have an account with Google, you can use it to sign in. Otherwise, tap Sign Up for YouTube!
4. Fill in the required information.

Play and Navigate a Video

Now that you're familiar with the YouTube interface, let's find a video and play it. The controls you'll use once a video is playing will look familiar, just like what you're used to in the Videos app.

To navigate to and play a video:

1. Open the YouTube app. If prompted to log in, do so. Note that you won't have access to all that YouTube has to offer unless you log in.
2. Click the Top Rated button at the bottom of the screen.
3. Tap any video to play it. The video should play in full-screen mode when the iPad is held in Landscape orientation. If a video is not playing in full-screen mode, pinch outward to have it fill the entire screen. Likewise, pinch inward to switch from full-screen mode to a smaller mode, shown in Figure 11-5.
4. Turn the iPad to view the video in Portrait or Landscape mode.
5. Pause, and then play the video.
6. Click the Top Rated button to return to the YouTube main page.

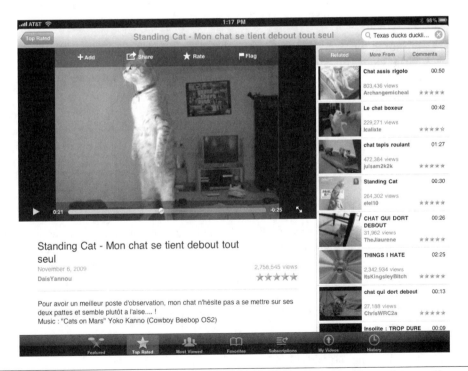

FIGURE 11-5   You can view videos in two ways, full-screen mode or this smaller mode, where you can also view related videos and have the option to share, rate, bookmark, or flag the video.

To access the YouTube controls while watching any video or while the video is paused:

1. Tap while in full-screen mode to access the available controls. They include Bookmark, Repeat, Play/Pause, and Skip (to the next video). You can also access the volume slider and use the Hi-Speed Scrubbing slider at the top of the page to quickly locate a specific part of a video.
2. Tap while in the smaller mode to access the available controls. They include: + Add (to add a bookmark), Share, Rate, and Flag, and options to play or move through the video with the slider provided. From this view you'll also see Related, More From, and Comments on the right side.

Shortcut If there's a specific event in a video you like, note how far into the video the event occurs. Then use the Scrubber Bar to quickly move there.

Search for a Video

You've seen the Search window in the YouTube interface, and it works just like any Spotlight Search window in any other iPad app. Just tap it to type in keywords for videos you'd like to see.

- Search for "Standing Cat – Mon chat" to see how to search for a specific video. Tap the video once to play it.
- Perform a broader search. In the Search box type **news bloopers**. Note all of the results. Read the ratings to decide which ones you'd like to view.
- Finally, type a username. Try mine, **JoliBallew**, with no spaces. You can then browse the videos uploaded by that YouTube user. Note that usernames are unique, so if you want to see all of the videos a friend has posted, simply ask for his or her username.

Bookmark a Video

Every so often you'll run across a video you know you're going to want to watch again. When that happens, you'll want to bookmark that video so it'll be easily accessible. Once you have bookmarked the video, you can access it from the Favorites button at the bottom of the YouTube interface. So first, find a video you absolutely love, and then

1. In full-screen mode, tap once to bring up the controls, and then, tap the Bookmark icon.
2. In the smaller screen mode, tap the video once to bring up the controls, and click the + (Add). Tap Favorites.
3. Tap the Favorites button to view your bookmarks and access them.

FIGURE 11-6 Tap the video to bring up the controls shown here.

Rate and Comment on Videos

Once you have created your YouTube account and signed in, you're ready to rate and comment on videos. Both are really easy, and both can be done from the smaller mode, discussed throughout this chapter.

To rate and comment on YouTube videos:

1. Locate a video to comment on or rate.
2. Tap the video screen while in the smaller mode, and tap Rate, shown in Figure 11-6. Tap the number of stars to apply to the video.
3. Tap Comments in the right pane to write your own comments. Tap in the Add a Comment window and begin typing. Click Send when finished.
4. You can also flag a video if you find it offensive. Flag is an option next to Rate.

Share a Video

You can tap Share, shown earlier in Figure 11-6, to email a link to a video to someone you think would enjoy it. Of course, you'll need to have Mail set up (see Chapter 4), and you'll need the email address of the person you'd like to send the link to, but you probably already have all of that. When your email is received, it'll look like this illustration.

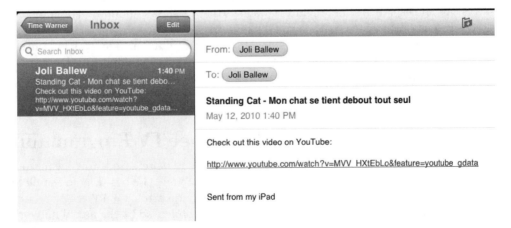

Explore Third-Party Apps

One of the greatest things about the iPhone and the iPod Touch, and ultimately the iPad, is and will continue to be third-party apps and the optional apps provided by Apple (like iWork). You can find apps in the App Store, as detailed in Chapter 7. While you may have previously focused on apps for social networking, increasing productivity, shopping, or finding your way around town, there are plenty of apps directed specifically at video and TV. There are two that are "must-have" apps for TV and movies that have already been released, and as time passes, you can be sure that more will be introduced.

Install the ABC Player for the iPad

The ABC Player for the iPad is a great third-party app available from ABC Television. You can use the app to watch TV shows that ABC makes available. Not all television shows are available, only some, but it's a great start for TV on the iPad. As time goes on, watch for other networks to release their own apps.

To install the ABC Player for the iPad:

1. Click the App Store icon on the Home screen.
2. Click the Spotlight Search window.
3. Type **ABC Player**.
4. Tap Free, and tap Get App.

Watch a TV Show from ABC

With the ABC Player installed, you can now watch a TV show on your iPad. Just open the app and look for the available shows. You can browse shows by Featured, Schedule, All Shows, Me, or Info. Figure 11-7 shows the All Shows option. When you tap a show, you can pick which episode you'd like to see.

Tap the arrow to play any show. It'll take a minute or so to load, but once it begins you'll have access to familiar controls (once the initial commercials have finished playing), including Play/Pause, view in wide screen, and the Scrubber Bar for moving forward or backward in the show.

Search for Additional Internet TV Programming

As noted, as time passes, new TV apps are sure to be released. You'll want to check occasionally to see if there are any that interest you. The best way to search for new apps from your iPad is to open the App Store, and search TV, TV programming, Watch TV, or Television. Look for apps that have been released by the actual networks, like NBC, FOX, CBS, TNT, and the like. Read the reviews before you download and install, to make sure they are worth the trouble, space, and so on.

FIGURE 11-7   ABC Player's All Shows option lets you view what's available and pick an episode.

Sign Up for Netflix

Netflix is a subscription service that, for under $10 a month, offers DVDs by mail that you can keep as long as you want, and a long list of movies and television shows you can watch instantly on your TV, computer, or iPad, if you have the right equipment and/or apps.

Netflix is something to seriously consider if

- You are always in range of a wireless network or you have an unlimited data plan from AT&T.
- You watch a lot of movies or television shows, and you want to watch those on your iPad.
- You want to watch network TV series you missed and series previously on premium channels like HBO and Showtime that you never had the opportunity to watch before.

- You don't want to purchase movies from iTunes, and you feel that the price for renting from iTunes is too expensive.
- You want to spend less than $10 a month to watch an unlimited number of movies and TV shows on your iPad (and you enjoy movies and television shows that have been out for a while).

You're not going to be able to watch newly released movies or TV shows on your iPad using the Netflix "Watch Instantly" options, so if that's what you're looking for, you'll probably want to stick with iTunes. Netflix offers new movies on DVD only, and it takes some time to get the production company's permission to offer TV shows and movies over the Internet as well as a bit of time to make that transition. However, if you're OK with the classics like *Guess Who's Coming to Dinner*, *Planet of the Apes*, *Doctor Dolittle*, and *Cool Hand Luke*, and if you're into really popular comedies like *Raising Arizona*, *When Harry Met Sally*, and *Arthur*, you can get your fill here.

Netflix fills a television void too. If you missed the first season of *Bones*, you can watch it on your iPad with Netflix. If you never got to watch Showtime's *Weeds* or *Dead Like Me*, you can watch it now. If you need to catch up on some of your favorite specials on The History Channel, there's an entire section dedicated to that. You can also watch made-for-TV movies, TV documentaries, miniseries, and even British TV. You can watch older episodes of *Mythbusters*, *King of the Hill*, *My Name Is Earl*, and a host of other shows. You'll certainly never run out of things to watch.

To watch a movie with the Netflix app, you'll need to sign up and sign in. This will require a credit card that can be billed each month. You can sign up from a computer or your iPad. To sign up for a free trial of Netflix to try out on your iPad:

1. Get the Netflix app from the App Store. It's free.
2. Tap the app to open it.
3. Under Not a Member? tap Click Here.
4. Fill out the required information and click Continue, as shown in the following illustration.

5. Input any additional information, as required.

Watch a Movie with Netflix

Watching a movie on Netflix is simple. From the Watch Instantly tab, locate the movie to watch, and tap Play:

1. Open the Netflix app.
2. Tap Watch Instantly.
3. Tap Genres.
4. Choose a genre from the list. (If you can't view all the genres, reposition the iPad to Portrait view.)
5. Browse until you've found a movie to watch.
6. Tap Play to start the movie, as shown here.

If you're not sure whether you want to watch a movie or not, tap the icon for the movie to get more information about it. From the pop-up that appears, you can see the cast, a summary, and the option to get even more information. An information page is shown in the next section.

Watch TV Shows with Netflix

Watching a TV show with your Netflix app is similar to watching a movie, but this time, from Genres, tap Television. Once in the Television section, browse to find a show you'd like to watch. As with Movies, you can tap Play to play it immediately, and as with Movies, you can also tap the icon for the show to learn more about it.

If desired, tap More Details to learn even more about the show, as shown in the following illustration.

There's a lot more to Netflix than what's detailed here, though. You can add movies and TV shows to an "instant queue," add them to your DVD queue, rate media you've watched, and more. After you've rated a few shows, Netflix will start to offer suggestions for shows you may like too, and often, it's right!

PART V

Productivity

12

Manage Contacts

HOW TO...

- Sync Contacts
- Open and explore the Contacts app
- Add a contact manually
- Add a picture for a contact
- Change the order in which contacts are listed
- Scroll and search to locate a contact
- Get a map to a contact's address
- Email a contact
- Edit a contact
- Share contact information

If you've ever used an email program, cell phone, instant messaging program, or even an old-fashioned Rolodex, you're familiar with contacts. A *contact* is a person or company that you…well, contact, via email, phone, SMS, MMS, letter, fax, or other medium.

Your iPad comes with a Contacts app that allows you to keep digital contacts. When you add a contact manually, you can input the usual information: email address, phone number, street address, zip code, and the like, but you can also add personal information such as birthdays, anniversaries, and even children's names. You can add a picture. Beyond adding the information, though, you can access contact information from various other apps, like Mail and Calendar. You can even have the Calendar app send you a reminder on a person's birthday or on your anniversary.

Add, Access, and Edit Contacts

The Contacts app is located on the Home screen of your iPad. You'll use this app to easily browse the contacts on your iPad. You may already have contacts if you've synced them from your computer, or if you've manually added them from Mail. You can also add contacts simply by touching the + sign and inputting information.

Sync Contacts

If you haven't synced contacts on your iPad, you can do so from iTunes on your computer. As with other syncing tasks, connect your iPad, select your iPad in the left pane, and configure your syncing preferences. iTunes enables you to sync contacts from various sources:

- **On a Mac** Sync contacts from Mac OS X Address Book, Yahoo! Address Book, and Google Contacts. You can sync with all of these at the same time if you like.
- **On a PC** Sync with Microsoft Outlook 2003 and 2007, Google Contacts, Windows Vista Contacts, Windows Address Book (Outlook Express), and Yahoo! Address Book. Unlike on a Mac where you can sync with multiple applications at the same time, on a PC, you can only sync with one of these at a time. You can merge the information, though; for instance, you can sync all of your Outlook Contacts, and then switch to Google and merge those contacts with the ones already on your iPad.

If you haven't synced any contacts yet, first, on your computer, clean up your Contacts list. Make sure the people in the list are people you still communicate with, that there aren't any duplicates, and that the email addresses are valid. Then, configure the settings as desired, and click Sync. Figure 12-1 shows the options from the Info tab of iTunes on a PC.

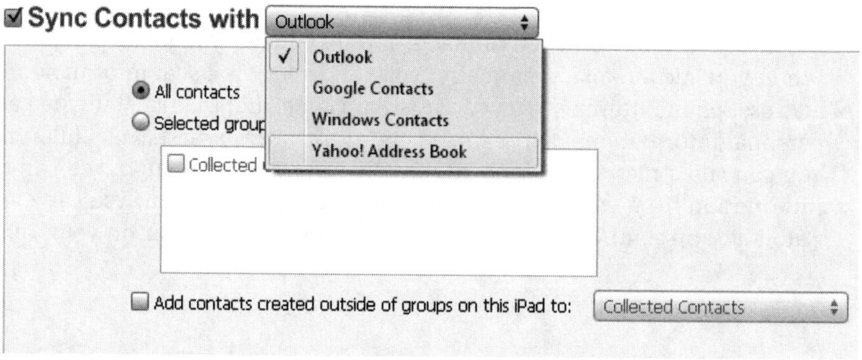

FIGURE 12-1 Connect your iPad, and in iTunes, click the Info tab to view syncing options for Contacts.

Open and Explore the Contacts App

The Contacts app is one of the more simple apps to use. It looks like the physical address book you're probably already familiar with, and includes alphabetical tabs to let you access a page quickly. The + sign lets you add a contact manually, and you can tap any existing contact and then Edit to add information if you desire. For now, though, let's just explore the app.

To open and explore the Contacts app:

1. Touch the Contacts icon on the Home screen.
2. If you have contacts in your Contacts list, use your finger to scroll through them.
3. Touch any contact to view it. See Figure 12-2.
4. Rotate the iPad 90 degrees to explore Landscape view.
5. Note the + sign. This is where you'll add a new contact.

Add a Contact

As noted, to add a contact you simply click the + sign in the Contacts app. When you do, an empty Contact card will appear, where you can add information to your heart's content. Make sure to add an address if you have one; later you can touch the address to open the Maps app and get directions to the contact's location.

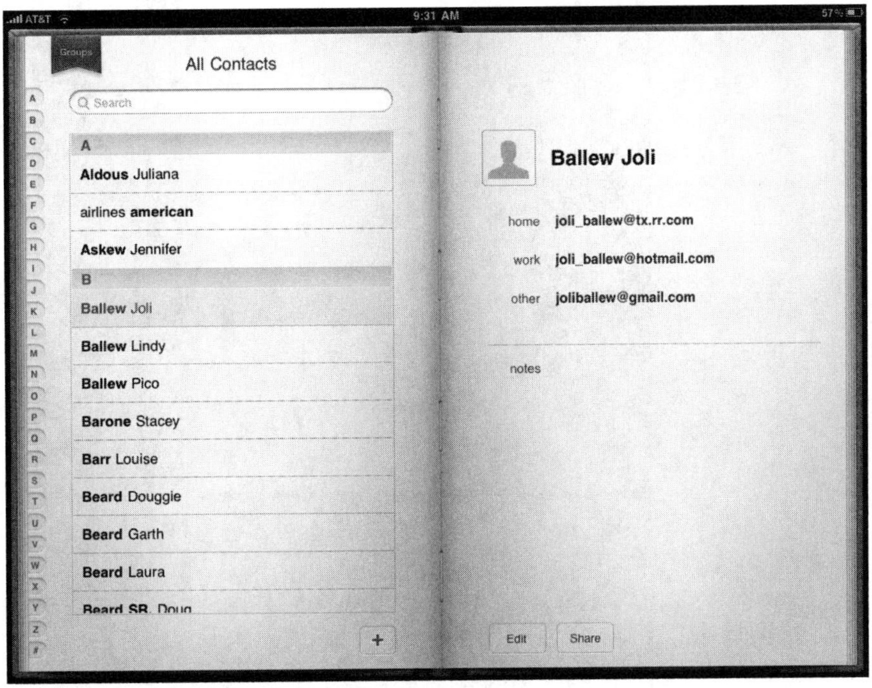

FIGURE 12-2 Contacts are listed alphabetically by the contact's last name, but you can make changes to this in Settings.

You Can Use MobileMe or Microsoft Exchange

You can set up a MobileMe on your iPad and enable Contacts. You can then sync contacts over the air with other MobileMe devices. You can also set up a Microsoft Exchange account, and obtain and sync contacts with your Exchange server at work.

To add basic contact information:

1. Open the Contacts app.
2. Click the + sign, located at the bottom of the page.
3. Fill in basic information, shown in Figure 12-3, including but not limited to:
   a. First and last name
   b. Phone number

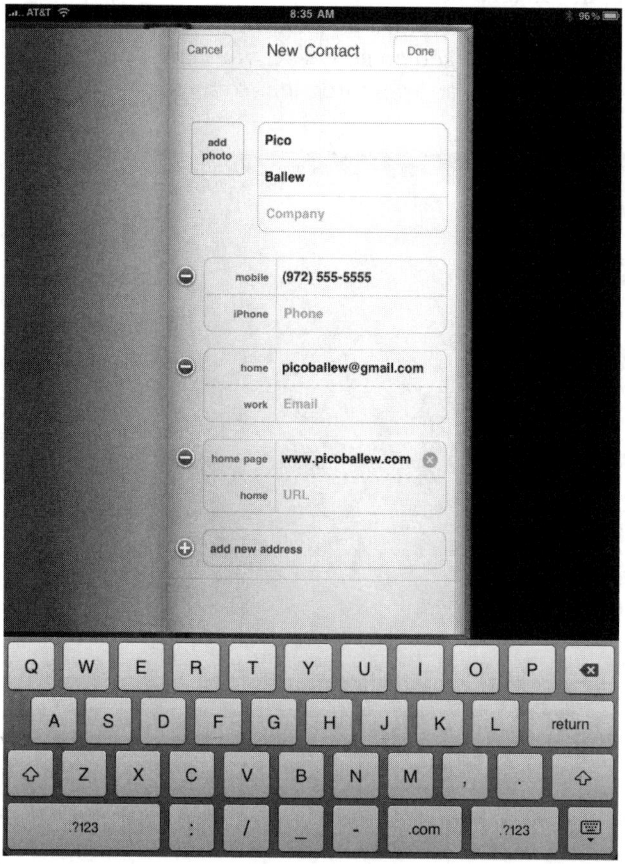

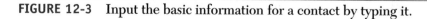

FIGURE 12-3   Input the basic information for a contact by typing it.

c. Email address
d. Street address
e. City, state, and zip

4. To add additional information, scroll down to the bottom of the Contact Card and click the green + sign next to add field. Note all the fields you can add, shown in the illustration, including but not limited to
   a. Prefix
   b. Phonetic First Name
   c. Phonetic Last Name
   d. Nickname
   e. Job Title
   f. Birthday

5. Depending on the option you choose in Step 4, you'll have the option to input information regarding that field.

6. You can click Done now, as shown here, or continue to the next set of steps to add a photo.

To add a picture for a contact:

1. With a Contact card open, tap Add Photo in the top-left corner.

To add a picture for a different contact, tap the contact name in the Contacts list and tap Edit.

2. Tap the folder that contains the picture to add.
3. Tap the picture to use.
4. If desired, drag to move and scale the picture. Note that you can also pinch to resize it.
5. Tap Use.
6. Tap Done.

Change How Contacts Appear in the List

By default, the names in the Contacts list are listed alphabetically, sorted by a person's last name. But the names are displayed in the list with their first name listed first. To us, this is not the optimal setup. If you like, you can change the order in which the contacts are sorted and/or how they are displayed. You do that from Settings:

1. Tap Settings on the Home screen.
2. Tap Mail, Contacts, Calendars.
3. If desired, under Contacts, next to Sort Order, tap Last, First to change it to First, Last.
4. If desired, under Contacts, next to Display order, tap First, Last to change it to Last, First.

Locate Contacts

You know you can scroll through your list of contacts to locate the one you want, but as your contact list grows, scrolling may not be the best way to locate the person you want. There are a few other ways to locate a contact. One is to tap the first letter of the contact's first or last name (depending on how you have your Contacts list configured) to skip to that part of the alphabet in your Contacts list. You can then locate the contact alphabetically, minus the scrolling. However, what may be the fastest way of all is searching for the contact.

To scroll or tap to find a contact:

1. In the All Contacts list, flick up or down to scroll the list.
2. Tap any letter on the left side to go to that section of the Contacts list.

Search to Locate a Contact

At the top of the Contacts list is a Spotlight Search window. You can use this window to type in a part of your contact's name, and view the results in a list. If you have four contacts with a first name of Brittany, you can type **Brit**, and then select the desired contact from the list.

To search for a contact:

1. In the Contacts app, locate the Search window.
2. Touch inside the Search window to bring up the virtual keyboard.
3. Type the first few letters of the name of the contact you'd like to find, as shown in this illustration.
4. Touch the contact to view the Contact card.

Get a Map to a Contact's Address

You can get a map to any contact's home or place of business quickly, provided you've previously input that information in the Contact card. Just locate the contact in the Contacts app and touch the address. Here's the step-by-step example:

1. Open the Contacts app.
2. Use any method you like to locate the contact.
3. Touch the contact to open their Contact card.
4. Touch the address.
5. Maps will open and you'll have the directions you wanted.

Note   For more information on using Maps, see Chapter 14.

Get in Touch with a Contact

The main reason you add contacts on your iPad is almost always to make it easier to email them. You may add yourself as a contact too, so that you can easily share your contact information with others, and you may add a contact just so you'll have easy access to a map to their home. However, for the most part, contacts you add are for emailing. In Mail, most of the time you only need to type a few letters of the contact's name and the information for that contact appears wherever it's needed (like the To line in an email).

Email a Contact

You have a couple of options for sending email to a contact. You can open the Contact card for a person you'd like to email in Contacts, and click their email address to open a new message in Mail, or you can open the Mail app and start a new email, and type part of the contact's name in the To line to add them.

To send an email to a contact from the Contacts app:

1. Open Contacts and locate the contact to email.
2. Tap their name to open their Contact card.

3. Tap their email address, as shown in the following illustration, to have Mail open automatically and insert the email address in the To line.

To send an email from the Mail app:

1. Tap Mail to open it.
2. Tap the Compose button.
3. Tap the + sign to locate a contact to add, shown in Figure 12-4, or, simply type the first letter of their first or last name to select them from another list that appears.

How to... **Add a Contact from an Email**

If you receive an email from someone you do not yet have in your contact list, tap the sender in the From line and tap Create New Contact. Alternately, you can tap Add to Existing Contact.

Note For more information on using email, see Chapter 4.

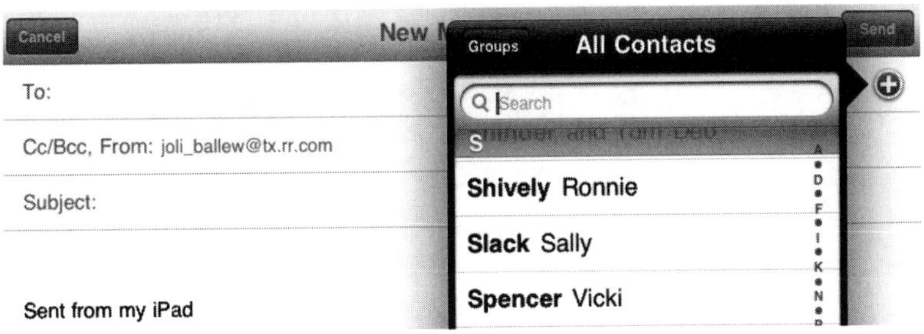

FIGURE 12-4   One way to select a contact from your Contacts list is to tap the + sign in an email and select the contact from a list.

Manage Contacts

You really don't have to do much to manage your contacts except update contact information when it changes, delete contacts you no longer need, and sync contacts to your computer. You can share a contact if you like, to send the information to someone else, but for the most part, your job is to keep the contact information up to date. Your iPad does the rest. It keeps your contacts alphabetized, enables you to easily access contacts from various apps, and makes syncing contacts with a computer (with iTunes) a breeze.

When contact information changes, you should edit the contact accordingly and in a timely manner. You never know when you may need to contact a person!

To edit a contact:

1. Open the Contacts app.
2. Locate the contact to edit.
3. Tap Edit.
4. Replace the desired information.

To delete a contact:

1. Open the Contacts app.
2. Locate the contact to delete.
3. Tap Edit.
4. Scroll down to the bottom of the page and tap Delete Contact, as shown here.

To share a contact via email:

1. Open the Contacts app.
2. Locate the contact to share.
3. Tap Share.
4. Mail opens to a new mail message. Complete the message and tap Send.

13

Manage Your Schedule

HOW TO...

- Open Calendar and explore views
- Create a Calendar event
- Add an alert for an event or set it to repeat
- Tap an event to edit it
- Navigate the Calendar
- Search the Calendar
- Add new calendars
- View a single calendar and show multiple calendars at once
- Subscribe to someone else's calendar
- Sync to verify that all calendars are updated

Perhaps (like us), you've given digital calendars a try, only to be turned off by how difficult it is to add and edit events, sync with your computer, or maintain the calendar in the long term. It's a big step—depending on a device to remember important dates like birthdays, anniversaries, interviews, and the like can be unnerving. It's difficult to completely let go of your written calendar. Those days just might be over, though. You know you can depend on your iPad; it has a long battery life, it doesn't crash or freeze up, and it's easy to sync with your computer. Starting today, you can make the transition. You can trust the Calendar app to maintain your schedule with minimal effort from you.

Explore the Calendar and Set Events

The Calendar app is available from the Home screen; tap it once to open it. If you haven't already synced calendar events through iTunes, an empty calendar awaits your first entry! Once in the Calendar app, you can explore different views, tap to see different calendars and calendar layouts, and add events.

To open the Calendar and explore the interface:

1. Tap the Calendar app on the Home screen.
2. At the top of the Calendar app, click Day, Week, Month, and List, as shown in the following illustration.
3. Turn the iPad 90 degrees to rotate from Landscape view to Portrait.

If you keep a calendar on your computer, and if you've already synced that calendar data, you'll see entries on your calendar. If you're a PC user, you may have already synced some data from your Microsoft Outlook Calendar. If you use a Mac, you may have synced data from iCal or Microsoft Entourage. If you have a Microsoft Exchange account, you can incorporate that and receive and respond to meeting invitations too, and you can enable calendar syncing if you use MobileMe. You'll need to enable both of the latter in the Settings app, under Mail, Contacts, Calendars.

Create an Event

If you're ready to immerse yourself in the Calendar, you'll start by inputting data. Think about all of the things you could input, and make a list of dates you'd like to keep track of:

- **Birthdays and anniversaries**   Create birthdays and anniversaries as once-a-year events, and set reminders for a couple of days before the date. Then, you'll have plenty of time to buy a present or card. Because you create a yearly event, you won't have to input it again.
- **Doctor and dental visits**   We all go to the doctor and dentist once a year for a checkup (or we should). Create an event for this so you won't forget to make that appointment when the time is near.
- **Goals**   Create an event that is really a goal, such as what you'd like to weigh at the start of next month, the month after that, and the month after that. Your goals may include how much you'll walk, run, or bike. Of course, goals can be many other things, but only you know what you input here. Whatever you add, it'll be easier to stay on top of the things you want to achieve.
- **Deadlines**   Create events that are common deadlines, such as when quarterly taxes are due. Create events for deadlines for work projects, home projects, or the like too.
- **Travel plans**   Create events for travel dates and include flight information, rental car information, and gate information. With the information in your calendar, you can easily access it no matter where you are.
- **Yearly events**   Create events for yearly events like Election Day, National Night Out, Tax Day, golf tournaments, marathons, and even the date your cell phone subscription renews.
- **Weekly events**   Create recurring events for things that happen each week, like going to an aerobics class every Tuesday night or meeting with your parents or kids every Thursday. If you try to plan additional events, you can easily see that you already have plans. You may even want to input information about your favorite TV shows, so you can try to watch them if you're out of town.

- **Children's events** Input your kids' soccer and baseball games, rehearsals, and recitals, and for best results, create a separate calendar for their events. You can always overlap your calendar with theirs, if you need to compare the two.
- **"Me" Time** While you're scheduling, pencil in some "me" time. Mark off a little time each week just for yourself.

Before you create an event, consider whether or not you need to create multiple calendars to organize them. You can create a calendar for your own schedule, a separate schedule for your kids, and a third just for work. You can merge the calendars when necessary too, so you can see all of your obligations. If you think you'd benefit from multiple calendars, read the section "Work with Multiple Calendars" later in the chapter first, and then return here.

Now, create entries for every event you can. Set reminders too, and open the Calendar each day to view those entries. Before you know it, you'll be totally organized! To add an event to the calendar and add alerts and reminders:

1. Open the Calendar app.
2. Locate the + sign at the bottom of the page.
3. Type the desired information:
   a. **Title** Tap to add a descriptive title for the event. If you're adding a birthday, for instance, type **Andrew's Birthday**.
   b. **Location** Tap to add a location, if applicable.
   c. **Start and End Times (or All Day Event)** Tap to configure the start and end times, or to create an all day event. Click Done after entering the desired information.
   d. **Repeat** Tap to set the event to repeat. Choose from None, Every Day, Every Week, Every 2 Weeks, Every Month, or Every Year. Click Done when finished. Use the End Repeat setting to determine when an event no longer needs to repeat.
   e. **Alert** Tap Alert to set an alert. Choose from None, 5 Minutes Before, 15 Minutes Before, 30 Minutes Before, 1 Hour Before, 2 Hours Before, 1 Day Before, 2 Days Before, or On Date of Event. Tap Done when finished.
   f. **Calendar** Tap Calendar to choose a calendar. What you see here will differ based on the calendars you have access to. Notice the colors associated with each calendar option. When you add an event to a specific calendar, it will appear on the calendar in that color. Click Done when finished. (If you only have one calendar, you will not see this option.)
   g. **Notes** Tap to type notes regarding the event.
4. After all the information is added, tap Done.

5. Notice the new event on the calendar, as shown in the following illustration. Tap Edit to edit the event, if desired.

Cancel	Edit Event	Done		12 Wednesday
				Finish Chapter 13

Finish Chapter 13

Home office

| **Starts** | Wed May 12, 2010 | > |
| **Ends** | Wed May 12, 2010 | |

Repeat   Never >

Alert   None >

Upload to FTP by 6 p.m.

Andrew's Birthday

Delete Event

Apr 25 - 1   May 2 - 8   [May 9 - 15]   May 16 - 22   May 23 - 29   May 30 - 5

Browse Events and Dates

Now that you've input some data, you can browse the calendar and your upcoming events. You can also browse the calendar for free time. There are several ways to browse the calendar and access events. You can

- Tap any event that you've already input to view the complete event. You can do this in any calendar, in Day, Week, Month, or Year mode.
- In Month view, double-tap any date to view that date in the calendar.
- In Day view, use your finger to scroll through events.
- Use your finger to scroll through dates using the bar that runs across the bottom of the Calendar app.
- In any view, tap an event to edit it. Note you can delete an event in the Edit window.

Search a Calendar

When you have a lot of information in Calendars on your iPad, you may find that you need to search for something on it (versus scanning and scrolling). Like other apps on your iPad, Calendar has a Spotlight Search window. Just type what you're looking for, and when it appears in the list, tap it to go to that event, as shown in the following illustration.

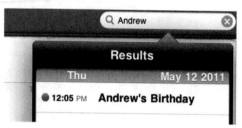

Work with Multiple Calendars

You may wear multiple hats. You could be a full-time employee, a mom or dad, a coach, a hobbyist, an athlete, and/or a caregiver. When you have multiple types of responsibilities and interests, you also have multiple schedules. That's where multiple calendars come in. To help you keep your priorities in order, you can create a calendar just for work, one just for your kid's games and your own athletic endeavors, one for the hours you're responsible for taking care of an aging parent, and another for "me" time.

If you'd rather put all of your personal responsibilities on one calendar, though, you can. There's still a reason for keeping two or more calendars, though. You can create another calendar for your children or a spouse. You may even create a separate calendar for your boss. You can add their events to a separate calendar, and view that calendar when you need to know where they are and what they are doing. Of course, with this plan you have to actively involve them, and make sure they input what they have planned, but they can do that on a computer that can then be synced to your iPad daily.

Each calendar you create stands alone. Each calendar has events listed in its own color, and each calendar can be viewed with any other calendar when needed. With multiple calendars on a single device, you can keep track of everything.

Create Additional Calendars for Your iPad

Creating a second or third calendar isn't something you do on your iPad. You create additional calendars in the calendar application you use on your computer. For instance, in Microsoft Outlook

1. Open the Calendar in Outlook.

2. Click the arrow next to New and click Calendar, as shown here.

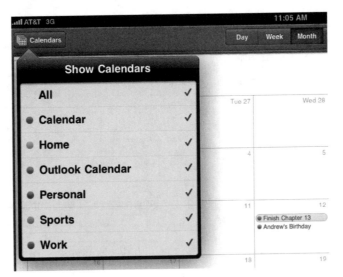

3. Type the name of the new calendar and click OK.
4. Sync your iPad to your computer, noting that syncing is enabled for Outlook in iTunes (from the Info tab).
5. Once the sync is complete, on your iPad:
   a. Tap Calendar.
   b. Click Calendars in the top-left corner.
   c. Note the new calendars and the colors associated with them. Our new calendars include Personal, Sports, and Work, as shown in the following illustration.

To view a single calendar and show multiple calendars at once:

1. In the Calendar app, tap Calendars.
2. Tap any calendar to show or hide it. If it has a check by it, the calendar will show, if not, it will be hidden.

Subscribe to Someone Else's Calendar

You can subscribe to compatible calendars on the Internet and have those calendar events included with the calendar you keep on your iPad. You'll find calendars everywhere and for almost anything, including calendars for your favorite sports teams, calendars for your kid's lunch program at school, calendars that detail work-related holidays, and more. Apple provides a number of free calendars if you'd like to try them out, including calendars for national holidays and sports events.

To subscribe to a calendar available from Apple:

1. Open Safari and navigate to icalshare.com.
2. Note the Calendar categories, shown in Figure 13-1.

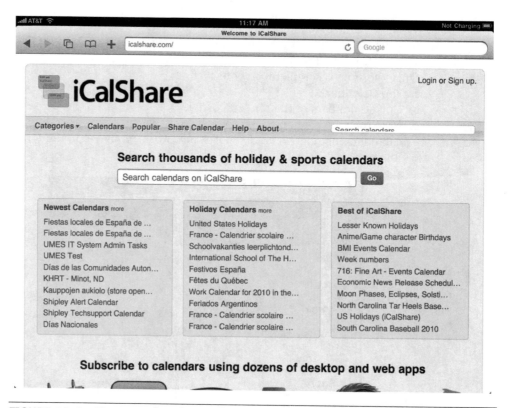

FIGURE 13-1   You can subscribe to all kinds of calendars from the iCalShare web site.

3. Locate a calendar you'd like to include, and tap it. We'll choose United States Holidays.
4. Tap Subscribe to Calendar.
5. Tap Subscribe.
6. Tap View Events to see the new entries.
7. To see all the entries, tap List. The results are shown in the following illustration.

Set Up and Verify Syncing

In order to truly trust your calendar, you need to verify that syncing works between your iPad and your computer. This involves creating events on your iPad, connecting your iPad to your computer, and verifying that events are copied back to the calendar program on your computer. You should also find out just where those events are stored on your computer, and then configure an appointment there and verify that it is transferred to your iPad when you sync. You should be able to create events at either place and sync them automatically each time you connect your iPad to your computer.

To verify that the events you create on your iPad are copied to your computer, and to locate them:

1. Connect your iPad to your computer.
2. Click your iPad in the source pane of iTunes.
3. Click the Info tab.
4. Verify that syncing is enabled for the application you use on your computer.
5. Click Sync.
6. Open the Calendar app on your computer.
7. Locate the calendars you've created on your iPad and verify that they are enabled in your Calendar app. In Outlook, two of our calendars look like what's shown in Figure 13-2.

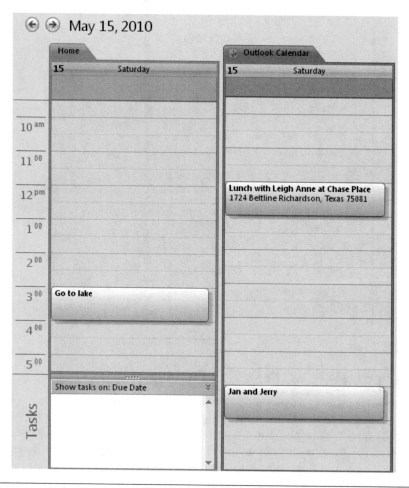

FIGURE 13-2 Calendar events from your iPad should also be available on your computer after you've synced them.

14

Use Maps

HOW TO...

- Open Maps and explore the interface
- Find your present location
- Explore all views—satellite, topography, street, and terrain
- Pinch and scroll to change views
- Find a location and drive there
- Explore Street View
- Find a nearby restaurant and walk to it
- Find a route using public transportation
- Share a location
- Find a business and get information about that business
- Mark a location
- Add a bookmark

The Maps app is one of the most awesome apps on the iPad, at least in our opinion, and (unlike the iPhone), the iPad has a large enough screen that you can actually use the app effectively. You can incorporate Maps with Google's Street View when available to view a picture of your destination, and access driving routes, walking routes, and public transportation routes easily. You can search for points of interest, landmarks, businesses, restaurants, or even a specific intersection. You can easily find your present location, and if a location isn't marked on a map, such as a friend's house or park, you can mark it yourself, and save it as a bookmark. You can even share destinations and locations with others via email.

You can use Maps with either version of the iPad. The Wi-Fi model finds your location using known Wi-Fi hotspots. This means that when you want to know where you are, your iPad will gauge this based on how close or far you are from any stable, known Wi-Fi hotspots. The Wi-Fi + 3G models use Wi-Fi hotspots too, but they also use GPS (Global Positioning System) and cellular towers to provide location information. Although it can all be rather complicated to explain, suffice it to say that you can use Maps no matter which iPad you own.

Explore the Maps App

You open the Maps app the same way you open any app, by tapping it once. There are several interface features to explore, and they are arranged familiarly with buttons and tabs. These include

- **Search**   Tap Search when you want to view something on the map, including your present location. In contrast, tap Directions to get directions from one place to another.
- **Directions**   Tap Directions to access two windows you can fill in to get directions from one place to another. You can get directions from your present location to a new location, or using any two addresses. (You don't have to input an address, though; you can input a restaurant name, street name, and more.) In between the two windows is an icon that enables you to reverse the route, if desired.
- **Location icon**   Tap the round Location icon to the left of the Bookmark icon to show your present location on a map. A blue dot appears to denote where you are.
- **Bookmarks**   Tap to see bookmarks you've saved and to access them. Bookmarks are like your Favorites list in Internet Explorer, or, well, Bookmarks in Safari. There are three tabs available in the Bookmarks window:
  - **Bookmarks**   A list of Bookmarks you've saved in Maps.
  - **Recents**   A list of places you've recently looked up with Maps.
  - **Contacts**   A list of the contacts you have in the Contacts app. You can tap any contact that has an address associated with it to access a map of their location or to get directions to it.
- **The Search window**   Type anything here to perform a search for it. You can type exact street names and addresses or generic ones, like Coney Island or The Statue of Liberty. See Figure 14-1.
- **Page turner/Dog ear**   Tap or pull back the bottom-right corner of the Maps interface so that you can see "underneath" the Maps interface, shown in Figure 14-2. Here, you'll find options to change the view and additional options:
  - **Classic**   To view a graphical representation of the map with street names, parks, and water included. See Figure 14-1.
  - **Satellite**   To view the location as it appears from the sky. You can pinch and double-tap to zoom in or out, as you can with other views. See Figure 14-2.
  - **Hybrid**   To view a map in Classic and Satellite view, together.

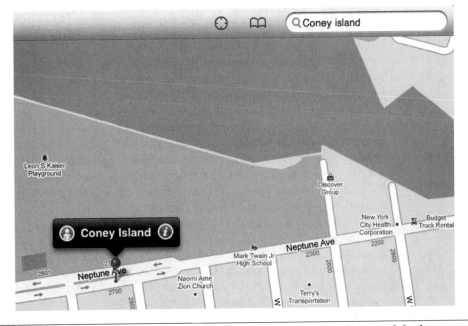

FIGURE 14-1   The Search window offers a place to type anything and find it on the map. This map is in Classic view.

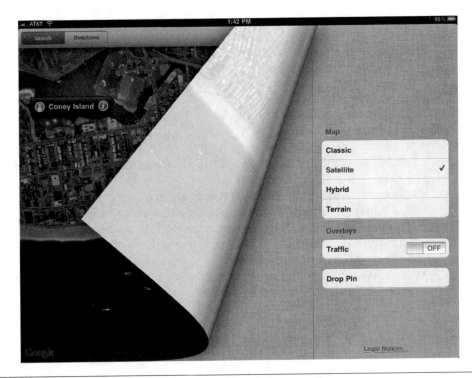

FIGURE 14-2   Additional options are offered "below" the current map.

- **Terrain**   To view the map in another graphical representation that includes terrain features, such as elevation.
- **Traffic**   To show traffic conditions, if available for the current map. Colors that denote traffic are red, yellow, and green.
- **Drop Pin**   To drop a pin anywhere on a map, tap this and then tap and hold where you'd like the pin to appear. A pin for Coney Island appears in Figures 14-1 and 14-2.

The best way to explore the Maps app is to first find your current location, and then, tap the various options for views to see how they look. Because you're probably familiar with your surroundings, you can easily recognize what's around you. Once the iPad knows your current location, you can easily browse nearby streets, businesses, and even the current traffic, if available.

To find your present location:

1. Open Maps.
2. Tap the Location icon, shown here.
3. If you're prompted to enable Location Services, close Maps, open Settings, and tap General. Turn Location Services from Off to On.
4. Tap the blue letter "i" to learn more about your location, including the address and the option to share your location with others, create a bookmark, and even view a picture, if available.

With a map on the page, you're ready to explore views. To switch views:

1. Touch the bottom-right corner of the map to turn the page and see what's underneath.
2. Touch any view option to see that view on the map.
3. Repeat to explore all views.
4. In any view, use your finger to scroll through the map. You'll learn more navigational techniques next.

While in any map and in any view, try out these navigational techniques:

- Pinch your fingers toward each other to zoom out of a map.
- Pull your fingers outward to zoom in on an area on a map.
- Tap twice to zoom in. (Pinch to zoom back out.)
- Reposition the iPad from Landscape to Portrait view and back by turning the iPad 90 degrees left or right.
- Tap and drag across the screen to see more of the map.

Go Places and Do Things

So you know where you are and how to navigate the map by pinching or scrolling, and by tapping to zoom in. Now it's time to actually use Maps to perform tasks. In this section you'll learn several things including how to get driving directions to a specific address, how to locate a business and restaurant on a map and view pictures of them, how to locate a nearby restaurant and get walking directions or directions using available public transportation, and how to locate a business, among other things. Once you've found a location, you can tap to see the Information screen, where you can get directions, a phone number, and other information regarding it. Finally, you'll learn how to mark a site on a map that isn't currently marked as a business, park, restaurant, landmark, and the like. You can mark your own house, where you work, a friend's house, a park, or anything else you like so that you can more easily share it or access it. By marking and then bookmarking your favorite locations, you'll have easy access to them later.

Find a Location and Drive There

You can replace all of your physical maps and map books with your iPad, provided you can access satellite information and the Internet from where you are (an iPad 3G model is ideal for this). You can type in any address to obtain driving directions to the address from your present location, and scroll through maps digitally to view the terrain or route. If you need directions from one place to another, but one of those places is not available in Contacts or any recent lists, you can type in two addresses too. This enables you to obtain directions from a starting point to an end point; from anywhere to anywhere.

To find an address and get directions to that address:

1. In Maps, tap Directions.
2. By default, the starting point is your current location. For best results, tap the Location icon to make sure Maps knows where you are before going any further. If you want to start from a different address, tap in that window and type a new address.
3. Tap in the second window to type the ending address. Note that you can type something other than an address, though. As you can see in Figure 14-3, I've searched for Chase Place, a local bar and grill.

FIGURE 14-3 It's easy to get directions using Maps, especially if you start from your current location.

4. At the bottom of the page, tap the driving icon. It looks like a car.
5. Click Start, as shown here, and then advance through the directions using the arrow buttons.

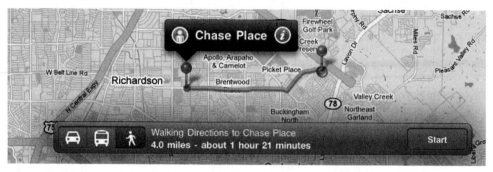

 You can open the Contacts app and touch a contact's address to get a map of that location.

Explore Street View

Street View is a view available via Google Maps that allows you to view pictures of a location or your destination. This feature provides 360-degree views of many locations across the world. You can access these images from the information window that appears in the pin associated with a location. When Street View is available, you'll see a thumbnail in the information window. To see the picture in full screen, tap the thumbnail, as shown here.

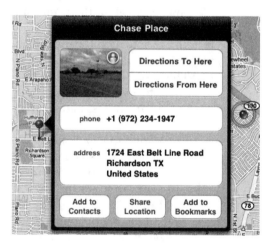

 You Can Use a Digital Compass to Find Which Way Is North

Tap the Location icon two times. The map will reposition itself to point north. To test it out, while holding the iPad, turn in a circle.

While in full-screen mode, you can drag your finger across the screen to see what's to the left and right of the location, or even what's across the street. When you're finished exploring, tap the small icon in the bottom-right corner to return to Maps, as shown here.

 To hide an information window, tap outside of it. To show it again, tap the pin on the map.

Find a Nearby Restaurant and Walk to It

Another way you can use Maps is to locate your current position in a city, and then search for nearby restaurants. To search, simply tap inside the Spotlight Search window and type **Restaurants**. Touch any restaurant result to view the phone number and address, and if available, the restaurant's web site. Once you find a restaurant you like, you can get directions to it easily. As with other Maps results, you can get driving directions, but you can also get walking directions or directions using public transportation.

To search for and find a nearby restaurant:

1. In Maps, click the Location icon to pinpoint your present location.
2. Touch inside the Spotlight Search window to bring up the keyboard.
3. Type **Restaurants**. Tap Search on the keyboard.
4. Tap any pin on the map to see the restaurant name, address, and to get directions.

To get walking directions to the restaurant:

1. In any restaurant's information page (which you access by tapping the pin for it), tap Directions To Here.
2. On the map, tap the icon to get walking directions. The icon looks like a man walking, as shown in this illustration.

Find a Route Using Public Transportation

You can also get directions using a route that incorporates public transportation. If you're in a city, and on foot, but the restaurant or business you need to get to is too far to walk, this is a good alternative. You find a public transportation route using the same method you use to find a walking route, except you tap the icon that looks like a bus instead of tapping the icon that looks like a man walking.

Once the route is on the screen, look for icons that detail how to get there. You'll see icons that show you where you must walk, and icons that tell you where you can ride. Tap the icon to see more information. Figure 14-4 shows an example.

FIGURE 14-4 Look for the bus icon to get information about the route you need to take.

Share a Location via Email

If you'd like to invite others to meet you at a location, you can click Share Location from the information page. You'll see the option Share Location on every information page, as shown in this illustration. Tap it and a new email will open, where you can complete the invitation.

Share
Location

Locate a Business

Chances are when you need the phone number or address of a business, you head to your computer or cell phone and not the stack of phone books piled up in your laundry room. Phone books are cumbersome (and often unavailable), and after you find the address and phone number you still have to drag out a map, call the business, or head back to your computer to get directions to it. That's all changed with Google Maps, always-on Internet, and computer technology. Now when you want to contact a business, you simply search for it online.

You can use Maps and your iPad to locate a business, obtain the phone number and address, and get directions, all with only a few taps of your finger.

To find a business and get a phone number, address, and directions:

1. Open Maps.
2. Tap the Search window.
3. Type the name of the business.
4. Locate the business on the map. Tap the small letter "i" to access the business's information page. A sample information page is shown in the following illustration.

5. Call the number, get directions, add to bookmarks, or share the location, as desired.

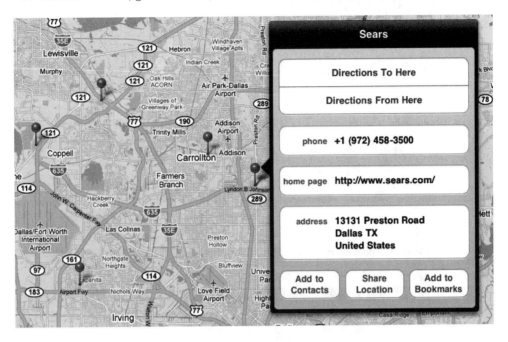

Shortcut Every pin on this page is a Sears store. Tap any pin for the address or phone number.

Mark a Location of Your Own

You know now that when you search for a restaurant or business, Maps sets down a pin in its location. You touch the pin to get more information about it, including directions. You probably also know that not all locations have pins. A brand new restaurant won't, for instance, since the information about it has not had time to get to the Internet servers responsible for providing the information to Google Services. There may not be a pin for the establishment where you work, and maybe not even for your home. You can add your own pins, though, simply by tapping and holding an area of the screen.

To mark a location (and save it as a bookmark):

1. Locate the location on a map.
2. Tap and hold to drop a pin.
3. Click the letter "i" to open the information page.
4. To name the location and save it, tap Add to Bookmarks, and name the bookmark as desired.
5. Tap Save.

Find a Landmark

You can locate (and often view) landmarks, points of interest, and even museums and art galleries, by searching for them in Maps. For instance, you can search Maps for University of Texas, Austin, and view the campus in Maps using Street View. You can have Maps locate your current location and type **Museum of Art** to locate the nearest art museum. You can even search for the White House or the Statue of Liberty, although we can't guarantee there's a picture of that available.

To find a landmark and attempt to view it in Street View:

1. In Maps, type the name of the landmark you'd like to view.
2. Tap the letter "i" to bring up the information page.
3. If a picture is available, click it. If a picture is not available but a web site is, click that. Although there's no picture of the Statue of Liberty available from Google Maps, you can access the web site and access photos and multimedia, as shown in the following illustration.

Bookmark a Location

It takes a little bit of effort to locate a place on a map. Generally you have to search for it, and on occasion you type in an address. It's not a big deal, but if it's a location you think you'll need to look up again, you may as well make a note of it. So, once you've located a site you want to revisit, you should bookmark it. A bookmark enables

How to... ## Access a Bookmark

After you've saved bookmarks, you have easy access to them:

1. Tap the Bookmarks icon in Maps.
2. Note the three tabs at the bottom of the Bookmarks window. Tap Bookmarks. See Figure 14-5.
3. Tap the bookmark to visit.

you to easily access the location again without having to search for it. Bookmarks act like Favorites for web sites. You click the bookmark and you're offered the location you marked. This makes it very easy to share a location later, or revisit it should you need to.

To add a bookmark for a location:

1. Locate any place in Maps you'd like to bookmark via search or dropping a pin.
2. Tap to open the information page.
3. Tap Add to Bookmarks.
4. Accept the name of the bookmark or type your own.
5. Tap Save.
6. Tap outside the Information window to close it.

FIGURE 14-5   The Bookmarks window offers a place to access saved bookmarks as well as recent places and contacts.

15

Use Notes

The Notes app is like having a legal pad with you all the time. It looks like the familiar legal pad you're used to, and once you write down a note, it stays there, just as a note on a legal pad would (meaning that you don't have to click Save and name the note). You can review notes you've written, and even if you stop taking notes to listen to music or check your email, when you come back to the Notes app, the note you were working on is there, ready to complete, just where you left off. You can easily delete a note, just as you can with a legal pad, and you can carry notes on your iPad with you anywhere you go, even to the grocery store.

Unlike a legal pad, though, the Notes app will let you know when you misspell something and suggest punctuation while you type. It'll even offer advice replacing misspelled words. And, unlike with a legal pad, you can email notes to others or to yourself, and you can sync notes to your computer using iTunes.

Creating a note is easy; you simply tap anywhere in a note and use the keyboard to write what needs to be written. The beauty of Notes is just that, the simplicity of it.

Create Notes

Think of all the things you write down in a day. You probably jot down phone numbers, grocery lists, to-do lists, and all kinds of reminders that need to be dealt with immediately, or at least within a couple of days. You may write down a recipe, a gift idea, or an ongoing list of items you need at the home improvement store. If you keep these notes on bits of paper, you will likely misplace them often. At the very least, your notes are mismanaged and in various places around your home, office, car, or purse, making them difficult to use efficiently.

You can use your iPad and the Notes app to get organized and to stay organized. You can type your most recent notes while working through this chapter, and make it a point to keep new notes on your iPad from here forward. When you choose to do this, you simplify your life by having everything in one place; everything is neat and orderly, and easily accessible. You'll never lose a note again.

First, open Notes and explore the available views:

1. Tap Notes on the Home screen.
2. View the Notes app in Portrait view. Note that there's a + sign for creating a new note, and icons at the bottom of the page. Now, turn the iPad sideways to view it in Landscape mode. You can see a list of any existing notes in this view too.

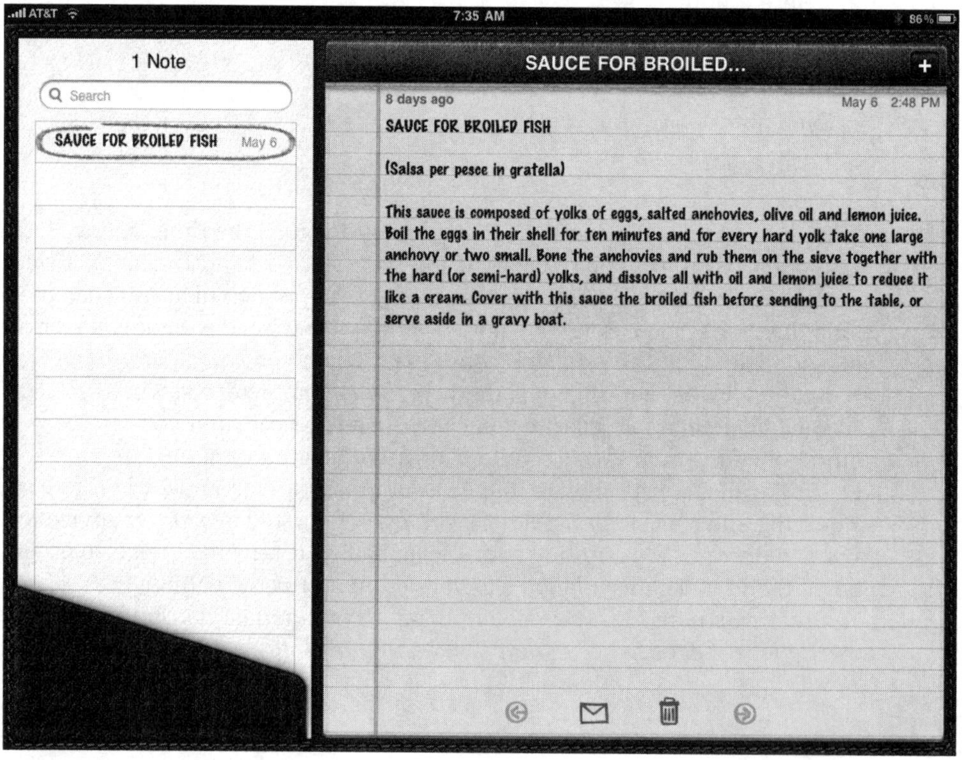

FIGURE 15-1 In Landscape mode you can see a list of notes in the source pane.

Did You Know?

Paste Is Supported in Notes

We did not type the text shown in the Sauce for Broiled Fish note. We copied the text from a free book titled *The Italian Cook Book* (by Maria Gentile), available from the iBookstore. Paste is supported in Notes.

To create a note:

1. If you've never created a note, simply tap inside the blank note already on the screen. If there's a note there already, tap the + sign to create a new note.
2. Use the keyboard to type. You do not have to save the note; it will remain in your Notes list until you delete it.

Correct Errors in Notes

Although the Notes you keep in the Notes app are often personal notes to yourself such as grocery lists and to-do lists, Notes will still track spelling and suggest punctuation for you as you type. When Notes finds spelling errors, it will underline them, giving you the option to fix them.

To see how spelling and punctuation correction works in Notes:

1. Open Notes and start a new note. (Click the + sign to create a new note.)
2. Use the keyboard to type a note, creating misspelled words while typing.
3. If you see an error, denoted by a squiggly line underneath a word, tap it to view the suggested correction.
4. Tap the correction to apply it. See Figure 15-2.

Use Advanced Notes Tools

The Notes app includes a few tools to help you type faster and incorporate data from other applications. The accelerated typing tools track what you write and suggest words, among other things. You can also use your finger to place the cursor anywhere in a note to edit it. You can also copy text from other apps, including Mail, Safari, Calendar, Contacts, and Maps to paste that text into a Note.

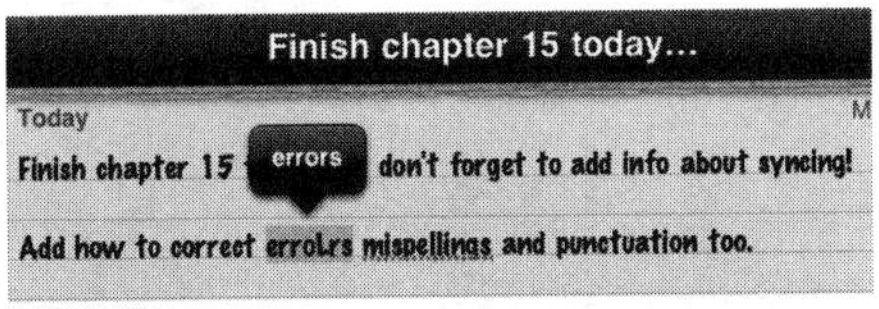

FIGURE 15-2   Squiggly lines in a note let you know something is wrong with the way a word is spelled or punctuated.

You'll learn about the available accelerated typing tools as you type. For instance, if, while typing, you misspell a word that the iPad's Dictionary knows, it will offer a suggestion. Also, as you type, Notes will suggest words for you, if it thinks it knows what you're trying to type. In either case, simply press the Space bar to accept the suggestion. If Notes makes a suggestion that isn't right, tap the X next to the suggested word (shown in the following illustration) to "teach" your iPad that this is not what you want, or just keep typing.

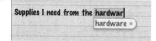

As with other apps, you can also tap and hold to select text, and then to cut, copy, or paste it. You can even tap Replace and choose a different word to input from the suggestions offered. And tapping produces the magnifying glass, which you can use to navigate to a specific word on the note. There's more on this later.

 There are typing tips scattered throughout this book, and available from the inside back cover.

Incorporate Text from Contacts and Maps

You know how to copy text and how to paste it. This has been covered throughout the book, in its own section of Chapter 4, and is also detailed on the inside back cover. You may not know that you can copy text from other apps and paste it into Notes, though. You can't paste pictures into a note, but you can paste text.

To copy an address from Maps and paste it in Notes:

1. Tap Maps and locate an address. For more information on Maps, refer to Chapter 14.
2. Tap the address from the Information window, and tap Copy, as shown here.

3. Close Maps and open Notes.
4. Tap inside an existing note or create a new note (and then tap inside it).
5. Tap Paste.

To copy an email address in Contacts and paste it in Notes:

1. Open Contacts and locate the contact to copy.
2. Tap the email address for the contact.
3. Tap Copy.
4. Close Contacts and open Notes.
5. Tap inside an existing note or create a new note (and then tap inside it).
6. Tap Paste.

Manage Notes

If you think about the Notes app as a glorified legal pad, it'll be easy to visualize deleting a note, locating existing notes, and editing notes. The Notes app offers a trash can icon on every note you create to make it easy to get rid of notes you no longer need. The source pane (available in Landscape view) makes it just as easy to locate notes you've previously written, and by dragging upward you can scroll notes that extend more than one page. Finally, editing a note is as simple as touching the note and typing.

 If you prefer Portrait view for your notes, use the left and right arrow keys at the bottom of the page to see other notes you've written.

To access previous notes and delete a note:

1. Locate the note to delete:
   a. In Portrait view, use the left and right arrow keys to find the note.
   b. In Landscape view, tap the note in the source pane.
2. Once you've found the note to delete, click the Trash Can icon, as shown here.

To edit a note:

1. Locate the note to edit.
2. To add something to a note:
   a. Tap inside the note where you'd like to start typing.
   b. Type the additional information.
3. To erase something that's on a note:
   a. Tap any note and hold briefly.
   b. Tap Select or Select All.
   c. Tap Cut to delete the selected text, noting that you can use the blue grab points to select more or less text.

4. To correct a single letter in a note or to add text in the middle of a note or sentence:
   a. Tap and hold until the magnifying glass appears.
   b. Drag the magnifying glass to the location to perform the edits.
   c. Use the Back button on the keyboard to erase letters one at a time, and use the keyboard to type.

Share Notes

There are several ways to share notes, and one of them is to sync them with your computer (in essence, sharing them with yourself). You sync notes the same way you sync music, contacts, and pictures; you connect your iPad to your computer and let iTunes manage the rest. You can then access the notes on your computer, and even change data on them. The next time you sync, the changes will be synced to the notes on your iPad.

There are other ways to share notes. Although you'll probably mostly create notes for your own personal use, you may occasionally want to share a note with others. Perhaps you've found the perfect banana cream pie recipe, have a phone number to share, or want to delegate a to-do list to your spouse. You can share these notes via email.

Finally, you can email yourself a note. That email can arrive just about anywhere you need it, including on your home computer, your email-enabled cell phone (such as a BlackBerry or iPhone), or even a handheld PDA you use for work. This is a great option when you need to get a note to another device quickly, and beats any other option that includes syncing the note to your phone and somehow transferring it using another method.

Sync Notes

If you use a compatible program on your computer (like Microsoft Outlook, for instance) that allows you to create and view notes, you can sync the notes you create on your iPad to your computer. Any changes you make to any notes, whether they are on your computer or your iPad, will be synced when you connect the two next time. You have to set up iTunes to sync Notes, as you do with other data.

To set up iTunes to sync Notes data and to sync existing notes:

1. Create a few notes on your iPad.
2. Connect your iPad to your computer.
3. When iTunes opens, click the iPad in the source pane.
4. From the Info tab, set Notes to sync automatically.
5. Select a source to sync notes with in the associated drop-down list, as shown in Figure 14-3.
6. Click Sync.

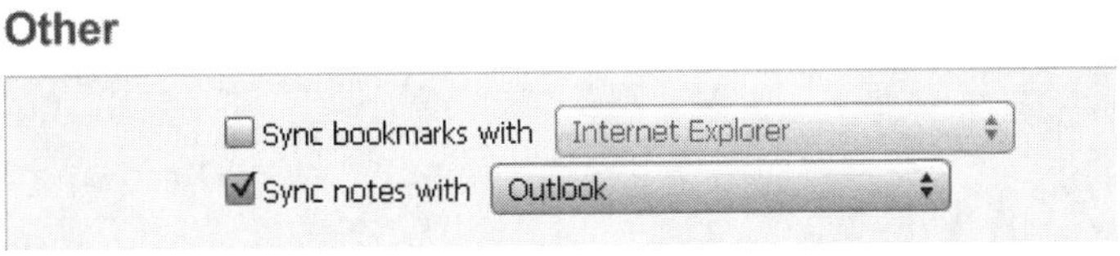

Other

☐ Sync bookmarks with   Internet Explorer ⇕
☑ Sync notes with   Outlook ⇕

FIGURE 15-3   You have to tell iTunes you want to sync notes.

To verify that syncing is working properly:

1. Disconnect your iPad from your computer.
2. Locate a note on your computer, open it, and make changes to it. As you can see here, we're using Notes within Microsoft Outlook.

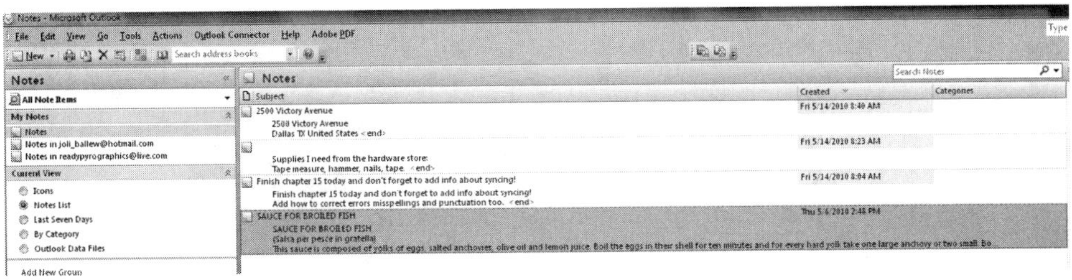

3. Save the changes.
4. Connect your iPad to the computer, and sync again.
5. On your iPad, open Notes to verify that changes to the note were applied and synced.

Email a Note

You may need to email a note to someone, or you may want to email a note to yourself to get it on another device (like a BlackBerry) quickly. Emailing a note is as simple as tapping the Mail icon in any note and filling out the new email that appears.

To send a note via email:

1. Make sure your iPad is connected to the Internet.
2. In Notes, open the note to email.
3. Click the Mail button.
4. Complete the email and tap Send.

PART VI

Accessibility and Security

16

Accessibility

HOW TO...

- Enable and explore VoiceOver
- Disable VoiceOver
- Enable and use Zoom
- Enable and use white-on-black display
- Enable and use mono audio
- Explore additional Accessibility options
- Enable and use closed captioning
- Explore hardware options

If you have any kind of disability, be it vision, hearing, or mobility, you can rest easy knowing that the iPad offers at least a few accessibility options. And, if you've purchased accessibility apps for an existing iPhone, those apps should work on the iPad too. There are several accessibility options that come with your iPad: VoiceOver, screen zoom, white-on-black display, mono audio, and closed-captioned content. Of course, the iPad's size is a boon too; because the device is bigger, it's easier for those with vision, hearing, and mobility disabilities to use. And there are a few things that you can use to help you use your iPad that aren't technically accessibility options, such as setting a minimum font size for emails or zooming in on faces during a Picture Frame slideshow.

There are also hardware options to explore. If you have trouble typing on the iPad's virtual keyboard, you can purchase Apple's optional keyboard dock or wireless keyboard. If you have a vision problem, the feel of the tactile keyboard may be just what you need to type effectively. Beyond Apple's keyboard options, though, watch for third-party keyboards that are compatible. You may find one that is more suited to your needs.

Did You Know?

The iPad Can Be Part of a Therapy Program or Perfect for the Elderly

The iPad is not a complex device. For those with cognitive disabilities, this is a plus. You tap to open an app, and you tap to make that app do something. This makes the iPad the perfect device for those with a brain injury, intellectual disability, or neurological impairments. This also makes it a great device for older individuals who are overwhelmed by the idea of using a computer. The iPad is not intimidating, and you never hear of one "crashing" or ceasing to work because you've pressed the wrong buttons or key combinations. iPads shouldn't get viruses either, and they don't need a lot of attention when it comes to updates and staying secure. It's just what the doctor ordered!

Although the iPad's speaker is pretty loud, there is still an option to connect external speakers. This means you can connect headphones too. If you have a hearing disability, one of these options may work for you.

Enable and Use VoiceOver

Your iPad includes VoiceOver, a feature that will read what's on the screen if you're blind or visually impaired (or learning a new language). Once VoiceOver is activated, to use it, you simply tap the screen. When you tap, you'll hear a description of the item under your finger and a black rectangle will appear (called the VoiceOver cursor). You can then drag, double-tap, or flick to control the iPad. VoiceOver speaks 21 languages, so you can have it speak to you in your native tongue, and it works with all of the applications built into iPad.

Note
VoiceOver only works with the built-in iPad apps and third-party apps that specifically support it.

VoiceOver offers a lot of features, too many to detail here. But it's all spelled out in the iPad User Guide, which is bookmarked in Safari. However, to help you get started, here are a few introductory steps you can take:

1. To enable VoiceOver, tap Settings, General, and then Accessibility.
2. Tap VoiceOver. See Figure 16-1.
3. Move the slider from Off to On.
4. Double-tap OK in the prompt.
5. Note the practice tips underneath the slider. Tap any item to have the item read out loud.

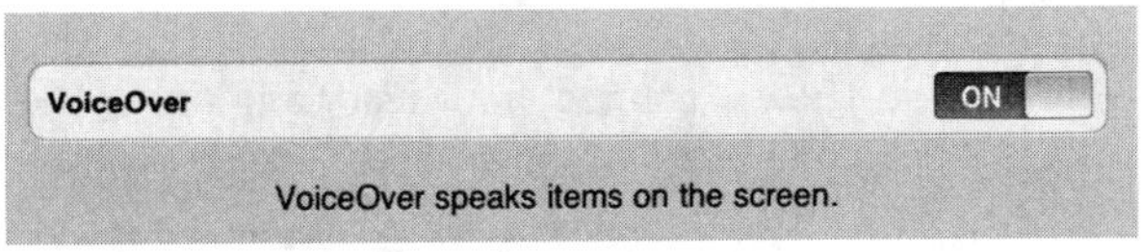

VoiceOver   **ON**

VoiceOver speaks items on the screen.

FIGURE 16-1   There are several Accessibility options in Settings, General.

6. Note the other settings. You can change the speaking rate, and change what VoiceOver relates when you type.
7. Press the iPad's Home button to exit Settings.

To disable VoiceOver, you'll have to use specific gestures to get back to the Settings options and the VoiceOver On/Off slider:

1. If you aren't on the Home screen that offers access to Settings, use three fingers to flick to that page or simply double-tap the iPad's Home button.
2. Tap Settings one time.
3. Double-tap to open Settings.

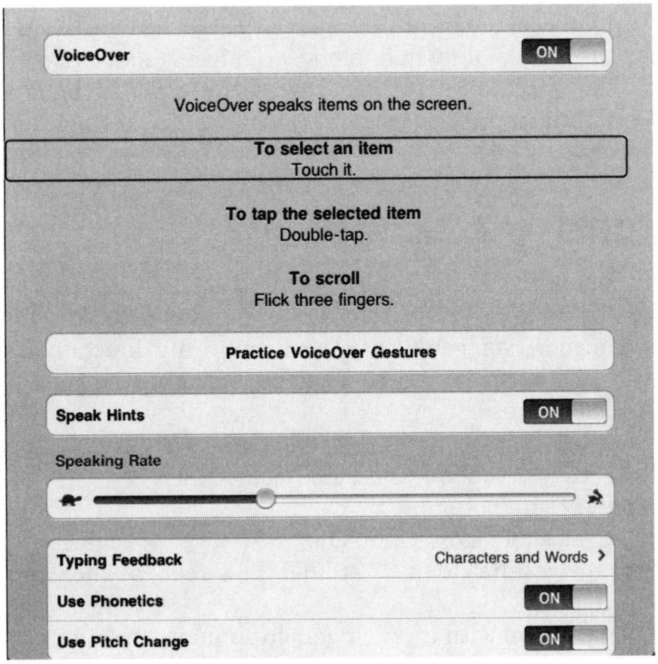

FIGURE 16-2   When using VoiceOver, you have to use new gestures to perform tasks, like using three fingers to scroll.

Enable VoiceOver in iTunes

To enable VoiceOver in iTunes, connect your iPad, and under the Summary tab, click Universal Access. Click VoiceOver, as shown here.

4. Turn the iPad to Portrait view to have access to the Accessibility settings.
5. Tap the Accessibility button once to select it, and twice to open it.
6. Tap the VoiceOver option once to select it, and then double-tap to access the slider.
7. Tap the slider once to select it. Double-tap to turn VoiceOver off.

Enable and Use Zoom

Another option if you are visually impaired is Zoom. Zoom lets you magnify the iPad's entire screen up to five times its original size, and it works with any application. Once you've zoomed in, you can move the screen in any direction to view what's on it. Zoom works with every app and in every screen, including the Unlock and Spotlight screens.

To enable and use Zoom:

1. Tap Settings, General, and then Accessibility.
2. Tap the Zoom option.
3. Move the slider from Off to On.
4. Note the gestures to move around the screen, as shown in the following illustration:
   a. Double-tap with three fingers to zoom in one time.
   b. Drag three fingers to move around the screen.

c. Double-tap with three fingers, and on the last tap, drag up or down to increase or decrease the zoom level.

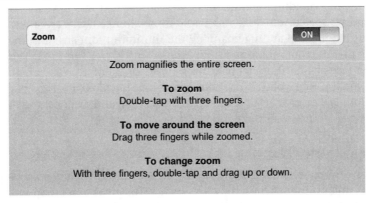

5. To disable Zoom, move the slider from On to Off in Settings | General | Accessibility, and Zoom.

Enable and Use White-on-Black Display

White-on-black display is a high-contrast display for the visually impaired. The name tells the story; when this feature is enabled, you'll see white letters on a black background. If colors and fonts make it difficult for you to read what's on the screen, try this option.

To enable and use white-on-black display:

1. Tap Settings, General, and Accessibility.
2. Tap the slider for White on Black.
3. Tap again to disable it.

Enable and Use Mono Audio

If you have a hearing disability that affects only one ear, you can enable mono audio. When you enable mono audio, you tell the iPad to combine the left and right channels of stereo audio so that the sound is identical for each ear. When you wear headphones, you can be sure that all parts of a recording are being broadcast identically to both ears.

To enable and use mono audio, tap Settings, tap General, tap Accessibility, and tap the slider for Mono Audio to enable it.

Explore Additional Accessibility Features

There are a handful of additional Accessibility features available from Accessibility, including Speak Auto-Text and Triple-Click Home. There are a few more scattered about the iPad, including changing the minimum font size for email messages, changing the font and font size in iBooks, and if you want to stretch it a little, zooming in on faces when showing pictures with Picture Frame. You can also set a maximum volume limit for your iPad (should your hearing aids distort or buzz if you play music too loudly), or change how quickly slides change in a slideshow so you'll have time to view the picture and make it out.

Speak Auto-Text

When you enable this feature, your iPad will automatically speak auto-corrections and auto-capitalizations when they are made. This gives you an opportunity to accept or reject those changes, and to note what changes have been made for you. You access this feature from Settings | General | Accessibility.

Triple-Click Home

You can enable this feature to have an easier way to turn some Accessibility features on or off by pressing the Home button three times. When you turn on this feature, you can configure it so that a triple-click toggles VoiceOver or White-on-Black, or set it to ask what you want to do. You access this feature from Settings | General | Accessibility.

Minimum Font Size for Email

From Settings, and then Mail, Contacts, Calendars, under Mail, set a minimum font size for email messages. Options include Small, Medium, Large, Extra Large, and Giant. Giant isn't as large as you might expect it to be, but at least it's quite a bit bigger, than say, Medium.

Change Font Size and Type in iBooks

When reading a book in iBooks, tap the Font button and tap Fonts to have access to the options. Tap the larger A to make the text larger, and if desired, select a new font. See Figure 16-3.

Show Faces in Picture Frame

In the Picture Frame settings, you have the option to zoom in on faces during the Picture Frame show. During a Picture Frame show, faces will be easier to see if they are zoomed in on. The iPad can't discern all faces and won't zoom in on everyone, but it will be able to zoom in on some of them.

You can only access this setting if the Transition is set to Dissolve, and it is not available if the transition is set to Origami. To configure this, from Settings in Picture Frame, set the Transition to Dissolve, and then move the slider for Zoom In On Faces from Off to On.

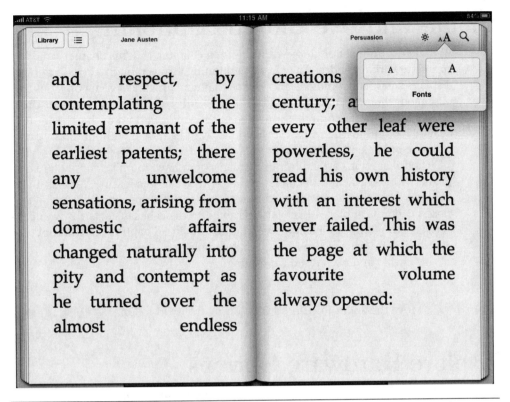

FIGURE 16-3   Some apps, like iBooks, offer the ability to change the size of the font easily.

Maximum Volume Limit in iPod

From Settings, in iPod, tap Off next to Volume Limit to set a volume limit with a slider and to lock it. If you opt to lock the volume limit, as shown here, you'll need to input a code before you can change it.

Slideshow Slide Duration

If the pictures in a slideshow move too quickly and you can't make out what's on each slide, change the slideshow duration to its maximum, 20 seconds.

Enable and Use Closed Captioning

We talked a little about closed captioning in Chapter 11. This chapter wouldn't be complete without addressing closed captioning again, though. Closed captioning displays subtitles on movies and videos that explain what's going on (if music is playing or there are creaking sounds on the stairwell), and also provides the dialogue for the movie or video in text provided at the top or bottom of the screen. If you are deaf or hard of hearing, this allows you to watch a movie without missing any of the dialogue or background noises.

Closed captions are built into media, so you have to make sure you're obtaining media with closed captions included in them to use this feature. Movies and podcasts with closed captioning are available at the iTunes Store. You won't yet find closed captions at places like Netflix, though. This is because Netflix would have to (basically) duplicate each movie, and insert closed captions in the copy. This is prohibitive in terms of time, cost, and technology.

To enable and use closed captioning:

1. Tap Settings, and tap Video.
2. Move the slider for Closed Captioning from Off to On.

Explore Hardware Options

As noted in the introduction, there are several hardware options you can employ to assist you in accessing your iPad. There are keyboards for typing, and you can attach speakers and headphones. If you're having trouble using your iPad or hearing what you play on it, consider these optional items. Watch for additional hardware devices in the future, including those that will allow users with more severe disabilities to access the iPad using third-party devices.

Explore Apple's Keyboard Dock

The Apple Keyboard Dock is useful if you have trouble physically using the on-screen keyboard because of its size, if you have a visual impairment that makes it difficult for you to see the keys on the screen, or if you need to feel the keys on the keyboard to ensure that you're pressing the proper keys while typing. Apple's iPad Keyboard Dock is $69 from the Apple Store, located online at www.apple.com.

The Apple Keyboard Dock offers the following features:

- The keyboard has special keys that activate various iPad features including the Home screen, Spotlight Search, display brightness, Picture Frame mode, and more.
- The keyboard comes with its own dock, which enables you to connect your camera (with the optional Camera Connection Kit), connect to your computer, and connect to a wall outlet (with the power adapter included with your iPad).
- The dock enables you to connect speakers.

There are a few downsides, though. There's no way to use the keyboard and dock with the iPad in Landscape view (unless you rig up some kind of stand yourself). You have to use Portrait view. This may pose problems for the visually impaired, who may prefer Landscape view. And because the keyboard is part of a docking station, you can't effectively use the keyboard and dock while sitting on the couch or while on a bus.

If you already have an Apple Bluetooth keyboard and you like it, you can use it instead of buying the new iPad Keyboard Dock. You won't have access to the iPad-specific keyboard features, but it is compatible.

Explore Speakers and Headphones

If you visit the Apple Store online to shop specifically for iPad accessories, you won't find speakers or headphones listed. You'll find the Keyboard Dock, VGA connector, and Camera Connection Kit, but no speakers or headphones. This is because just about any speakers and headphones will work with the iPad, and you likely already have something you can use. If you want to buy either from the Apple Store, though, simply search the store for what you want.

A search for speakers provides all kinds of options including

- Rechargeable mini-speakers perfect for traveling
- Speaker systems perfect for viewing movies at home

Watch for additional speaker-related items that may be released later, like iPad speaker docks, Bluetooth speaker systems, and speakers designed specifically for gamers.

Before purchasing Bluetooth devices or docks, verify that they are compatible with the iPad.

A search for headphones provides plenty of options too including:

- Small, in-ear ear buds
- Travel headphones
- Over-ear or on-ear headphones
- Behind-the-head headphones

And speaking of headphones, as you know, you can use stereo Bluetooth headphones with the iPad, but there are also headphones made specifically for the iPad, iPhone, and iPod, which include remote controls and a microphone built onto the cable. Apple's latest In-Ear headphones, for instance, include an iPad-compatible remote built into the cable that controls volume, play, pause, and track skip, and also includes a microphone. This remote functionality might be just what you need.

17

Security

HOW TO...

- Protect your iPad with a passcode
- Enable restrictions
- Configure parental controls
- Sign out of iTunes, the App Store, and web sites
- Secure Safari
- Avoid phishing scams
- View usage data settings
- Use MobileMe for additional security

There are a few features available on your iPad to help you secure it, like the ability to create a passcode that must be entered to unlock your iPad and the option to disable apps, including Safari, YouTube, iTunes, and others. You can also set parental controls to disallow movies, music, and other media that has a specific rating you select.

You can do things to keep you and your iPad safe too, including signing out of iTunes and the App Store when you aren't using them (as well as other web sites), and disabling Safari's AutoFill option, which automatically inputs personal data like your name and address. You can also enable fraud warning for Safari and learn how to protect yourself from phishing scams. You can even sign up for MobileMe ($99/year for you or $149 for a family), which offers a service called Find My iPad and enables you to wipe all the data off your iPad remotely, should it ever be lost or stolen, for extra protection.

By far, though, the best thing you can do is to keep track of your iPad. If you have to leave it in a car, at least put it in the trunk. And if you have to leave it in a hotel room, consider putting it in the hotel room's safe. Even when your iPad is in your home, you should keep it hidden from people you don't know, like handymen and the like. You know people are going to want your iPad; who wouldn't?

Use a Passcode

You can set a passcode for your iPad. A *passcode* is a four-digit number that must be input to unlock your iPad once it's locked due to inactivity or after you press the Sleep/Wake button to manually lock it. When a passcode is applied, you must know the passcode to get to the data on the iPad, and to use it.

To enable Passcode Lock and create your own passcode:

1. Tap Settings.
2. Tap General.
3. Tap Passcode Lock.
4. Tap Turn Passcode On.
5. Type a four-digit passcode, and type it again to verify.
6. Once the Passcode is enabled, you can configure additional options, shown in Figure 17-1.
   - **Change Passcode** Tap to change your passcode. You must know your old passcode to change it to a new one.
   - **Require Passcode** Tap to choose Immediately, After 1 Minute, After 5 Minutes, After 15 Minutes, After 1 Hour, or After 4 Hours of Inactivity.
   - **Picture Frame** To require a passcode (or not) when showing pictures with Picture Frame.
   - **Erase Data** To opt to erase all data on the iPad after ten failed passcode attempts.

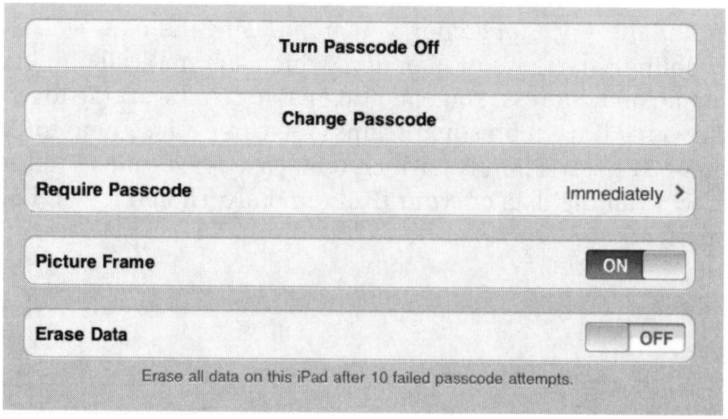

FIGURE 17-1 Enable and set a passcode and configure passcode preferences.

Enable Restrictions

When you enable restrictions, you have the option to allow or disallow access to specific apps and content. When you disallow specific apps, those apps disappear from the Home screen. For instance, if you disallow Safari, only Mail, Photos, and iPod will appear across the bottom of the Home screen, as shown here, and Safari will be unavailable.

You can allow or disallow the following features:

- **Safari**   When this option is disabled, the user cannot access Safari to surf the Internet.
- **YouTube**   When this option is disabled, the user cannot access the YouTube icon to watch YouTube videos.
- **iTunes**   When this option is disabled, the user cannot open the iTunes app, and thus, can't make any iTunes Store purchases.
- **Installing Apps**   When this option is disabled, the user cannot install any apps from the App Store.
- **Location**   When this option is disabled, the user cannot use Maps or another location-based app to pinpoint or broadcast their location. Location data is not provided. These options are shown in Figure 17-2.

You can also enable and disable specific content:

- **In-App Purchases**   Some apps offer an option to make additional purchases to add features or to upgrade the app. When you disable this feature, you disable the option to purchase upgrades, features, and additional apps.
- **Ratings For**   Choose the country you want to draw ratings from. If you're in the United States, make sure United States is selected. Tap it to select something else.
- **Music and Podcasts**   In the United States, music and podcasts can be rated Explicit. Tap this setting to access a switch that toggles Explicit content playback on or off.

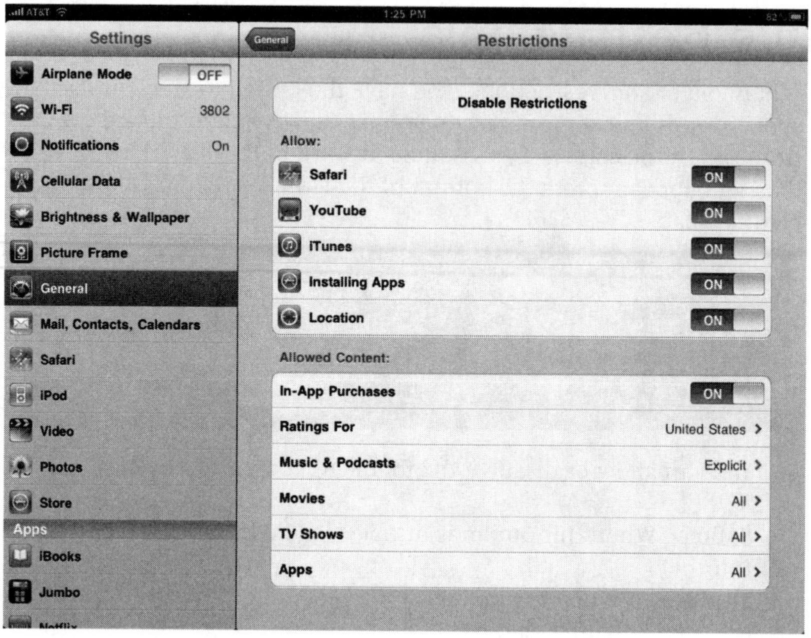

FIGURE 17-2   Once you enable restrictions, you're in control of what apps can be used and what content can be accessed.

- **Movies**   Tap Movies to set the type of movies you'll allow to be played. As shown here, you can allow or disallow all types.

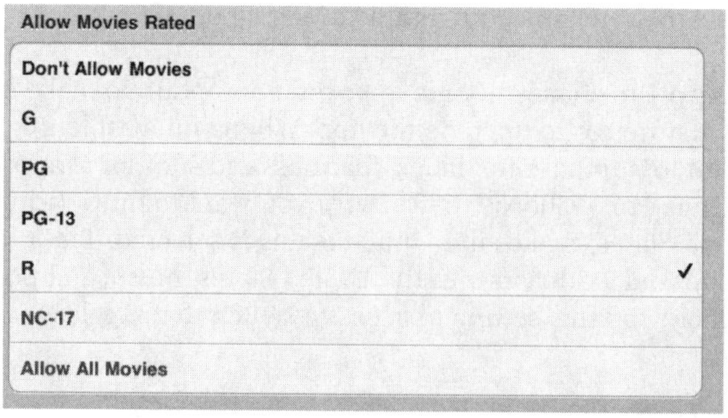

- **TV Shows**   Tap TV Shows to choose what kinds of TV shows to allow. You may want to disallow TV – MA for instance. (MA stands for Mature Audiences.)
- **Apps**   Tap Apps to enable and disable apps based on their age-appropriateness.

Did You Know?   **iBooks and the iBookstore Are Unrestricted**

There are no restrictions on the iPad for books from the iBookstore. That's because there is no ratings system for books.

To enable restrictions and configure allowed and disallowed content (and you can perform similar steps to disable restrictions once enabled):

1. Tap Settings, and tap General.
2. Tap Restrictions.
3. Tap Enable Restrictions.
4. Input a passcode and input it again to verify it.
5. Move the slider for any item app to allow or disallow.
6. Tap any option under allowed content to change what's allowed and what isn't. Tap the Restrictions button to return to the Restrictions page.
7. When finished, press the iPad's Home button.

Sign Out of Stores and Web Sites

If you've created a web clip for an email provider (such as one from Yahoo!), and you've told that provider to keep you logged in for two weeks, then anyone with access to your iPad also has access to your email. All they have to do is tap the web clip on your Home screen. The same is true of sites like Facebook. If someone gets access to your iPad and taps your Facebook web clip, they can change your status or send messages to their heart's content. If you want to be really secure but don't want to apply a passcode, you'll want to sign out of these types of sites when you're finished using them. Figure 17-3 shows the option to log out of Facebook on the Account drop-down menu.

Additionally, you can easily log out of the App Store and iTunes by tapping your account at the bottom of just about any page, as shown here.

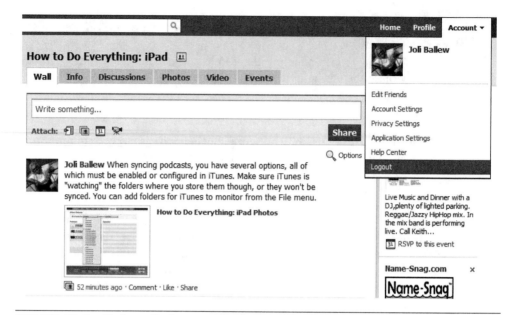

FIGURE 17-3 To be safe, log out of web sites when you're finished using them.

Be Careful on the Internet

As you learned in Chapter 3, Safari is what you use to surf the Internet on your iPad. You can lock down Safari to make it more secure in Settings, Safari. You can also preview a web link before you click it, to make sure that you're actually going to the site you want to, and not a fraudulent site set up to look like a real one. Finally, you can monitor your data usage so you can see how much data you're using, and keep track of how much more data you can use if you're on a limited plan.

Secure Safari

By default, Safari is set to show features of the web, such as some movies, animation, and web applications. You may wish to change the security settings to help protect your iPad from possible security risks on the Internet. You configure security settings under Settings, Safari. Options include

- **AutoFill** Disable this option to keep Safari from automatically inputting contact info, and usernames and passwords.
- **Fraud Warning** Enable this option to have Safari warn you when visiting web sites reported as fraudulent.
- **JavaScript** Disable this option to disable JavaScript on web pages, which lets web programmers add sophisticated elements to a page, but can also be potentially exploited by hackers and computer viruses.

- **Block Pop-ups**   Enable this option to block pop-ups that could possibly appear when you close or open a web page.
- **Accept Cookies**   Disable or change this option to keep Safari from accepting cookies from web sites. Cookies tell web sites your preferences when you visit, like your name, what you like to purchase or look for while on the site, and similar, generally harmless, information. The web site puts a cookie on your iPad so the web site can remember you the next time you visit. This allows web pages to be customized for you. Note that some web pages won't work correctly if you completely disable cookies.
- **Clear History**   Tap to clear the history of web pages you've visited.
- **Clear Cookies**   Tap to clear all cookies from Safari.
- **Clear Cache**   Tap to clear the browser cache. The browser cache stores things like pictures, so the pages will open faster the next time you visit them. If a page doesn't show new content, it's offering the page cache. Clear the cache to pull new data from the page.

Avoid Phishing

Phishing is a term used when an unscrupulous person tries to get you to input personal information by tricking you into thinking the web site or web form you're using is official, when in reality, it isn't. You may be familiar with phishing emails. The email says that your bank account, PayPal account, instant messaging account, or something similar has been compromised, and you need to visit the company's web site to fix the problem. If you go to that site, you're asked for information including name and address, social security number, birth date, and even bank account numbers, usernames, and passwords. The bad guys then use that information to purchase things using your account or to steal your identity.

There are also phishing web sites. These are links to other web pages that appear on a web page that imply they'll take you to an official web site, but once you're there, you become suspicious because the page seems a little off or the web address doesn't match the address you expect.

Before you visit any web site from an email or another web page, if you feel suspicious of the page, you can preview the web address before going there. Here's an example. This email looks as if it's from Amazon.com, a valid online company, but how can you be sure that the link in the email will take you to www.amazon.com, and not some phishing web site like www.westealyouridentity.com? Easy, just tap and hold to view the web address of the link. In this illustration, notice that the web link starts with http://www.amazon.com, which indeed is a valid web page for Amazon. (If it didn't start with amazon.com, you'd have to be suspicious.)

You can perform the same test on any web page in Safari. Simply tap and hold to see where the link will really take you.

Monitor Data Usage

If you have an iPad 3G and a limited-use cellular data plan with AT&T, you know that when you're close to meeting your cellular usage data limit for the month, AT&T will let you know with a message on your iPad. You can check your usage any time, though, from Settings:

1. Tap Settings.
2. Tap General.
3. Tap Usage.
4. You can easily see your Sent and Received Cellular Network Data usage, and reset the statistics.

Cellular Network Data	
Sent	33.5 MB
Received	384 MB
Last Reset: Never	
Reset Statistics	

Consider MobileMe

If you've signed up for MobileMe, you may already be aware of the built-in security features available to you through it. If you've been on the fence about signing up with MobileMe, it may be these features that help you commit. MobileMe is pricey, though—$99 a year for a single person and $149 for a family—but it just may be worth it if you keep a lot of sensitive data on your iPad or if anyone in the family tends to lose things.

Here are a few MobileMe features related to security:

- The Find My iPad feature helps you locate your iPad if you lose or misplace it. You'll need to enable this in the Mobile Me settings, and should your iPad ever be misplaced, you can visit me.com to get its approximate location.
- You can display a message on your iPad to help someone return it to you if it's lost.
- The Remote Passcode Lock feature lets you remotely lock your iPad. If your iPad is stolen while it is unlocked, you can easily lock it. You can even create a new or replacement four-digit passcode if you think someone knows yours.
- The Remote Wipe feature lets you erase all content and settings on your iPad if it's stolen. This resets all settings to their original value and erases all your information, data, and media.

PART VII

Appendixes

A

Settings

The Settings icon enables you to customize your iPad's apps and set preferences. This is where you'll go to change your wallpaper, configure settings for Safari, and configure preferences for Picture Frame, among other things. There's a wide range of settings to choose from and lots of preferences you can set. You can configure preferences and settings in the following categories: Airplane Mode (iPad Wi-Fi + 3G only), Wi-Fi, Notifications, Cellular Data (iPad Wi-Fi + 3G only), Brightness & Wallpaper, Picture Frame, General, Mail, Contacts, Calendars, Safari, iPod, Video, Photos, and Store. Each time you change a setting here, it is applied immediately.

Although we've introduced many of these settings in this book, this Appendix outlines what you can do within each category of settings. The list is organized by what you *can do* while you're in a specific category; it is not simply a list of settings and how to enable or disable them (which was covered throughout this book).

Airplane Mode

When you are on an airplane, you'll often be advised when you can use "approved devices." The iPad is one of those approved devices, provided that you disable the wireless features of the device. Airplane Mode is only available on the iPad Wi-Fi + 3G model.

Airplane options include the ability to:

- **Turn Airplane Mode on or off**   As the name implies, to turn Airplane Mode on or off.

Wi-Fi

You configure Wi-Fi settings to state how the iPad should use local Wi-Fi networks to connect to the Internet. You'll want to leave Wi-Fi enabled when you know you'll be accessing the Internet from your home network or a wireless hotspot. If no Wi-Fi networks are available, or you turn Wi-Fi off, the iPad will connect to the Internet over your cellular data network (on iPad Wi-Fi + 3G only), if it's available and if you subscribe to a cellular data service.

Wi-Fi options include the ability to:

- **Turn Wi-Fi on or off**   To turn Wi-Fi on or off.
- **Join a Wi-Fi network**   To join a Wi-Fi network in range. You first select a network from the list, and then you may be required to enter a password.
- **Set the iPad to ask if you want to join a new network**   To be notified when networks are available (or not).
- **Forget a network, so the iPad doesn't join it automatically**   You want to "forget" networks you know you'll never use, because your iPad works through all of the networks when looking for one. This uses battery power and takes time. It's best to keep the list short, and only filled with networks you recognize. To do this, tap next to a network you've joined before, then tap Forget This Network.
- **Join a closed Wi-Fi network**   To join a Wi-Fi network that isn't shown in the list of networks. To enter a network manually, tap Other, then enter the network name and other required information, such as a password.
- **Adjust settings to connect to a Wi-Fi network**   To change settings for your current Wi-Fi network.

Notifications

If you've installed any apps from the App Store that use the Apple Push Notification service, you'll have access to Notifications settings. Otherwise, you won't see this in Settings. Using this service, apps can alert you about new information, even when the application isn't running. Most notifications play a sound, offer text, or place a number on the app's icon on the Home screen. To maximize battery life, you can turn these notifications off.

Notifications options include the ability to:

- **Turn all notifications on or off**   To turn off all notifications (or turn them all on).
- **Turn sounds, alerts, or badges on or off for an application**   To turn off notifications for a specific app. (Note that "badges" are the notifications that appear on an icon, such as the number of new status updates.)

Cellular Data

Cellular Data settings are available only on the iPad Wi-Fi + 3G model. They enable you to change settings related to your current cellular data network, and turn cellular data and/or roaming on or off.

Cellular Data options include the ability to:

- **Turn the cellular data network connection on or off**   To turn on or off access to the cellular network. You may want to turn off cellular network access when you've reached your monthly quota of bandwidth, and turn it back on at the beginning of your next payment cycle.
- **Turn data roaming on or off**   To turn data roaming on or off. Data roaming may cost extra if you're out of the country. It's best to leave this off if you do not fully understand your cellular data plan.
- **View your account information**   To see or change your account information.
- **Change APN Settings**   To change settings related to your cellular data plan, including your username and password, if applicable.
- **Add a SIM PIN**   To add a PIN to lock your micro-SIM card. If your iPad is stolen, a thief could possibly pull the SIM card and obtain data from it.

Brightness & Wallpaper

Use Brightness settings to adjust the screen brightness and Wallpaper settings to personalize your iPad's Home screen wallpaper and the picture you see when you unlock your iPad.

Brightness & Wallpaper options include the ability to:

- **Adjust the screen brightness**   To change the screen's brightness using a slider.
- **Set whether your iPad adjusts screen brightness automatically**   To enable or disable Auto-Brightness. When Auto-Brightness is enabled, your iPad will adjust the brightness automatically using the built-in ambient light sensor.
- **Set wallpaper**   To select a wallpaper for the Lock screen, Home screen, or both.

Picture Frame

You can use your iPad as a digital picture frame. You can enhance this by also incorporating the optional dock to hold the frame in place on a mantle or table. Picture Frame mode lets you also apply transitions in between photos, and choose what photos to display. You can even zoom in on faces and shuffle photos when playing them.

Picture Frame options include the ability to:

- **Select a transition**   To choose the type of transition to use between photos.
- **Zoom in on faces during a Picture Frame show**   To zoom in on faces during a show using Picture Frame. This option will appear grayed out unless you've opted for the Dissolve transition.
- **Shuffle**   Turn shuffle on or off. Randomizes the order in which photos are displayed.
- **Choose what pictures to show**   To select a folder or all photos to use when Picture Frame is playing.

General

General settings include those related to the date and time, security, network, and other things that affect every part of your iPad. This is also where you can find information about your iPad, or reset your iPad to its original state. The General settings offer subcategories that, when selected, offer even more options. Listed next are the subcategories and what they include.

About

Click About to get information about your iPad including but not limited to total storage capacity; space available; number of songs, videos, and photos; serial number; and software version.

Usage

The Usage setting is available on the iPad W-Fi + 3G model only. Click the Usage category to obtain information about your battery and the amount of cellular data you've sent and received.

Usage options include the ability to:

- **Show battery percentage**   To display the percentage of battery charge next to the battery icon on the Home screen. On iPad Wi-Fi models, this setting is available on the General settings menu, above the Reset option.
- **See cellular network data**   To view the amount of data sent and received over the cellular data network (on iPad Wi-Fi + 3G only) since the last time you reset your usage statistics.
- **Reset your usage statistics**   To clear accumulated data and statistics.

Sounds

Click Sounds to make changes to settings related to sounds.

Sounds options include the ability to:

- **Adjust volume**   To change the volume of the current song, podcast, audiobook, or video, drag the slider. You can also use the volume buttons on the side of your iPad.
- **Set alert and effects sounds**   To turn specific sounds on or off. You can enable or disable sounds when you do the following:
  - Get an email message
  - Send an email message
  - Have an event that you've set to alert you
  - Lock the iPad
  - Type using the keyboard

Network

Network settings enable you to access and change settings related to the various networks you use, including Wi-Fi and VPNs.

Network options include the ability to:

- **Add a new VPN configuration**   To add a new VPN Configuration. (You'll have to drill down into VPN settings to access this command.)
- **Change a VPN configuration**   To change a VPN's configuration settings.
- **Turn VPN on or off**   To turn VPN on or off.
- **Delete a VPN configuration**   To delete a VPN.
- **Access Wi-Fi Settings**   To access Wi-Fi settings detailed earlier.

Bluetooth

Your iPad can connect to Bluetooth devices like headphones and keyboards. Bluetooth devices allow you to listen or type without wires. There are three options for Bluetooth:

- **Turn Bluetooth on or off**   To turn on and off Bluetooth capabilities.
- **Search for devices**   To watch while your iPad searches for Bluetooth devices, once Bluetooth is enabled.
- **Connect to a device**   To pair your iPad with a Bluetooth device in range. You first select a device from the list, and then you may be required to enter a password.

Location Services

Your iPad can keep track of where you are, provided you have Wi-Fi enabled. Your location is gleaned from information available from local Wi-Fi networks, and the iPad Wi-Fi + 3G model also uses cellular networks and GPS to determine your location. You can turn Location Services on or off.

Location Services options include the ability to:

- **Turn Location Services on or off**   To turn location services on or off.

Tip   Turn Location Services off when you're not using it to maximize battery life.

Auto-Lock

Locking your iPad turns the display off. There's a button on the outside of your iPad for locking it. You can turn the display off to maximize battery life, but it will lock itself after a few minutes of idle time anyway. Locking the iPad also keeps it safe from unintended operation, by preventing taps on the screen from activating an app. You can also require a passcode when you're ready to unlock your iPad. Passcode features are not enabled by default. By setting a passcode, you can prevent your iPad from being accessed without your permission, as detailed in the next section.

Auto-Lock options include the ability to:

- **Set the amount of time before the iPad locks**   To change how long the iPad is idle before it is locked automatically. You also have the option of disabling Auto-Lock.

Passcode Lock

You can secure your iPad by requiring a Passcode Lock. When you enable this feature, each time you unlock your iPad you have to input this code. This keeps it safe from unauthorized users.

Passcode Lock options include the ability to:

- **Set a passcode**   To enter a four-digit passcode.
- **Turn Passcode Lock off**   To turn the Passcode Lock off (and on again).
- **Change the passcode**   To change the passcode.
- **Set how long before your passcode is required**   To set how long your iPad should be idle before you need to enter a passcode to unlock it.
- **Picture Frame**   To require a passcode (or not) when showing pictures with Picture Frame.
- **Erase data after ten failed passcode attempts**   To turn on this feature (or to turn it off later). If you turn on this feature, after ten failed passcode attempts, the iPad will erase all your information and media.

Restrictions

Restrictions on the iPad are kind of like parental controls on other devices. You can set restrictions for the content that can be played on the iPad, as well as hiding and thus disabling applications like YouTube or iTunes. There aren't a lot of restrictions you can place on the iPad, but the ones that are available can be quite useful.

Restriction options include the ability to:

- **Turn on restrictions**   To enable restrictions. You'll have to create and enter a four-digit passcode.
- **Turn off restrictions**   To disable restrictions.
- **Set application restrictions**   To hide and disable individual apps including Safari and iTunes.
- **Set allowed content**   To set restrictions on the type of content that can be played or purchased.

Home

You can configure what you want to happen when you double-click the Home button on your iPad. It can go to the Home screen, the Search screen, or the iPod app.

Home options include the ability to:

- **Set whether double-clicking the Home button shows iPod controls**   To turn iPod controls on or off by double-clicking the Home button. This feature works even when the iPad is locked or the display is off.
- **Set what categories appear in search results**   To set what categories appear in Search results. Tap an item to deselect (or reselect) it.
- **Set the order of search result categories**   To reorder the category list, drag beside a search category to move it to a new place in the list.

Date and Time

There are settings available to personalize the date and time information on your iPad. Depending on the model and the settings already configured, you can change the time format, choose to have the time set automatically, set the time zone, and set the date and time manually. For instance, on a Wi-Fi + 3G model, when you change the setting for Set Automatically from On to Off, two additional settings appear, Time Zone and Set Date & Time; if you change it from Off to On, those two settings disappear.

Date and Time options include the ability to:

- **Set whether the iPad shows 24-hour time or 12-hour time**   To turn 24-Hour Time on or off.
- **Set automatically**   To have the iPad set the time automatically.
- **Set the time zone**   To set a time zone.
- **Set the date and time**   To set the date and time.

Keyboard

You can change various settings for the keyboard and set preferences for how you type. For instance, you can turn on or off the Auto-Capitalization feature if you'd rather not have the iPad automatically capitalize the beginning of sentences.

Keyboard options include the ability to:

- **Turn Auto-Correction on or off**   To turn Auto-Correction on or off.
- **Turn Auto-Capitalization on or off**   To turn Auto-Capitalization on or off.
- **Set whether Caps Lock is enabled**   To turn Enable Caps Lock on or off.
- **Turn the "." shortcut on or off**   To turn the "." shortcut on or off. (The "." shortcut lets you double-tap the space bar to enter a period followed by a space when you're typing.)
- **Set up international keyboards**   To add and configure keyboards for multiple languages.

International

Your iPad comes with various international settings. With these, you can set the language for the iPad, turn keyboards for different languages on or off, and configure similar preferences for your preferred language.

International options include the ability to:

- **Set the language for your iPad**   To choose the language you want to use.
- **Set up international keyboards**   Access to the same international keyboard settings that you can access under Keyboard. To add and configure keyboards for multiple languages.
- **Set date, time, and telephone number formats**   To choose your region.

Accessibility

Accessibility options make it easier for a person with a visual, mobility, or hearing disability to use the iPad.

Accessibility options include the ability to:

- **Have what's on your iPad's screen read to you**   Enable VoiceOver.
- **Zoom in on your iPad's screen**   Enable Zoom.
- **Use a high-contrast screen**   To use the white-on-black screen mode.
- **Use Mono Audio**   To combine stereo audio channels so that identical sound is heard in both channels.
- **Speak Auto-Text**   To have the iPad speak auto-corrections and auto-capitalizations to you.
- **Triple-Click Home**   To enable a feature that allows you to triple-click the Home button to toggle some Accessibility features.

Resetting Your iPad

You will change the default values for various settings on your iPad as you use it. You'll likely reorder the Home screen, add words to the Dictionary while typing, or change Network settings. You can reset these by resetting specific apps on your iPad. You can also reset your iPad, and delete everything on it, restoring it to factory settings.

Resetting iPad options include the ability to:

- **Reset all settings** To reset all settings. This only applies to settings on the iPad, not your data (like contacts, calendars, and media).
- **Erase all content and settings** To completely reset your iPad and delete all of the data on it.
- **Reset network settings** To reset only the network settings.
- **Reset the Keyboard Dictionary** To reset the Keyboard Dictionary.
- **Reset the Home screen layout** To reset the Home Screen Layout.
- **Reset the location warnings** To reset Location Warnings.

Mail, Contacts, Calendars

You'll use the Mail, Contacts, Calendars settings to set up email accounts and MobileMe. You can also customize preferences for these accounts and related features, including Contacts and Calendar.

Accounts

This is where you configure the email accounts and calendar subscriptions on your iPad. You can change your account settings, stop using an account, or even delete an account.

Account options include the ability to:

- **Change an account's settings** To choose an existing account and make changes to it.
- **Stop using an account** To disable an account.
- **Adjust advanced settings** For email accounts, configure options such as mailbox behaviors and settings for incoming messages.
- **Delete an account from iPad** To delete an account completely. If you want to use the account again, you'll have to re-enter it. If you aren't sure, disable the account instead.

Fetch New Data

Fetch and Push are detailed in Chapter 4. You can enable or disable Fetch and Push here.

Fetch options include the ability to:

- **Turn Push on**   To turn on Push.
- **Set the interval to fetch data**   To set how often you want to fetch data.

Mail

You can configure lots of Mail settings. You can create a new a signature for all outgoing emails, set the minimum font size for email messages, set a default email account, and more.

 To change the sounds associated with Mail, in Settings, go to the General options, under Sounds.

Mail options include the ability to:

- **Set the number of messages shown on the iPad**   You can opt to see the most recent 25, 50, 75, 100, or 200 messages.
- **Set how many lines of each message are previewed in the message list** To change email preview options; specifically, how many lines of text you'd like to preview (up to five lines).
- **Set a minimum font size for messages**   To set a font size from Small, Medium, Large, Extra Large, or Giant.
- **Set whether the iPad shows To and Cc labels in message lists**   To show or hide the To/Cc labels.
- **Set whether the iPad confirms that you want to delete a message** To confirm you want to delete a message (or not).
- **Set whether the iPad automatically loads remote images**   To load remote images (which will cause the email to take longer to load) or to turn off this feature. (You can manually load the images while reading the email if you want to see them.)
- **Set whether the iPad sends you a copy of every message you send** To always send a blind carbon copy (Bcc) to yourself each time you send an email.
- **Add a signature to your messages**   To add, change, or delete the automatic signature for outgoing messages.
- **Set the default email account**   To set your default email account. The default account is the one that will be used automatically each time you compose an email in another application, like Maps or Photos.

Contacts

You can change how your contacts are sorted.

Contacts options include the ability to:

- **Set how contacts are sorted**   To change the sorting option for contacts. You can sort contacts by first name or last name.
- **Set how contacts are displayed**   To change the display order for contacts. You can display contacts by first name or last name.

Calendar

The Calendar helps you keep track of appointments and important dates. You can change how the Calendar sends you alerts, among other options.
Calendar options include the ability to:

- **Set alerts to sound when you receive meeting invitations**   You can turn this on or off. You may need to be alerted for each meeting invitation, or you may not.
- **Set how far back in the past to show your calendar events on iPad** To select a period of time for how far back to show events on your calendar.
- **Turn on Calendar time zone support**   To enable Time Zone Support. When this option is enabled, the Calendar always displays your event dates and times using a specific time zone. When this option is turned off, event dates and times are determined by the time zone of your current location.

Safari

There are a few things you can configure regarding Safari. You can choose a specific Search engine, enable AutoFill, and change Security settings. There are also "Developer" settings that you can likely ignore.

General

General options include the ability to:

- **Select a search engine**   To select the search engine you want to use. Options include Google and Yahoo!.
- **Enable AutoFill**   To set Safari to automatically fill out web forms. Safari uses data that you've previously entered into web pages to fill in forms.
- **Show the Bookmarks Bar**   To permanently show a bar with bookmarks on it in Safari.

Security

Security options include the ability to:

- **Change security settings** To turn Fraud Warning on or off; to enable or disable JavaScript; to block or allow pop-ups; to set whether Safari accepts cookies; to clear the history of web pages you've visited; to clear all cookies from Safari; and to clear Safari's cache.

Developer

If you want to know when a web page has errors, and if you're interested in resolving those errors because you develop apps or web sites for the iPad, the debug console can help.

Developer options include the ability to:

- **Turn the Debug Console on or off** Get help regarding web page errors using the Debug Console.

iPod

The iPod app is the app you use to play music. You can configure various settings for the iPod, including playing all songs at the same sound level and setting a volume limit, among other things. Some of these options must be made at your computer.

iPod options include the ability to:

- **Set iTunes to play songs at the same sound level** Enable Sound Check.
- **Use EQ to customize the sound** To select an equalizer from a list of predefined settings.
- **Set a volume limit** To set the maximum volume for the iPod and to lock it, if desired.
- **Display song lyrics and information about podcasts** To display lyrics and information when applicable.

Video

Video settings offer options that apply to all video content, including rented movies. Some of the things you can configure include enabling closed captioning and wide-screen.

Video options include

- **Set where to resume playing** To set where videos that you previously started watching begin. You can resume playing from the beginning or where you left off.
- **Turn closed captioning on or off** To turn closed captioning on or off.

- **Set the TV output signal to NTSC or PAL**   If you're using the iPad with a video output accessory, use this setting to determine what video format you'll output. If you're in the United States, NTSC is the correct choice. Elsewhere, try PAL.
- **Turn Widescreen on or off**   To turn Widescreen on or off when using video output accessories. Turn this on to preserve the wide-screen aspect ratio when watching a video made specifically for the wide screen.

Photos

The settings in Photos are those related only to slideshows.
Photos options include

- **Set the length of time each slide is shown**   To specify the length of time each photo in a slideshow should appear before the next photo appears.
- **Set whether to repeat slideshows**   To repeat slideshows once they are completed. Turn repeat on to repeat, or off to end.
- **Set photos to appear randomly or in order**   To randomly shuffle photos in a slideshow.

Store

The Store settings offer a place to change or create an iTunes Store account.
Store options include:

- **Sign into or out of an account**   To enter your username and password to enter, and to sign out if desired. While signed out, users have the option to create a new iTunes account.
- **View your iTunes Store account information**   To type your password and other Store information.

 You may have more categories listed. For instance, if you've downloaded iBooks, it'll be listed, as will various other apps you acquire. Not all apps place a listing here, though.

B

Troubleshooting

You may not know that you can call Apple at 1-800-My-Apple and get help. You can call for help about setting up email, using Safari, or downloading an app. We've called a couple of times and it's a short wait on hold, the people who answer the phone are easy to understand and are extremely helpful, and they'll even call you back if they need more time to resolve your problem or if you're disconnected. So, if you'd rather simply call someone than look through this Appendix, help is just a phone call away.

You can also get help on the Internet. Visit www.apple.com/support/ipad/ if you'd rather look there. The Support pages can help you set up and use all of the apps available on the iPad, including Wi-Fi, Mail, and more. There's no way we can include here everything that can go wrong and what to do about it, so that may be a good place to look if you don't see what you're looking for. At Apple's Support site you can access troubleshooting guides, discuss your problem with other iPad users, and troubleshoot problems that are less common than the ones here.

To use this Appendix, locate the heading that relates most closely to your problem, and read the information in that section to resolve it. The sections include

- I am having a problem related to email
- I can't get connected to the Internet
- I have a hardware problem
- I have a backup, sync, update, or restore question
- I have a problem not listed here

I Am Having a Problem Related to Email

There are two separate issues with regard to email:

- You have previously set up email and sent and received email successfully, but are now having a problem.
  or
- You have just set up an email account and are receiving errors and/or cannot send or receive email.

I Used to Be Able to Get My Email, But Now I Can't

There could be a few things going on here: First, you must be connected to the Internet to get your mail. This may mean that Wi-Fi or cellular data needs to be enabled, and that you need to be within range of a free Wi-Fi network or within your provider's data coverage area. So first, open Safari and see if you're connected to the Internet. If you aren't, take steps to resolve that problem first.

If you're connected to the Internet, consider or try the following:

- Verify that you have enough battery power. If your battery is low, plug it in to charge it, and after 10 or 20 minutes, try again.
- If you get email on your iPad and on another device like an iPhone, BlackBerry, or computer, you may experience difficulty downloading your mail at the exact same time as another device. That's because the mail server could be busy sending your mail to one of your other devices and can't accommodate your request right now. Wait. Your mail may come in shortly.
- It may be that your iPad's Mail app is frozen or "stuck." This is unlikely, but try to close Mail and then open it again. If you can't close Mail, press and hold the Sleep/Wake button. When the red slider appears, press and hold the Home button. This will close Mail. Reopen Mail to see if the problem is resolved.
- Open Settings, and then Mail, and verify that you haven't accidentally deleted or disabled your email account(s). While there, consider letting Mail show 200 recent messages.
- If your iPad uses a cellular data network (iPad Wi-Fi + 3G only), turn off Wi-Fi. This will force the iPad to connect to the Internet through the cellular data network. This will resolve the problem if its cause is due to the local Wi-Fi network connection or its settings. Note that if you're in a pinch and you use a web-based email account such as Gmail, Yahoo mail, or Hotmail, you can check your email using Safari.

I've Set Up a New Email Account, But I'm Not Getting Any Mail

Setting up a new Mail account, especially if it's not one of the supported email accounts like Google or Yahoo!, can be trying. It's easy to make a mistake when you input the required data, like POP mail server names. Even with an account that's supported, you can easily misspell your password or email address. If there are any errors in your email setup, you won't be able to send or receive email. If you've set up a new email account and can't send and/or receive email:

- Work through the troubleshooting tips outlined in detail in the previous section. Make sure your battery has enough power to get your email; if you get email on another device such as an iPhone or computer, wait a few minutes to see if both are trying to access the mail servers at the same time; if Mail is frozen, close and reopen the app; and if you use a cellular data plan, disable Wi-Fi for a moment to rule out a problem with the wireless network. Finally, reboot your iPad, just in case. Sometimes this resolves problems immediately.
- If none of those actions resolve the issue, you'll need to verify your settings for your Mail accounts:
  - Click Settings, and click Mail.
  - Tap the problematic account.
  - Review the information for the POP servers, username, password, and so on. If necessary, call your provider to verify you have the correct settings.
- If you still can't get your email to work, contact your service provider and ask them to walk you through it. If they don't yet support the iPad, ask them for the following information and write it down very carefully:
  - Incoming mail server host name
  - Outgoing mail server host name
  - Your account type, such as IMAP or POP
  - Any special requirements such as whether you need to enable secure logon or type a special port number
- If you have a cellular data plan, and you can receive email but not send it, in your email account's SMTP settings, turn on the additional email server, cwmx.com. Configure this to Use SSL. Repeat, and configure the second to not use SSL.
- Finally, search for people on the Internet who have had similar problems. Not all accounts are supported yet, but with the right amount of finagling, you can likely get it to work.

I Can't Open an Email Attachment

Your iPad can only open certain types of attachments. They are listed here. If the attachment is a file type not listed here, it may not open.

Your iPad supports the following attachment types:

File Name	File Type
.bmp	Bitmap
.doc	Microsoft Word
.docx	Microsoft Word
.gif	Graphics Interchange Format
.htm	web page
.html	web page
.jpg	JPEG
.key	Keynote
.numbers	Numbers
.pages	Pages
.pdf	Preview, Adobe Acrobat
.png	Portable Network Graphics
.ppt	Microsoft PowerPoint
.pptx	Microsoft PowerPoint
.rtf	Rich Text Format
.tiff	Tagged Image File Format
.txt	Text document
.vcf	Contact information
.xls	Microsoft Excel
.xlsx	Microsoft Excel

I Can't Get Connected to the Internet

If you can't connect to the Internet on a Wi-Fi only iPad, it's one of two things. Either you don't have Wi-Fi enabled or you aren't within range of and connected to a Wi-Fi network. To resolve this problem, enable Wi-Fi in Settings, under Wi-Fi. There you'll see if networks are available, and you can attempt to connect to them.

If you can't connect to the Internet on a Wi-Fi +3G iPad, it's one of a few things. You may not have Wi-Fi enabled, or you may not be within range of and connected to a Wi-Fi network, as detailed earlier. Try to connect using the methods outlined there.

If you are unsuccessful connecting to a Wi-Fi network, you can try using your cellular data connection. For this to work:

- You must have signed up with AT&T for cellular data service.
- You must have Cellular Data enabled in Settings.
- You must be inside your provider's coverage area.

I Have a Hardware Problem

If you're having a problem with your hardware, first, make sure everything is connected properly and fully charged. Most of the time if a cable is involved, the problem is that it's not firmly connected. If the problem persists, turn on and off the device.

As with all troubleshooting steps, make sure you have enough battery power, and that you have the proper features enabled on your iPad. If you're having trouble connecting a Bluetooth device, for instance, make sure that Bluetooth is enabled in Settings, General, and that the device to connect is turned on and ready. If you're trying to pull pictures from a digital camera using the Camera Connection Kit, make sure the camera is turned on and set to the proper position (often Play). Often hardware problems can be resolved by putting in fresh batteries too, as is often the case with keyboards.

My iPad Doesn't Respond and Is "Frozen"

If your iPad isn't responding and seems to be "frozen," there are several things you can try:

- If your screen won't rotate, verify the Screen Rotation Lock is not engaged.
- If an application seems to be the cause of the iPad's unresponsiveness, press and hold the Sleep/Wake button. When the red slider appears, press and hold the Home button. This should close the current application. Your iPad may be just fine after that. Sometimes third-party apps are "buggy," and cause the iPad to freeze up. If you think this is the case, it's best to uninstall or delete the app.
- If the battery is low on power, charge the iPad by connecting it to a wall outlet using the power adapter.
- If the previous options don't work or are not the issue, you'll need to turn off the iPad and turn it back on. Press and hold the Sleep/Wake button, and when the red slider appears, drag the slider to turn off the iPad. Then press and hold the Sleep/Wake button to turn the iPad back on.
- As a last resort, reset the iPad. Resetting won't cause data loss if you choose the right option; it's like rebooting a computer. Press and hold the Sleep/Wake button and the Home button simultaneously for 10 seconds. When the Apple logo appears let go. The iPad will reset.

I'm Trying to Install Some Hardware, But a Message Says the Accessory Is "Not Supported by iPad"

The iPad only works with specific supported devices. Each device you purchase should say "compatible with the iPad" or something similar. If it does not, it may not work with your iPad. However, if you're sure the device is supposed to be compatible, or if it has previously worked with your iPad, check the cables and connections to verify that it is connected properly. If a setting needs to be enabled, like Bluetooth, enable it, and if possible, try to connect the device to another iPad to verify the device itself is not defective. If possible, try a different compatible cable. (Finally, if you receive an error that the device won't work, dismiss the error message and see if the device will work anyway.)

I Have a Problem with My Battery or the Battery Icon

If you see any error messages related to the battery or if your iPad won't charge, consider the following problems and solutions:

- If the battery is completely drained or is extremely low on power, it probably won't boot up, even if it's plugged into a wall outlet. Let the iPad charge (preferably connected to a wall outlet, not a computer) for 10 or 20 minutes and see if this resolves the issue.
- If the iPad is plugged in to a wall outlet but won't charge, try the following:
  - Test the outlet with another device to make sure the outlet is working properly.
  - Verify that all connections to the outlet and the iPad are secure.
  - Make sure you're using an Apple power adapter. Third-party adapters can cause problems.
- If the iPad won't charge while plugged in to a USB port on a computer:
  - Test the USB port with another device to make sure it's working properly.
  - Try a different USB port. The USB port you use must be a USB 2.0 type in order to charge the iPad. Older USB ports (1.0) will work for syncing data, but they don't provide enough power to charge the iPad.
  - Don't use a USB hub. Plug the iPad directly into a USB port.
- If the iPad still won't charge, turn it off and plug it in to a working wall outlet using the included power adapter. Wait an hour or so and try to turn it on again.

I Have a Backup, Sync, Update, or Restore Question

Backing up, syncing, updating, and restoring are all very important tasks with regard to your iPad. You should back up your iPad regularly, sync data between your computer and iPad often, and occasionally, check for updates. There are many reasons to do this, but one is to have a backup in case your iPad is lost, stolen, or broken. You can use your latest backup to restore your iPad, if you replace it with a new one.

I Want to Back Up My iPad in Case Something Happens to It

You use iTunes and your computer to create backups for your iPad, which includes your iPad's operating system, your apps, the settings you've configured, application data, and various other data that is directly related to the iPad. The backup doesn't include items you sync that are stored on your computer and that you've transferred to your iPad, though, such as songs, pictures, and videos, or songs, pictures, and videos you've pulled from the Internet and synced to your computer. This data is backed up via syncing through iTunes. So there are two tasks to backing up your data:

- Connect your iPad to your computer to back it up.
- Connect your iPad to your computer to sync it.

You can do both at the same time by simply connecting your iPad to your computer. If, after connecting your iPad to your computer, iTunes does not show that it (1) backs up your iPad and (2) syncs it, then in iTunes, click the iPad in the source pane of iTunes, and click each tab to verify that the items you want to be synced are selected. Then, click Sync.

To manually create a backup:

1. Connect your iPad to your computer.
2. Make sure your computer is connected to the Internet.
3. Right-click your iPad in the source pane of iTunes. (Mac users, CTRL + click.)
4. Click Backup.

For extra security, you can set iTunes to encrypt your backups. When you encrypt your backups you assign a password. You'll have to input the password to restore the data later. If you use a password, make sure you write it down and keep it in a safe place. Here's how to encrypt your backup:

1. Connect your iPad to your computer.
2. In iTunes, select iPad in the source pane.
3. In the Summary pane, tick Encrypt iPad Backup.
4. Select a password, then click Set Password.

I Created a Backup and Now I Want to Use That Backup to Restore My iPad

If you've created a backup using iTunes, you have a copy of your settings, application data, your iPad's operating system, and various other pertinent data that make your iPad run, and run the way you want. And if you've synced your iPad with your computer, you have a backup of all of your media too. You can restore from these two backups should you ever need to. You can restore the data to your existing iPad, or, if the iPad was lost, stolen, or damaged, you can restore to a new iPad.

To restore iPad from a backup:

1. At the computer where you manage your iPad, connect to the Internet.
2. Connect your iPad to the computer.
3. In iTunes, right-click on a PC or CTRL-click on a Mac on the iPad in the source pane, then choose Restore from Backup from the menu that appears.
4. Choose the backup that you want to restore from the pop-up menu, then click Restore. If the backup is encrypted, you'll need to enter your password.
5. When the restore is complete, sync your iPad.

I Want to Sell My iPad or Give It to Someone Else, and Need to Delete All My Data and Personal Information

This is easy to do. Simply connect your iPad to your computer, and from the Summary tab in iTunes, click Restore. This will restore your iPad to factory settings. Once the restore is complete, do not sync your iPad. You can also do this directly on the iPad under Settings, General | Reset | Erase All Content and Settings.

I Want to Make Sure My iPad's Operating System Is Up to Date

Once in a while, Apple makes an update available for your iPad. You can easily check for updates by connecting your iPad to your computer, and in iTunes, from the Summary tab, clicking Check for Update.

I Have a Problem Not Listed Here

There are a few problems that stand alone; perhaps you can't get your iPad to sync, or an application appears on the screen too small. Although we can't list everything here that you could encounter, here are a few common problems and their solutions.

I Can't Sync My iPad

If you can't sync your iPad, try the following:

- Charge the iPad's battery from a wall outlet for about 20 minutes.
- Reboot your iPad.
- If you have another cable to connect your iPad to your computer, try it. If the cable has been damaged, syncing can't occur.
- Restart your computer.
- Unlock your iPad if it has a passcode applied.
- Check iTunes for an update.
- Make sure you're syncing to the same computer you typically use to sync your iPad.

An Application Appears too Small

This often happens because you've acquired an app created for an iPhone or iPod Touch and it hasn't been updated for use with the iPad's larger screen. You can try tapping the "2x" button in the bottom-right corner of the screen to zoom in or look for an updated version at the App Store.

I Deleted an App, Movie, Book, or Other Data from My iPad and Now I Want It Back

Connect your iPad to your computer. Click your iPad in the source pane of iTunes. Click the appropriate tab, Apps, Movies, Books, or the like. Tick the option to sync these items, and in the list beneath, tick the apps to put back on your iPad. Click Sync.

I Can't See the Virtual Keyboard

This happens when the iPad is paired with a Bluetooth keyboard, or if it's connected to the iPad Keyboard Dock. To show the virtual keyboard, press the Keyboard key on the Keyboard Dock, or press the Eject key on a Bluetooth keyboard.

Index